AN INTRODUCTION T
AUTOMATA THEORY

COMPUTER SCIENCE TEXTS

COMPUTER SCIENCE TEXTS

AN INTRODUCTION TO AUTOMATA THEORY

M. W. SHIELDS
BA, PhD
Lecturer, Electronic Engineering Laboratories,
The University of Kent at Canterbury

BLACKWELL SCIENTIFIC PUBLICATIONS

OXFORD LONDON EDINBURGH

BOSTON PALO ALTO MELBOURNE

Editorial offices:
Osney Mead, Oxford OX2 0EL
(*Orders:* Tel. 0865 240201)
8 John Street, London WC1N 2ES
23 Ainslie Place, Edinburgh EH3 6AJ
52 Beacon Street, Boston
Massachusetts 02108, USA
667 Lytton Avenue, Palo Alto
California 94301, USA
107 Barry Street, Carlton
Victoria 3053, Australia

First published 1987

Printed and bound in Great Britain

DISTRIBUTORS

USA and Canada
Blackwell Scientific Publications Inc
PO Box 50009, Palo Alto
California 94303
(*Orders:* Tel. (415) 965-4081)

Australia
Blackwell Scientific Publications
(Australia) Pty Ltd
107 Barry Street
Carlton, Victoria 3053
(*Orders:* Tel. (03) 347 0300)

British Library
Cataloguing in Publication Data

Shields, M.W.
An introduction to automata theory.
1. Machine theory
I. Title
001.53′5 QA267

ISBN 0–632–01756–2
ISBN 0–632–01553–3 Pbk

Library of Congress
Cataloging-in-Publication Data

Shields, M. W. (Mike W.)
An introduction to automata theory.

Bibliography: p.
Includes index.
1. Machine theory. I. Title.
QA267.S47 1987 511.3 87–27740
ISBN 0–632–01756–2

To my Mother,

this little book is respectfully dedicated.

Contents

Preface

Welcome to the machine.

PINK FLOYD
Wish you were here

This book is based on a course of ten one-hour lectures given by the author to third year computer science and computer systems engineering students at the University of Kent. Ten hours is not very much, certainly not enough to present the usual material on automata theory – the Chomsky hierarchy and the related hierarchy of machines, Turing computability and so on – and so I decided to teach some elementary structure theory. My aim was to show that *systems*, of which students had some experience, were capable of mathematical manipulation of a fairly non-trivial kind, that they are not obdurate monoliths approachable only by the dubious intuition of the 'real programmer'. In other words, I attempted to present automata theory as a rudimentary *formal theory of systems*.

Thus, within its domain of application, it provides a means for *formal specification* via flow tables or state graphs and, considering these as notations for specification, automata provide a *formal semantics* for them. There are also standard techniques for *implementation* in hardware (and software). The objects with which automata are implemented may be interpreted as automata themselves and we have notions of structural relationships between automata which give us means of formalising the notion of a *correct implementation*.

It is received wisdom that non-trivial systems should not be constructed or conceived as a homogeneous whole but rather constructed out of interconnected modules. Automata theory possesses various formal notions of *composition* which enable complex systems to be constructed out of simpler ones.

There is a converse problem of *systems partitioning*: breaking a rough specification into modules which may then be refined. We devote several chapters to the problem of *decomposing* automata. It is satisfying to see to what extent we can deduce information about how a system may be decomposed from an associated lattice of congruences.

This book does not demand a great deal of mathematical sophistication from the reader, who is merely required to be comfortable with set theory and be capable of following a reasoned argument.

There is a set of exercises at the end of each chapter. Most of these are very simple and are designed to illustrate some aspect of the text. Some involve a step-by-step development of further results. There are also notes at the end of each chapter, describing extensions to the material and giving suggestions for further reading.

The author would like to thank Martin Guy for his helpful suggestions (but not for his coffee), Dan Simpson for his comments and Dominic Vaughan of Blackwell Scientific Publications for his patience. I would particularly like to thank Steve Smith for undertaking the gargantuan task of reformatting my original troff source.

Of course, any errors remaining in the text remain the responsibility of the author.

Mike Shields

Chapter 1

Great Aunt Eugenia and Other Automata

You'll get more out of me and a machine than you will out of twenty labourers, and not so much to drink, either.

GEORGE BERNARD SHAW
Man and Superman

1.1 ON MACHINES

This book is about machines. The word *machine* can evoke several different pictures in peoples' minds. Mention it to a mechanical engineer, for example, and he will visualise some vast, brutish agglomerate of pulleys and cogwheels and boilers. The word has an entirely different connotation to a programmer (as in the redolent phrase, 'The machine's down again'), while to a houseperson, it would, I suppose, summon up visions of vacuum cleaners or tumble-action spin driers or (if he/she were Russian), tractors.

We shall be using the word in an *abstract* and *mathematical* sense; the word 'machine' will here denote a mathematical entity. The advantage of such an abstract approach is generality. Our results may be used in many apparently unrelated cases; what they will have in common is that in each case the same notion of machine will apply.

The more fundamental mathematical entities were usually contrived to reflect something in the real world. Whole numbers, for example, arose from the need to describe and predict the sizes of aggregates. The idea of 'machine' that we shall be using abstracts from that of a discrete, finite state, input/output device. Such a device has only a finite number of possible internal configurations. It has a specific collection of stimuli that may be applied, such as the pressing of a button or the insertion of a coin, and a finite collection of responses, for example the appearance of characters on a screen or the arrival of a packet of biscuits in a slot. Examples are: processors, programs, protocols and even (in a limited sense) people.

Such devices may be abstractly modelled by our abstract machines. But the abstract machines may themselves always be implemented by hardware and software, as we shall see. Indeed, one of the uses of abstract machines is in the design of digital hardware.

The familiar mathematical entities may usually be manipulated in some way. For example, numbers may be added or multiplied or factorized into a product of primes. Machines may also be combined to make other machines, or decomposed into simpler machines.

Why should this interest a computer scientist ?

What we are presenting here are the rudiments of a *theory of systems*. Computer science is, at the time of writing, beset by the '*software crisis*', a failure to produce software at a price, with a reliability and in a quantity sufficient to meet the needs of a voracious and increasing market. Part of the trouble is that the subject is, as yet, a craft rather than an engineering discipline. If it is ever to crawl out of the dark ages, it will need to acquire an appropriate mathematical theory of systems, as the traditional engineering disciplines have done.

Two candidates for such a theory of systems are presented in Chapters 11 and 12. They are both still subjects of extensive research.

The topics we discuss in this book reflect requirements for such a theory: the need for a notation for specification and a formal semantics for such a notation (Chapter 2); the ability to transform specification into implementation (Chapter 3); well-defined structural and behavioural relationships that permit exact comparison between systems and hence allow us to define what it means for an implementation to meet a specification (Chapters 4 and 5); the ability to compose systems together to make more complex ones (Chapter 6); the ability to partition systems to obtain a scheme of interacting modules (Chapters 7 and 8); and a mathematical theory of structure to support partitioning (Chapters 9 and 10).

Before elaborating on this – and certainly before we begin to look at precise definitions – we shall consider a couple of examples.

1.2 EXAMPLE: GREAT AUNT EUGENIA

An esteemed colleague, Dr F. X. Reid, is encumbered with a Great Aunt of advanced age, wealth and senile dementia. He reports that she responds to few stimuli; to be more precise, she reacts to three things only: ghetto-blasters* roaring out in the street outside her home, so-called video nasties† and gin‡, when a bottle of it is waved under her nose.

---

* Since I still have my sanity, it is my fervent hope that these things become obsolete and that accordingly the phrase lapses from polite use. It is in this hope that I now define the term for the sake of future generations. A ghetto-blaster is a vociferous object carried around by persons of no morals or taste to cause grief and annoyance to innocent citizens in public places.

† In a similar vein, and for a similar reason, let me explain that a video nasty is the cinematic equivalent of the ghetto-blaster.

‡ I trust that this word will not require a gloss.

These will have differing effects on her, depending on her mood. Reid tells me:

'She's a devil to get to wake up in the morning. Try anything you like – wave the gin under her nose, play "The Ghoul That Ate Guildford" – it doesn't make the slightest bit of difference. She just snores like fury and goes on sleeping, for weeks, sometimes. The family have had to buy one of those "ghetto-blasters" – that's the only thing that gets through to her.

'Mind you, she's a sweet-tempered old dear once she's woken up. Take "video nasties", for instance. She would never *dream* of doing anything as un-Victorian as watching one of the things in that mood. But if some young lout comes swaggering past the window with a "ghetto-blaster" then, my word ! She gets very irritable and starts a long harangue about bringing back ear-cropping. I'm afraid that if you offer her a bottle of gin while she's in a good mood, then that's it. She just starts swigging it and becomes embarrassingly maudlin.

'When she's in one of her irritable moods the only thing that will make her good-tempered is to watch a video nasty, though given the somewhat unpleasant cackling noise she makes, one wonders sometimes whether it's worth it. More inane cacophony doesn't help her temper or reduce her obsession with ears, but the worst of it is if she gets her hands on the gin. Glug-glug, down it goes, and there's only one word for her after that: "unspeakable".

'It doesn't matter whether she's being maudlin or unspeakable, it's still bad news for any noisy, inadvertent serenader that strolls past. She has this 1945 German army surplus luger, you see – well, I won't go on, but let's just say that I hate to think what we've had to hand over in out-of-court settlements. And she always ends up in an unspeakable mood afterwards. What we tend to do is get her to watch "The Martlesham Buzz-Saw Massacre". It doesn't sober her up, of course, and the cackling gets on one's nerves a little, but at least she's not unspeakable any more.'

'But doesn't she ever eat ?' I asked him.

'None of us have ever seen her. She seems to live on gin. I don't want you to get the wrong idea, though. Even she has a limit to the amount she can put away. Give her a second bottle and within a few minutes there she'll be, collapsed onto the bed (or the floor, whichever is nearer), dead to the world.'

All this is beginning to sound like the preamble of a 'brain-teaser' and so, to make the resemblance complete, I will add a question:

[Q1] Suppose Great Aunt Eugenia is in an unspeakable mood. How may she be rendered equable ?

As with most problems that are stated verbally (not to say verbosely), a good strategy is to present the data in a more coherent and organized form. Great Aunt Eugenia may be summed up as in Table 1.1.

Table 1.1. Great Aunt Eugenia

Moods	*Stimuli*			*Responses*		
	ghetto-b	video	gin	ghetto-b	video	gin
asleep	genial	asleep	asleep	wake	snore	snore
genial	irritable	genial	maudlin	harangue	refuse	drink
irritable	irritable	genial	unspeakable	harangue	cackle	drink
maudlin	unspeakable	maudlin	asleep	snipe	cackle	collapse
unspeakable	unspeakable	maudlin	asleep	snipe	cackle	collapse

In the table, each row corresponds to one of her five moods. The left-hand part of the table shows how a stimulus can cause her mood to change. For example, if you want to know what happens if she is offered gin when asleep, look at the intersection of the row marked 'asleep' and the column labelled 'gin'. There, you'll find the word 'asleep' – the offer has no effect. If, on the other hand, you want to know what her reaction is, look at the intersection of the 'asleep' row with the 'gin' column in the right-hand part of the table. You will see that all she does in that case is snore.

From the table it is also easy to work out the successive effects of a sequence of stimuli. Suppose, for example, that she is asleep, and that in turn we (i) play some loud rock music near to her window, (ii) offer her a bottle of gin, and (iii) repeat the rock music.

The effect of (i) will be for her to wake and become genial. In that mood, the effect of (ii) will cause her to drink and become maudlin. In the maudlin mood, she will respond to (iii) by taking pot-shots at us and her mood will become unspeakable. Thus, given the *input sequence*:

ghetto-b gin ghetto-b

and given that initially she is asleep, we will get the *output sequence*:

wake drink snipe

and her final mood will be 'unspeakable'.

[Q1] asks us to find an input sequence that will 'drive' the old lady from an unspeakable mood to one of geniality. Rather than trying to work this out from the table, it is easier to consider the same information presented pictorially, as in the diagram of Fig. 1.1.

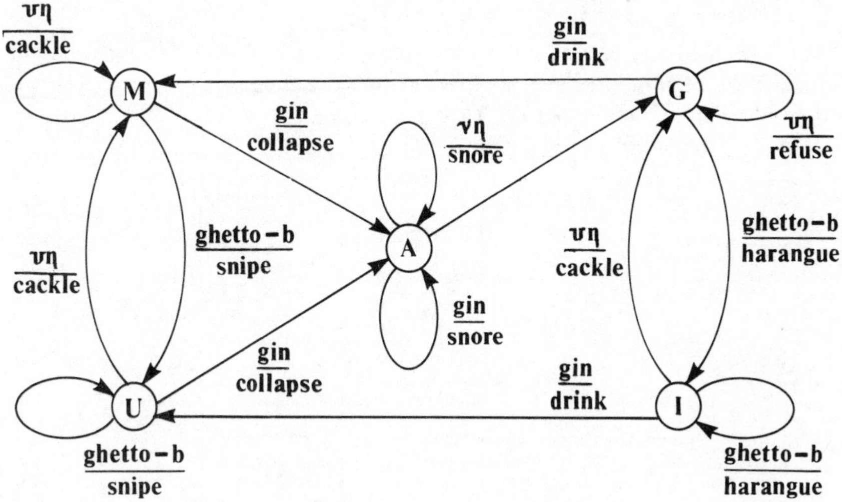

Fig. 1.1. A graphical representation of Table 1.1

The relationship between the two should be clear enough. To each mood, there is a circle, labelled by the mood. If s and s' are any two moods, and in mood s an input x will cause a change of mood to s' and produce an output y, then there is an arrow from s to s' labelled $\frac{x}{y}$.

One can see the effect of sequences of inputs by playing a *token game* on this graph. Place a counter on the initial mood. For any given input, there is exactly one arc leading from the marked mood having that input as a label. Move the token along that arc, reading off the output from the lower label on the arrow. The new position of the token will indicate her new mood.

So, to find sequences that will change her mood, we look for connected sequences of arrows that will take us, if we follow them, from the first mood to the second. If you look at the diagram, you'll see that one such sequence goes from 'unspeakable' to 'asleep' along an arrow marked $\frac{gin}{collapse}$ and from 'asleep' to 'genial' via an arrow marked $\frac{ghetto\text{-}b}{wake}$.

So one answer to question [Q1] is:

[A1] Give the old girl a bottle of gin and let her sleep it off !

1.3 EXAMPLE: PIPELINES

We can also use tables such as Table 1.1 to describe the input/output behaviour of finite storage devices. In this example, we consider a three-frame binary pipeline buffer. This can hold up to three binary digits. Its action is illustrated in Fig. 1.2.

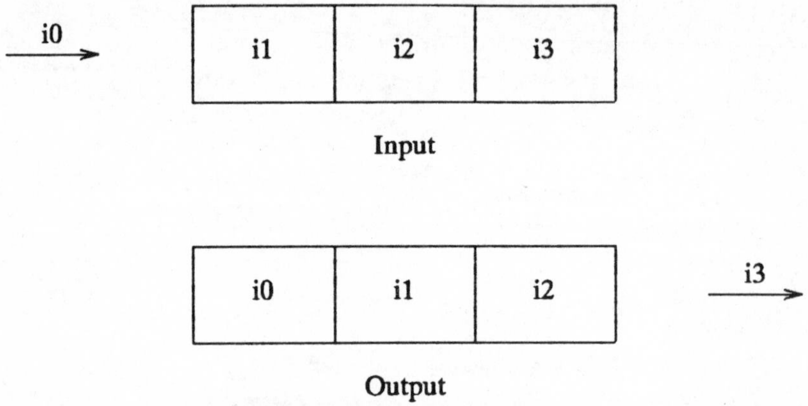

Fig. 1.2. Action of the pipeline

The action is simple enough. Binary digits are pushed in from the left and the contents of the pipeline are shifted one frame to the right. The contents of the rightmost frame emerge as output. The device acts as a three-frame shift register, eternally in shift mode.

The full definition of the input/output behaviour of the pipeline is given in Table 1.2.

Both Great Aunt Eugenia and the pipeline can be described in roughly the same way, by a table or graph describing how she or it responds to stimuli.

It should be easy to see how we might define an n-frame pipeline for any given finite number n. As an exercise, you might ask yourself how you might go about defining the general n-frame pipeline. We shall do this in Section 6.3.3.

One way of doing this that will have immediately occurred to anyone who has had even a brief acquaintance with digital hardware, is to glue several single-frame pipelines together, so that the output of each becomes the input of the next (except for the last frame, of course). We may say that the pipeline *decomposes* into three single frames or that it

Table 1.2. A three-frame pipeline

Contents	*Inputs* 0	1	*Outputs* 0	1
000	000	100	0	0
001	000	100	1	1
010	001	101	0	0
011	001	101	1	1
100	010	110	0	0
101	010	110	1	1
110	011	111	0	0
111	011	111	1	1

may be *composed* out of them. Less obviously, perhaps, Great Aunt Eugenia may also be decomposed, and because her case is less obvious, we shall find it more useful to discuss it.

1.4 DECOMPOSING GREAT AUNTS AND OTHER RELATIONS

The alert reader will realise that we are not really being ghoulish in giving this section its title – we are using the word 'decomposition' in the sense of the last paragraph.

We may see that there are *two* aspects to her moods that one might call the *physiological* and the *psychological*. She has three physiological states – asleep, drunk and sober – and two psychological states – in a pleasant or a foul temper. Each of her moods is a combination of two of these, as illustrated in Table 1.3.

Table 1.3.

Mood	*Physio-*	*Psycho-*
asleep	asleep	–
genial	sober	pleasant
irritable	sober	foul
maudlin	drunk	pleasant
unspeakable	drunk	foul

We may 'construct' Great Aunt Eugenia from two smaller and simpler 'Aunts', one of whom is concerned only with effects on her physiological state and the other of whom has only psychological states.

The two are connected 'in series'. Stimuli are presented to the first Aunt, the physiological Aunt, who changes state accordingly and sends an appropriate stimulus to the second Aunt who also changes state and produces an output. The net effect is a change of both states and an output.

For example, suppose the two Aunts are in states 'sober' and 'foul' respectively. From Table 1.3, we can see that this corresponds to a mood of irritability. Now suppose that we wave a bottle of gin under the nose of the physiological Aunt. From Table 1.1, we can see that in such circumstances, Great Aunt Eugenia would take the gin and drink it and that her mood would change to 'unspeakable'. Table 1.3 shows that 'unspeakable' corresponds to 'drunk' and 'foul'. If the composite Aunt is to behave like the 'real' Aunt, then the physiological Aunt must change state to 'drunk' and signal the psychological Aunt not to change state but to take the gin and drink it.

Two ideas are being illustrated here. One of them is the idea of decomposition; in some circumstances we may implement a machine with a network of smaller ones. The other idea is that of implementation itself. In this case, we are talking about implementing a Great Aunt with a composite of Lesser Aunts, but we might equally well be interested in implementing the old lady physically, using logic circuitry, perhaps, or a programming language.

In either of these cases, it is surely legitimate to ask, 'Does my circuit [or whatever it is] correctly implement the abstract machine ?' We should not be permitted to answer such a question unless the phrase 'correctly implement' has been given a precise meaning.

This may be resolved into questions about the relationships between machines and between their input/output behaviour.

Let us elaborate on this. We have said that any machine M may be 'implemented' by a digital circuit C. C may itself be viewed as an abstract machine M_C. Because M and M_C are both abstract mathematical objects, we may give a *precise* definition of what we mean by one implementing the other. Furthermore, because this definition is precise, and because M and M_C are finite, we may *verify* that the implementation is correct.

The verification of correctness of both software and hardware depends on our being able to express precisely what we mean by correctness. This in turn must take place within a theory that is capable of describing the objects in question. The part of automata theory that we shall be considering in this book may be considered a theory of this kind in miniature, but one that is intimately related to modern theories of systems.

1.5 AUTOMATA THEORY IN GENERAL

In this section, we shall describe briefly aspects of automata theory not covered in this book. The first concerns *formal languages*.

Computer scientists will be familiar with the BNF mechanism for describing the syntax of a programming language. For example:

<*name*> ::= <*B*><*N*><*F*>

<*B*> ::= *Backus*

<*N*> ::= *Naur* | *Normal*

<*F*> ::= *Form*

generates the two phrases for which 'BNF' is reputed to stand. In general a formal language is a set of sequences of symbols belonging to the *alphabet* of the language (in programming languages, these are the 'basic symbols').

A set of BNF definitions determines what is known as a *formal grammar*. In general, a formal grammar (or phrase structure grammar) consists of:

(a) A set of so-called *terminal symbols* from which 'sentences' of the grammar are made ('cat', 'it', 'microprocessor', in English; 'GOTO', ';', 'THEN', in a typical programming language).

(b) A set of so-called *non-terminal symbols* (such as '<noun-phrase>', '<adverbial-clause>', in English; '<program>', '<statement>', in a typical programming language).

(c) A set of *production rules* (also known as *rewrite rules*). These determine transformations of sequences of terminal and non-terminal symbols by the substitution of subsequences for subsequences. For example, in the BNF grammar given above, one production rule says that any occurrence of <*N*> may be replaced by the string *Naur* or *Normal*.

(d) A distinguished non-terminal called the *start symbol*.

Starting with the start symbol, we may use the production rules to transform it into sequences of terminal and non-terminal sequences. A sequence derivable in this way that consists only of terminal symbols is a *sentence* of the grammar. The set of all such sentences is called the *language* of the grammar.

The study of formal languages was initiated by Noam Chomsky, who was interested in the structure of natural languages such as English. He classified formal grammars into what is known as the Chomsky hierarchy, in descending order of complexity; recursive languages (Type 0), context sensitive languages (Type 1), context free languages (Type 2) and regular languages (Type 3).

It has subsequently been shown that for each class of languages, there exists a class of automata such that a language is of type x if and only if it may be accepted (successfully parsed) by a machine of type x. In Chapter 2, we shall look at three of these classes of machines, namely Turing machines (Type 0), pushdown automata (Type 2), and finite state acceptors (Type 3).

A second area of application of automata theory is in the theory of *computable functions*. The central object here is the Turing machine, mentioned above as type 0 acceptors, which are named after the mathematician Alan Turing who invented them.

Turing actually invented the machine to solve a problem in mathematical logic: given a formal theory, is there a procedure for determining whether or not a given well-formed formula is a theorem of that theory? To answer this question, it is necessary to clarify the notion of a decision procedure. It is an algorithm which, when applied to an input formula, would stop after a finite amount of time and give an answer, either 'yes' or 'no'.

Turing's formalisation of the notion of algorithm was ingenious and intuitively striking. He considered what actually goes on when one is carrying out a computation on paper. This, he argued, is a process in which a sequence of symbols is manipulated in one of a finite number of ways according to a finite set of rules. The Turing machine abstracts from this observation. It is a machine acting on an infinite tape on which there may be symbols. In a manner depending on the currently scanned symbol and the machine's internal state, it will overwrite the tape and shift it either to the right or left. This models the human performing a calculation, crossing numbers out and replacing them with other ones according to the rules of an algorithm.

It is now accepted that a function is computable if and only if it may be implemented by a Turing machine.

As for the decision problem, it turned out to be unsolvable – no such decision procedure can exist. This turned out to be a consequence of another unsolvable problem. Turing showed that there could be no algorithm which could determine whether or not a given Turing machine would ever finish computing or not.

There will be more to say on Turing machines in the next chapter.

1.6 CONTENTS OF THE BOOK

Chapter 2 introduces the formal definition of machines and explains how their input/output behaviour may be described by functions from input streams to output streams. We also look at some related machines and their uses. In particular, we sketch a description of finite-state acceptors and pushdown automata in relation to formal languages and we also briefly look at Turing machines and computability.

Chapter 3 looks at hardware and software implementations of machines.

Chapter 4 considers the question of what it means for something to *be* an implementation of a machine and looks at some general structural relationships between machines.

Chapter 5 examines behavioural relationships. In particular, we pose the question, 'Under what circumstances may two machines be considered equivalent?' This leads to the notion of a reduced machine and the related and important idea of SP partition.

Chapter 6 considers two ways of combining machines together to make new machines; combining them to run synchronously in parallel, and combining them so that the output of one is piped into the input of the other. We then show that these two operations satisfy certain algebraic laws.

Chapters 7 and 8 consider the converse problem of decomposing a machine into two machines combined in parallel or in series. In both cases, the decomposition depends on the existence of SP partitions.

Chapter 9 looks at the set of SP partitions of a machine. These turn out to constitute an algebraic system called a lattice. We show that there is a collection of 'prime' SP partitions from which all others may be obtained by 'multiplying primes together', and gives methods for finding these 'primes' and performing the 'multiplication'.

Chapter 10 begins by looking for necessary and sufficient conditions for the existence of a serial decomposition into three machines. The discussion turns into an examination of the relationship between the lattice of SP partitions of a machine M and that of a machine which is a serial component of M. It turns out that this relationship is such that all information about serial and parallel decomposition into more than two machines may be obtained from the lattice of M.

Chapters 11 and 12 look briefly at two modern theories of distributed systems, net theory and the calculus of communicating systems.

EXERCISES

1 Great Aunt Eugenia's behaviour is beginning to worry the family and they have decided to intervene. They have observed that a fairly heavy meal interferes with her capacity for gin. By hypnotic suggestion and shock therapy, she has been conditioned so that when she is inebriated and offered food, she will eat it and her mood will change to the sober state corresponding to the previous intoxicated state. Draw a state graph and construct a flow table to describe the New Eugenia.

2 Suppose that the pipeline of Section 1.3 is in state $s_1 s_2 s_3$ and is given the sequence of inputs $i_1 i_2 \cdots i_n$. What will be its final state and what sequence of outputs will appear ?

3 Now that uranium has been discovered in large quantities in the small kingdom of Dystopia, the country suddenly has lots of good friends internationally, not to mention a great deal of cash. In order to dispose of this embarrassing surplus, the Dystopians have decided to completely automate their railway system. Being rather old fashioned, the Dystopians are great admirers of the British and therefore intend to base their new system on British Rail. In particular, their new *robot porters* are to be modelled according to the behaviour of a typical BR porter.

After a great deal of investigation, most of it under the leadership of Dr F. X. Reid, the committee charged with the formal specification of the robot porter has come up with the following:

'The British railway porter seems to move constantly between four different states: if he is not hiding somewhere, he is either sullen or what the British call "bloody-minded" – a term indicating hostility and wilful obstructiveness – but may be brought to a state of loathsome obsequiousness by being offered money.

'This being has a very small repertoire of actions, to whit: running away, swearing, shrugging the shoulders, sneering, moving into sight at the slightest suggestion of a tip and holding out his hand for the money, sniffing, accepting tips either ungraciously or with the touching of his forelock and *very occasionally* carrying someone's luggage – though after such unaccustomed exertion, he always goes into hiding to recover.

'The creature will refuse to react to any stimulus unless it be: being hailed by a traveller, being asked to carry something and being offered a tip. We should add that it distinguishes between large tips and small ones.

'Finally, the dynamics of the British Railway porter may be described by the following table [Table 1.4]. The few abbreviations should be self-evident.'

Table 1.4

	hail	ask	smalltip	largetip	hail	ask	smalltip	largetip
bloody	hiding	hiding	bloody	sullen	escape	sneer	sniff	sniff
sullen	bloody	bloody	bloody	obseq.	swear	swear	sneer	touch-f.
hiding	bloody	hiding	bloody	sullen	sneer	sneer	appear	appear
obseq.	sullen	hiding	sullen	obseq.	swear	carry	take	touch-f.

Construct a graphical representation of the robot porter and use it to answer the following questions.

(a) Suppose you are on a station platform with a very heavy suitcase and there is not a porter in sight. Describe a sequence of actions which will result in a porter appearing and agreeing to carry the case.

(b) Assuming that 1 Dystopian Corona constitutes a small tip and that 5 Coronae constitutes a large tip, what is the least you need spend ? What is the most ?

4 Dystopia's neighbour and rival, Dementia, frequently quarrels with her, but Dementia-watchers in Dystopia have come to realise that Dementia's diplomatic activity is, like everything else Dementian, conducted on very rigid lines. The following flow table (Table 1.5) almost speaks for itself. In the table, the states are: angry (A), simmering (S), tolerant (T) and friendly (F). Inputs are: offer some compromise (c), sign treaty of everlasting peace (p), expel Dementian diplomats (e), mobilise the army (m). Outputs are: accept the compromise (α), denounce as a Dystopian trick (δ), claim that the whole thing was really a Dementian initiative (κ), offer to send the Dementian table-tennis team on a 'friendly' tour (τ), expel Dystopian diplomats (ε), make a nuclear attack on Dystopia (ν), invade Dystopia (ι) and mobilise the army (μ).

(a) Suppose you are the Dystopian Foreign Minister. Dementia seems to be in a friendly mood. Your Prime Minister tells you, however, that this is because they are feeling pleased with the espionage of their local 'diplomats'. He tells you that he intends to expel some of these diplomats and that if the Dementians follow suit, he will expel some more and mobilize the army. Would you agree with this strategy ?

Table 1.5

	c	p	e	m	c	p	e	m
A	S	A	A	A	α	δ	ε	ν
S	T	T	A	A	α	δ	ε	ι
T	T	S	S	A	α	κ	ε	μ
F	F	T	S	A	α	τ	ε	μ

(b) Suppose that the Dementian's current state is not known. Give a sequence of three actions which are guaranteed to leave the Dementians tolerant, whatever their starting state.

(c) You are a Dementian plant in the Dystopian Foreign Ministry and you have been given the task of causing the Dystopians to provoke a nuclear war. Give a sequence of three actions which will do this whatever the initial mood of the Dementians is. Note: the army may only be mobilized once.

Chapter 2

Sundry Machines

Exit the wealthy worker 12345/c nye molesworth and all the machines go *A puff-a grab-sizzle-grunt-scree-ow-gosh-sizzle-screeeeee-ect.*

GEOFFREY WILLIAMS
Whizz for Atomms

2.1 AUNTS AND PIPELINES

In Chapter 1, we looked at examples of what we called machines (we shall also sometimes use the more august term *automata* – singular, *automaton*). You may have noticed that a machine is uniquely determined by five pieces of information:

(a) its states or moods;
(b) its inputs or stimuli;
(c) its outputs or responses;
(d) a rule describing how inputs cause the machine to change state;
(e) a rule saying what output will occur in any given state and for any given input.

We also saw that we could present any given machine using a table or labelled directed graph.

But what actually *is* a machine ? Is it a table or a graph ? Well, in a way, yes. If you were to write down a precise, mathematical description of what a 'table' of the kind displayed in the previous chapter actually is, for example, the result would be pretty close to the accepted mathematical definition of a machine.

Let us try to introduce this gently. A machine is determined by the five things listed above, so we shall define a machine to be a list (S,I,O,δ,β) where S represents the collection of states, I represents the collection of inputs, O represents the collection of outputs, δ stands for the rule that defines state changes and β represents the rule that determines outputs.

Now, we are not only saying that there are five ingredients to a machine, but we are giving them in a specific order, in which the first item will always be the state no matter what it is called. For example, if we were perversely to say that 'M is the machine (δ,S,I,β,O)', then δ would represent the states of M, S its inputs and so on.*

By the way, a list of five elements separated by commas and enclosed by parentheses is called an *ordered quintuple*.

So, a machine is an ordered quintuple of things, (S, I, O, δ, β), but what are S, I and so on ?

Well, S, I and O may be considered to be *sets*.† Furthermore, we shall require that they be finite, non-empty sets.

This leaves δ and β. What are they ? Let's take δ first.

A moment's thought should convince you that we know everything about δ if we know what the new state will be if we give M the input i when it is in state s. In other words, for each pair, (s, i), a new state s' is determined, depending only on s and i – and the fact that s is the state and i is the input. Again, we must be careful about writing them in order, so that we know that the first element in the *ordered pair* is always to be taken as the state and the second as the input, otherwise things could get confusing – if $s, i \in S \cap I$, for instance.

So δ can be regarded as a *function* which maps each (s, i) to a new state $\delta(s, i)$. The set of ordered pairs (s, i) with $s \in S$ and $i \in I$ is simply the *Cartesian product* of S with I, $S \times I$. Thus, δ is a function:

$$\delta : S \times I \rightarrow S$$

Likewise, we know everything about β if we know what output M will give on input i in state s. Each pair (s, i) determines an output o. β may also be regarded as a *function*:

$$\beta : S \times I \rightarrow O$$

which maps each (s, i) to an output $o = \beta(s, i)$.

And that's that ! To quote an answer to the exam question in which a certain bibulous relative made her first public appearance; 'Great Aunt Eugenia, like so many ladies of her age, is a Mealy Automaton'.

2.2 MEALY AUTOMATA

2.2.1 Definition

A *Mealy type sequential machine* is an ordered quintuple $M = (S, I, O, \delta, \beta)$ where:

---

* However, see convention (2.2.3).

† A review of the set theory that we shall be using is to be found in the appendix.

(a) S is a finite, non-empty set of states;
(b) I is a finite, non-empty set of inputs;
(c) O is a finite, non-empty set of outputs;
(d) $\delta: S \times I \rightarrow S$ is the state transition function;
(e) $\beta: S \times I \rightarrow O$ is the output function.

2.2.2 Example

We shall illustrate this by defining Great Aunt Eugenia in the above style. Eugenia is a machine (S, I, O, δ, β) where the sets and functions are given below.

$$S = \{asleep, genial, irritable, maudlin, unspeakable\}$$

$$I = \{ghetto\text{-}b, video, gin\}$$

$$O = \{wake, snore, harangue, refuse, drink, cackle, snipe, collapse\}$$

$$\delta(asleep, ghetto\text{-}b) = genial \quad \delta(asleep, video) = asleep$$
$$\delta(asleep, gin) = asleep$$
$$\delta(genial, ghetto\text{-}b) = irritable \quad \delta(genial, video) = genial$$
$$\delta(genial, gin) = maudlin$$
$$\delta(irritable, ghetto\text{-}b) = irritable \quad \delta(irritable, video) = genial$$
$$\delta(irritable, gin) = unspeakable$$
$$\delta(maudlin, ghetto\text{-}b) = unspeakable \quad \delta(maudlin, video) = maudlin$$
$$\delta(maudlin, gin) = asleep$$
$$\delta(unspeakable, ghetto\text{-}b) = unspeakable \quad \delta(unspeakable, video) = maudlin$$
$$\delta(unspeakable, gin) = asleep$$
$$\beta(asleep, ghetto\text{-}b) = wake \quad \beta(asleep, video) = snore$$
$$\beta(asleep, gin) = snore$$
$$\beta(genial, ghetto\text{-}b) = harangue \quad \beta(genial, video) = refuse$$
$$\beta(genial, gin) = drink$$
$$\beta(irritable, ghetto\text{-}b) = harangue \quad \beta(irritable, video) = cackle$$
$$\beta(irritable, gin) = drink$$

$\beta(maudlin, ghetto\text{-}b) = snipe \quad \beta(maudlin, video) = cackle$

$\beta(maudlin, gin) = collapse$

$\beta(unspeakable, ghetto\text{-}b) = snipe \quad \beta(unspeakable, video) = cackle$

$\beta(unspeakable, gin) = collapse$

2.2.3 Convention

When we need to talk about several machines, we shall use subscripts or apostrophes. We make the rule that the subscript or apostrophe is inherited by the components of the machine. Thus the machine M_3 will be the quintuple $(S_3, I_3, O_3, \delta_3, \beta_3)$ and the machine M' will be $(S', I', O', \delta', \beta')$. This convention will save us the bother of having to write out the sets and functions each time.

There are two common ways of specifying a Mealy automaton, by its *flow table* and its *state graph*. We have already seen examples of these in Chapter 1, but it does no harm to look at the things again, now we know what machines are supposed to be.

2.2.4 Example

We illustrate with the following Mealy machine, M, where:

$$S = \{1,2\} \quad I = \{a, +, ;\} \quad O = \{?, !\}$$

and the functions δ and β are given by:

$$\delta(1,a) = 2 \quad \delta(1,+) = 1 \quad \delta(1,;) = 1$$

$$\delta(2,a) = 1 \quad \delta(2,+) = 1 \quad \delta(2,;) = 1$$

$$\beta(1,a) = ! \quad \beta(1,+) = ? \quad \beta(1,;) = ?$$

$$\beta(2,a) = ? \quad \beta(2,+) = ! \quad \beta(2,;) = !$$

The flow table is illustrated below; it is almost self-explanatory. It consists of two tables side by side. In each table, rows are labelled by states and columns are labelled by inputs. If $s \in S$ and $i \in I$ then in the left hand table, the entry in the intersection between row s and column i is $\delta(s, i)$ and the corresponding entry in the right hand table is $\beta(s, i)$. Note the conciseness of the flow table representation compared with the explicit definition of states and function given previously. Note also that in

Table 2.1. The flow table of a Mealy machine

	a	+	;	a	+	;
1	2	1	1	!	?	?
2	1	1	1	?	!	!

the table input and state sets are given explicitly. Is the same true for the output set ? Is it true if β is required to be surjective ?

The state graph of M is pictured in Fig. 2.1. It is a labelled directed graph in which:

(a) there is a node for each element s of S, labelled s; and

(b) if $i \in I$ and $s \in S$ with

$$\delta(s,i) = s' \text{ and } \beta(s,i) = o$$

then there is an arc from s to s' labelled $\frac{i}{o}$.

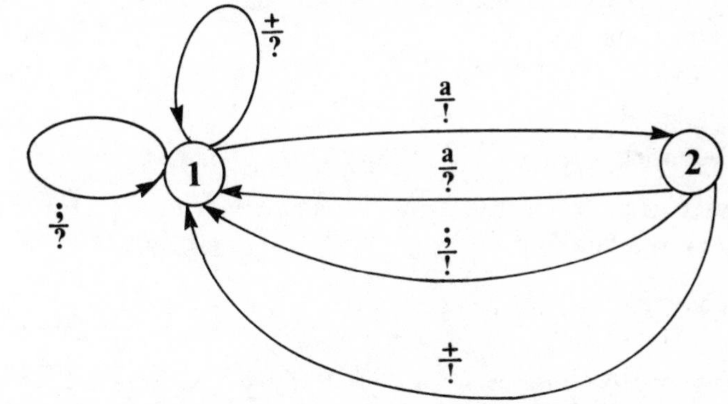

Fig. 2.1. The state graph of a Mealy machine

Intuitively, the machine operates as follows. From a given state s, a sequence of inputs

$$i_1 i_2 ... i_n$$

is given to the machine. These cause it to change state from $s_0 = s$ successively to states $s_1, s_2, ... s_n$, where for each $k \in \{1,..,n\}$:

$$s_k = \delta(s_{k-1}, i_k).$$

For Mealy machines, an output occurs during each transition, that is, we obtain a sequence of outputs $o_1 o_2 ... o_n$, where for each $k \in \{2,..,n\}$:

$$o_k = \beta(s_{k-1}, i_k).$$

Thus, for a given initial state and a sequence of inputs there is defined a sequence of outputs.

The example Mealy machine above was constructed as a simple parser. The two outputs may be thought of as representing a condition of error ('?') or absence of error ('!'). Starting in state 1, the machine gives no '?' output so long as the input sequence is of the form

$$a + ... + a \, ; \, a + ...$$

where there may be zero or more '+'s occurring in sequences separated by ';'. Try it.

We may see, then, that a machine determines, for each starting state, a *function* between the set of all possible input sequences and the set of all possible output sequences.

Let us be more precise.

2.2.5 Definition

Suppose X is a non-empty set. We define a *string* (or *word* or *sequence*) over X to be a function

$$x : \{1,...,n\} \rightarrow X$$

for some positive integer n. n is called the *length* of x and denoted $lnth(x)$. If $n = 0$, then we make the convention that $\{1,...,n\} = \varnothing$ and the unique function $x : \varnothing \rightarrow X$ will be denoted ε and called the *null* or *empty* string. Thus $lnth(\varepsilon) = 0$.

The set of strings over X is denoted X^*.

The informal notion of a string, say in ALGOL or BASIC, is of a sequence of characters. We may think of x as denoting the sequence $x(1)...x(n)$ and indeed shall use this way of talking about strings. Thus, by 'the string $a_1...a_n$', we mean the function x whose domain is $\{1,...,n\}$ and such that $x(i) = a_i$ for $i = 1,...,n$.

Note also that each element $a \in X$ determines a unique string x with $lnth(x) = 1$ and $x_1 = a$. To save time, we shall call this string 'a'.

Strings may be familiar to you as a programming language datatype. If so, then you will remember that there are a number of operations and relations on strings. One important operation is *concatenation*. Suppose $x, y \in X^*$, then their concatenation, written $x.y$ is the string z with $lnth(z) = lnth(x) + lnth(y)$ satisfying:

$$z(i) = \begin{cases} x(i) & \text{if } i \leq lnth(x) \\ y(i - lnth(x)) & \text{if } i > lnth(x) \end{cases}$$

Note that for every string $x \in X^*$, $\varepsilon.x = x.\varepsilon = x$.

Less formally and, perhaps, more comprehensibly, if $x = a_1 \cdots a_n$ and $y = b_1 \cdots b_m$ then $x.y = a_1 ... a_n b_1 ... b_m$.

Now that we have a more precise idea of what a sequence is, we can be more precise about the operation of machines. For example, a sequence of inputs is an element of I^*. If $x \in I^*$ then, as we have seen, from a given state s, M determines a string $y \in O^*$ and a new state $s' \in S$. We write $\delta^*(s,x) = s'$ and $\beta^*(s,x) = y$. Formally, we may define these functions *recursively*. If x is a string, then either $x = \varepsilon$ or $x = a.x'$, with $a \in X$ and $x' \in X^*$.

2.2.6 Definition

Let M be a Mealy machine. Let $s \in S$, $a \in I$ and $x \in I^*$. We define functions $\delta^* : S \times I^* \to S$ and $\beta^* : S \times I^* \to O^*$ by:

$$\delta^*(s,\varepsilon) = s \quad \delta^*(s, a.x') = \delta^*(\delta(s,a), x')$$

$$\beta^*(s,\varepsilon) = \varepsilon \quad \beta^*(s, a.x') = \beta(s,a).\beta^*(\delta(s,a), x')$$

2.2.7 Example

We take M to be Great Aunt Eugenia, and work out her response to the sequence *ghetto-b gin ghetto-b* from state *asleep*, described informally in Chapter 1.

$$\begin{aligned} &\delta^*(\textit{asleep}, \textit{ghetto-b gin ghetto-b}) \\ &= \delta^*(\delta(\textit{asleep}, \textit{ghetto-b}), \textit{gin ghetto-b}) \\ &= \delta^*(\textit{genial}, \textit{gin ghetto-b}) = \delta^*(\delta(\textit{genial}, \textit{gin}), \textit{ghetto-b}) \\ &= \delta^*(\textit{maudlin}, \textit{ghetto-b}) = \delta^*(\delta(\textit{maudlin}, \textit{ghetto-b}), \varepsilon) \\ &= \delta^*(\textit{unspeakable}, \varepsilon) = \textit{unspeakable} \end{aligned}$$

while for outputs:

$$\begin{aligned}
&\beta^*(\mathit{asleep}, \mathit{ghetto\text{-}b\ \ gin\ \ ghetto\text{-}b}) \\
&= \beta(\mathit{asleep}, \mathit{ghetto\text{-}b}).\beta^*(\delta(\mathit{asleep}, \mathit{ghetto\text{-}b}), \mathit{gin\ \ ghetto\text{-}b}) \\
&= \mathit{wake}\ \ \beta^*(\mathit{genial}, \mathit{gin\ \ ghetto\text{-}b}) \\
&= \mathit{wake}\ \ \beta(\mathit{genial}, \mathit{gin}).\beta^*(\delta(\mathit{genial}, \mathit{gin}), \mathit{ghetto\text{-}b}) \\
&= \mathit{wake\ \ drink}\ \ \beta^*(\mathit{maudlin}, \mathit{ghetto\text{-}b}) \\
&= \mathit{wake\ \ drink}\ \ \beta(\mathit{maudlin}, \mathit{ghetto\text{-}b}).\beta^*(\delta(\mathit{maudlin}, \mathit{ghetto\text{-}b}), \varepsilon) \\
&= \mathit{wake\ \ drink\ \ snipe}\ \ \beta^*(\mathit{unspeakable}, \varepsilon) \\
&= \mathit{wake\ \ drink\ \ snipe}\ \ \varepsilon = \mathit{wake\ \ drink\ \ snipe}
\end{aligned}$$

As we saw in Section 1.5, automata theory derives from a number of sources and various types of machine have been defined according to their intended application. This book would be incomplete without *some* reference to other types of machine, and some of them are described in the following sections.

On the other hand, we are chiefly concerned with the structure of Mealy machines and so we do not spend *too* much time on the others. Accordingly, our treatment of them will be somewhat terser than that of Mealy machines.

For more details, the reader is directed to the notes at the end of the chapter.

2.3 MOORE MACHINES

The second type of machine we look at resembles the Mealy machine except that in *this* case, output occurs *after* a transition and depends only on the new state of the machine.

2.3.1 Definition

A *Moore type sequential machine* is an ordered quintuple $M = (S, I, O, \delta, \lambda)$ where:

(a) S is a finite, non-empty set of states;
(b) I is a finite, non-empty set of inputs;
(c) O is a finite, non-empty set of outputs;
(d) $\delta: S \times I \to S$ is the state transition function;
(e) $\lambda: S \to O$ is the output function.

Informally, a Moore machine works as follows. If it is in a state $s \in S$ and an input $i \in I$ is given to it, then it will change state to $s' = \delta(s, i)$ after which it generates the output $\lambda(s')$.

We may also define a Moore machine using flow tables and state graphs. The main differences reflect those between the two types of automata. As output depends merely on state, in the flow table the output table has only one column. Similarly, in the state graph the outputs are associated with states rather than transitions. In the graph,

(a) there is a node for each element s of S, labelled $\frac{s}{\lambda(s)}$;

(b) if $\delta(s, i) = s'$ then there is an arc from s to s' labelled i.

The behaviour of Moore machines may be described formally as for Mealy machines.

2.3.2 Definition

Let M be a Moore machine. Let $s \in S$, $a \in I$ and $x \in I^*$. We define functions $\delta^* : S \times I^* \rightarrow S$ and $\lambda^* : S \times I^* \rightarrow O^*$ by:

$$\delta^*(s, \varepsilon) = s \quad \delta^*(s, ax') = \delta^*(\delta(s, a), x')$$

$$\lambda^*(s, \varepsilon) = \varepsilon \quad \lambda^*(s, ax') = \lambda(\delta(s, a)).\lambda^*(\delta(s, a), x')$$

2.4 STATE MACHINES

Mealy and Moore machines abstractly model input/output devices and, as we shall see in Chapter 3 in the case of Mealy machines, may be used in the design of digital devices. In the next two types of machine that we consider here, the main interest is in their state-transition behaviour. The first, the state machines are Mealy and Moore machines without outputs; the second, the pushdown automata, are state machines provided with memory in the form of a stack.

In both cases, any input sequence drives the machines from a given initial state to some final state. With each machine is associated a set of 'good' states. Thus, we may distinguish a set of input sequences which drive the machine to 'good' states. This set is the *language accepted by the machine*.

The reader may have met a concrete example of such a phenomenon in the guise of a syntax checker. This infuriating creature takes in a sequence of input symbols (the basic symbols of your program) and announces whether the sequence is a good string (the program parses correctly) or not. In the latter case, if you're lucky, it gives a list of error messages. If you're *really* lucky, these are pertinent and comprehensible.

Now to business.

2.4.1 Definition

A *state machine* is an ordered triple $M = (S, I, \delta)$, where S, I and δ satisfy

(a) S is a finite, non-empty set of states;

(b) I is a finite, non-empty set of inputs;

(c) $\delta : S \times I \to S$ is the state transition function.

State machines may be described in flow tables and state graphs just as Moore and Mealy machines. For example, Table 2.2 gives the flow table of a state machine. Similarly, we may define the state change defined by a sequence of inputs:

$$\delta^*(s,\varepsilon) = s \qquad \delta^*(s, ax') = \delta^*(\delta(s,a), x')$$

We may now amplify the remarks made at the beginning of this section about the connection between state machines and formal languages. A formal language with alphabet A is a set $L \subseteq A^*$. State machines act as *recognizers* for certain types of language.

2.4.2 Example

We illustrate with a machine derived from that of example 2.2.4, which we explained would continue to deliver an output ! when started out in state 1 provided that the sequence of inputs continued to be of the form :

$$a + \ldots + a\,;\, a + \ldots$$

We shall modify it so that

(a) it has no outputs;

(b) there is a special *initial state* and a special *final state*. These are such that if the machine is started up in its initial state and given an input sequence, then the machine will end up in its final state if and only if the input is of the form a; or $a + \ldots + a$;

(a) means that the machine will be a state machine. To achieve (b), we introduce two new states 3 and 4. 3 will be a 'fail' state: as soon as a syntax error occurs, the machine is sent into state 3. 4 is the final state. It is obviously reachable from state 2 via a ';' transition. Since any further input would cause a syntax error, all further transitions from state 4 would lead to state 3. The machine is given in Table 2.2.

Table 2.2. The flow table of a state machine

	a	$+$	;
1	2	3	3
2	3	1	4
3	3	3	3
4	3	3	3

We may then define the set of strings accepted by M from 1 with final state 4 to be the set:

$$\mathbf{L}(M) = \{x \in I^* \mid \delta^*(1,x) = 4\}.$$

This example illustrates a connection between automata and formal languages. To be precise, define.

2.4.3 Definition

A *recognizer** is an ordered triple $\mathbf{R} = (M, s_o, F)$, where
(a) M is a state machine;†
(b) $s_o \in S$ is the *initial state* of $\mathbf{R}$;
(c) $F \subseteq S$ is the set of *final states* of $\mathbf{R}$;

Given a recognizer, we may define the language it accepts, just as for the above example.

2.4.4 Definition

Let $\mathbf{R} = (M, s_o, F)$ be a recognizer. The language accepted or recognized by $\mathbf{R}$ is defined to be:

$$\mathbf{L}(\mathbf{R}) = \{x \in I^* \mid \delta^*(s_o, x) \in F\}.$$

There is an important theorem, due to Kleene, that says that a language may be accepted by a recognizer if it is *regular*. Regular languages are defined as follows.

* Recognizers are also known as Deterministic Finite State Automata. We prefer to reserve the word 'automata' to mean machines in general.

† In general, M will be a partial state machine, that is $\delta(s, i)$ may not be defined for some values of s and i. As our interest in acceptors is peripheral and since we wish to keep things simple, we will not go into this here.

2.4.5 Definition

Let A be a set.

(a) If $L \subseteq A^*$ is finite then L is regular

(b) If $L_1, L_2 \subseteq A^*$ are regular then so is $L_1 \cup L_2$.

(c) If $L_1, L_2 \subseteq A^*$ are regular then so is $L_1 L_2 = \{x_1 x_2 \mid x_1 \in L_1 \text{ and } x_2 \in L_2\}$.

(d) If $L \subseteq A^*$ is regular then so is L^*, where $L^* = \bigcup_{n=0}^{\infty} L^n$ and $L^0 = \{\varepsilon\}$ and $L^{n+1} = L.L^n$.

For example, if we set **R** = $(M, 1, \{4\})$, with M as in example 2.4.2, then **L(R)** = $\{a+\}^*.\{a;\}$.

2.5 PUSH-DOWN AUTOMATA

All the machines we have looked at so far have had a finite amount of memory; each could be in one of a finite number of internal states at any time. This is reflected in the limitation of the kind of language that finite state acceptors accept.

They could not, for example, accept a language of algebraic expressions involving multiply-nested parentheses; the question as to whether a ')' symbol is acceptable depends partially on the number of '(' that have already been read and so the machine would need to have at least that number of states. Since there is no limit to the number of '('s one might need in an expression* the machine would need to have an unbounded number of states.

The next class of machines we look at have additional memory, in the form of a *push-down stack*. It would be capable of parsing an expression with nested parentheses. Every time it received an open parenthesis it would push it onto the stack and every time it received a close parenthesis it would pop the stack, unless the stack were empty. In this case, the machine would halt and a syntax error be reported.

2.5.1 Definition

A non-deterministic push-down automaton (pda) is a 7-tuple $P = (S, I, V, \delta, s_o, v_o, F)$, where:

(a) S is a finite, non-empty set of *states*;

* Ask any LISP programmer.

(b) I is a finite, non-empty set of *inputs*;
(c) V is a finite, non-empty set of *stack symbols*;
(d) δ is the *push-down function*, $\delta : S \times V \times (I \cup \{\varepsilon\}) \to \underline{P}(S \times V^*)$,* where $\delta(s, v, i)$ is a finite set for each (s, v, i);
(e) $s_o \in S$ is the *start state*;
(f) $v_o \in V$ is the *start symbol* (initially, the only symbol on the stack);
(g) $F \subseteq S$ is the set of final states.

There are a number of important differences between pda's and the machines we have looked at so far. First, we have memory in the form of a stack. We shall use strings $X \in V^*$ to denote contents of the stack, where it is to be understood that if $X = a_1 \ldots a_n$, then a_1 is the symbol at the top of the stack, a_2, the symbol beneath it and so on. We shall write $Top(X)$ to denote the top of the stack, and $Rest(X)$ to denote the rest of the stack whose contents are X. Thus, in our example, $Top(X) = a_1$ and $Rest(X) = a_2 \ldots, a_n$. If the stack is empty, that is, $X = \varepsilon$, then we shall set $Top(X) = \varepsilon$ and $Rest(X) = \varepsilon$.

Next, we note that δ depends on three parameters (s, v, i) and maps each such triple to a set. The significance of this is as follows. The behaviour of the machine is determined by three things; the current state, s, the current input, i, and the symbol that is currently at the head of the stack, v. If $(s', X) \in \delta(s, v, i)$, then the machine *may* change state to s' and replace the symbol at the top of the stack by X. We wrote 'may'. The machine may change state to any state s' with $(s', X) \in \delta(s, v, i)$; the choice is purely random. Hence the name 'non-deterministic push-down automaton'.†

Also note that state changes may take part without any input, that is, state changes determined by $\delta(s, v, \varepsilon)$. But no changes may take place if the stack is empty, for δ is not defined for such a contingency.

Now let us formally define the behaviour of a pda. We note first of all that the internal 'state' of a pda is determined by two things, the state, $s \in S$ and the current contents of the stack, $X \in V^*$. We call a pair (s, X) a *configuration* of the machine. A sequence of inputs will drive the machine through a sequence of configurations as we shall explain.

We shall write $(s, X) \vdash^x (s', Y)$ to denote that the input sequence x may drive the machine from configuration (s, X) to configuration (s', Y).

---

* If X is a set, then $\underline{P}(X)$ denotes its powerset. See appendix.

† Of course, we may define a class of deterministic push-down automata, in which δ is a function, but these are not as interesting as the non-deterministic variety.

2.5.2 Definition

Let $s, s', s'' \in S$, $i \in I$, $x \in I^*$ and $X, Y \in V^*$ with $X \neq \varepsilon$, then:

(a) If $(s', Y) \in \delta(s, Top(X), \varepsilon)$, then $(s, X) \mid\!-^{\varepsilon} (s', Y.Rest(X))$.

(b) If $(s', Y) \in \delta(s, Top(X), i)$, then $(s, X) \mid\!-^{i} (s', Y.Rest(X))$.

(c) If $(s, X) \mid\!-^{a} (s', X')$ and $(s', X') \mid\!-^{x} (s'', X'')$ then $(s, X) \mid\!-^{a.x} (s'', X'')$.

For any $s, s' \in S$ and $x \in I^*$ and $X, X' \in V^*$, $(s, X) \mid\!-^{x} (s', X')$ if and only if this fact may be deduced using (a), (b) or (c). Thus, for example, $(s, X) \mid\!-^{x} (s', X')$ is not defined if $X = \varepsilon$.

A string x is *accepted* by the pda if and only if there exists $s_f \in F$ and $X \in V^*$ such that $(s_o, v_o) \mid\!-^{x} (s_f, X)$. $\mathbf{L}(M)$, the language accepted by M is the set of all strings accepted by M.

It is known that a pda accepts a language if and only if it belongs to the class of languages called the *context-free* languages. We have no time to go into this here,* but it is also known that every regular language is context-free but not vice versa. The usual example of a context-free language which is not regular is $\{a^n b^n\}$, where n ranges over the positive integers.

2.6 TURING MACHINES

A Turing machine may be thought of as a state machine with memory in the form of a tape divided into squares, each of which is either blank or contains a special *tape symbol*. The machine has a reading head which scans the tape and according to the current state and currently scanned symbol will:

(a) overwrite the tape symbol;

(b) move the tape either to the right or to the left;

(c) change its internal state.

However, it may be the case that no change is possible. This will certainly happen if a tape move will cause the reading head to go off the end. Actually, the tape is supposed to be infinite to the right, so only left moves can be impossible. But also, it is possible that a transition is not defined for some configuration of machine and tape, that is, the function that defines transitions is, in general, *partial*. Configurations from which no move is possible are known as dead or final configurations.

Turing machines were devised as an abstract model of computation. If a sequence of tape symbols is regarded as representing a number or sequence of numbers, then a machine may be regarded as executing an

---

* See, for example, Rayward-Smith (1983).

algorithm which takes as input the initial tape sequence and whose output is represented by the sequence present on the tape when the machine reaches a dead state – if it ever does. As we shall see shortly, this may never happen.

There are several things to note. Firstly, it is generally accepted that functions are computable if and only if they may be implemented by Turing machines. Other notions of computability have since turned out to be equivalent to computability by Turing machines. The postulate that '*computability = Turing computability*' is known as *Turing's Thesis*.

Secondly, there is no guarantee that the machine will ever stop. (Any reader who has inadvertently programmed an infinite loop will be used to this idea.) The important point here is that there can be no procedure for determining whether or not this will happen in any given case. This state of affairs is known as the 'Undecidability of the Halting Problem'. We will not go into details here, except to remark that if there *were* such a procedure, then, by Turing's thesis, it would be computable using a Turing machine – where inputs are suitably encoded descriptions of Turing machines. The trick, roughly, is to modify this machine so that it loops on deciding halting and halts otherwise. The machine is then given a description of itself as input. The result is paradoxical; hence no such machine can exist.

Finally, we have observed that we can use encoded descriptions of Turing machines as input to other machines. Turing described what he called a *Universal* machine, which could take an encoded description of any Turing machine and simulate it. This Universal machine is an abstract model of a a computer – invented a decade before the first computers were built!

Let us now formalise all this.

2.6.1 Definition

A (deterministic) Turing machine is a 4-tuple (S, T, δ, s_o), where:

(a) S is a finite, non-empty set of *states*;

(b) T is a finite, non-empty set of *tape symbols*, including the symbol #, which represents the 'contents' of a blank square;

(c) δ is a *partial* function $\delta: S \times T \to S \times T \times \{\mathbf{R}, \mathbf{L}\}$;

(d) $s_o \in S$ is the *initial state*.

2.6.2 Definition

A configuration is a 4-tuple, (x,s,t,y), where $x \in T^*$ represents the sequence of symbols to the left of the reading head, $s \in S$ represents the current state, $t \in T$ represents the symbol on the tape square currently under the reading head and $y \in T^*$ represents the contents of the tape to the right of the reading head. Since the tape extends infinitely to the right and only a finite number of squares will not be blank, we assume that $y \neq y'.\#$ for any y'. That is, we represent the contents of the tape by a finite sequence ending in a non-blank character.

c is an *initial configuration* if it is of the form (ε, s_o, t, y), some t, y.

Now we shall formally define a *move* or *transition* of the machine.

2.6.3 Definition

Let c, c' be configurations. We define what it means for c to move to c' in one step, written as $c \mid\!- c'$.

(a) If $c = (x,s,t,y)$ and $\delta(s,t) = (s', t', \mathbf{R})$, then $c \mid\!- c'$ if $c' = (x.t', s', t'', y')$, where $t''.y' = y$ if $y \neq \varepsilon$ and $t'' = \#$ and $y' = \varepsilon$ if $y = \varepsilon$.

(b) If $c = (x,s,t,y)$ and $\delta(s,t) = (s', t', \mathbf{L})$, then $c \mid\!- c'$ if $c' = (x', s', t'', t'.y')$, where $x'.t'' = x$ if $x \neq \varepsilon$. If $x = \varepsilon$, then c is a dead state. In general c is a dead state if $c \mid\!- c'$ for no c'.

Let us explain (a). The transition function requires that the current square be overwritten by t' and then that the tape be moved to the right. Thus, the current square now becomes the leftmost part of the left part of the tape, which accordingly becomes $x.t'$. If the right part of the tape is not blank, then $y = t''.y'$. The rightmost part moves under the reading head making t'' the new currently scanned symbol. The right part now has t'' stripped from it and becomes y'.

2.6.4 Definition

We say that there is a *computation* from c to c' if $c \mid\!-^* c'$, where

(a) $c \mid\!-^* c$;

(b) $c \mid\!-^* c'$ if there exists c'' such that $c \mid\!- c''$ and $c \mid\!-^* c'$.

We may now explain how Turing machines determine functions.

2.6.5 Definition

Let M be a Turing machine, then M determines a partial function $f_M:T^* \to T^*$, such that $f_M(x)$ is defined and equals y if M has a computation $(\varepsilon, s_o, \#, x) \mid\!-^* (x', q, \#, y)$, some x', q, where $(x', q, \#, y)$ is a dead state.

Functions such as f_M are known as computable functions.

EXERCISES

1 Implement Great Aunt Eugenia as a Moore automaton. Can you discover a general construction that would implement a given Mealy machine as a Moore machine ?

2 Consider the machine whose flow table is given in Table 2.1. Give the output sequence when the initial state and input sequences are:
(a) 1 and $a\ +\ ;\ +\ a$
(b) 2 and $a\ +\ a\ :\ a\ ;\ a\ ;$
(c) 1 and $a\ +\ a\ :\ a\ ;\ a\ ;$

3 Prove that $\varepsilon.x = x = x.\varepsilon$ for all strings x.

4 The state table in Table 2.3 describes a simple robot that can be made to traverse a maze. It has sensors that register if there is something immediately ahead of it (input 'obs') or nothing ('free'). It responds by either turning through 90° to the right or left or moving forwards.

Construct the state graph of this automaton and explain informally the principles according to which it works. Describe the behaviour of the robot given that initially it is placed in the maze of Fig. 2.2:
(a) at the spot marked A facing north;
(b) at the spot B facing west;
You may assume that it moves one square at a time.

The next few exercises refer to example 2.4.2.

5 Prove by induction on n, that for any n; $\delta(1,(a+)^n) = 1$. Prove that $\delta(1,a;) = 4$. Deduce that for any n, $\delta(1,(a+)^n.a;) = 4$ and hence $\{a+\}^*.\{a;\} \subseteq \mathbf{L}(M)$.

6 Show that if $x \in I^*$ and $\delta(1,x) = 3$, then for every $y \in I^*$, $\delta(1,x.y) = 3$. Conclude that if $\delta(1,x) = 3$, then for no y do we have $x.y \in \mathbf{L}(M)$.

Table 2.3. A simple robot

	obs	free	obs	free
S1	S2	S1	left	forwards
S2	S3	S2	left	forwards
S3	S4	S3	left	forwards
S4	S5	S4	right	forwards
S5	S6	S5	right	forwards
S6	S1	S6	right	forwards

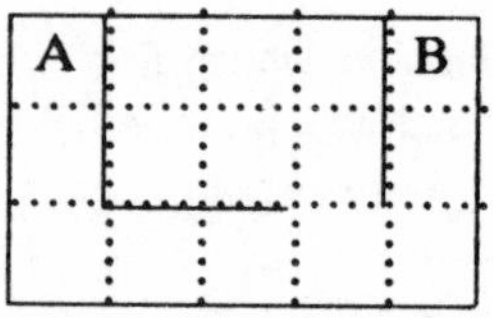

Fig. 2.2. A simple maze

7 Use **6** to show that if $i.x \in \mathbf{L}(M)$, with $i \in I$, then $i = a$ and that if $a.i.x \in \mathbf{L}(M)$, then either $i = +$ or $i = ;$. Show that if $a;.x \in \mathbf{L}(M)$, then $x = \varepsilon$. Show that if $a{+}x \in \mathbf{L}(M)$ then $x \in \mathbf{L}(M)$.
Conclude that if $x \in \mathbf{L}(M)$, then either $x = a;$ or there exists $y \in \mathbf{L}(M)$ such that $x = a{+}y$.

8 Use **5** and **7** to prove that $\{a+\}^*.\{a;\} = \mathbf{L}(M)$.

NOTES

The material in this book is largely drawn from the first few chapters of Hartmanis & Stearns (1966).

There is a copious literature on grammars and acceptors. Rayward-Smith (1983) provides a good introduction to finite state acceptors and push-down automata. His (1986) treats Turing machines, computability and complexity. Conway (1971) gives a lively account of experiments on Moore machines and Kleene's theorem. For a fuller account, the reader could consult Salomaa (1973) or Hopcroft & Ullman, (1969).

Chapter 3

Implementing Finite Automata

You can, if you like, talk about designing a machine...that would 'read' any book in five minutes, the equivalent of five years or ten years' 'reading' being obtained by merely turning a knob. This, however, is the cheap soulless approach of the times we live in. No machine can do the same work as the soft human fingers.

MYLES NA GOPALEEN
on 'Book-handling'

3.1 INTRODUCTION

The theory of Mealy automata provides us with a notation for abstractly specifying certain kinds of systems; finite-state, discrete, input/output systems. One of the tests of any specification notation is the ease with which specifications may be implemented. In this chapter, we shall see that any Mealy machine may be readily implemented in digital logic circuitry.

We also present a scheme for software implementation in a toy language called AUTRAN.*

3.2 IMPLEMENTING FUNCTIONS

It is likely that, whether you realise it or not, you already know how to implement Mealy automata with only one state. In that case, M determines a single function $f_M : I^* \to O^*$ given by $f_M(x) = \beta^*(s, x)$, where s is the unique state of M. Also, since we must have $\delta(s, i) = s$ for all i, we can see that for $a_1, \ldots, a_n \in I$,

$$f_M(a_1 \ldots a_n) = \beta(s, a_1) \ldots \beta(s, a_n)$$

Thus M may be implemented by a black box which gives an output $\beta(s, i)$ to a given input i.

* AUTRAN will be very objectionable to some people because of the presence in it of GOTO statements, but it is superior to the vast majority of programming languages in that it possesses a formal semantics.

Let us now consider an arbitrary function $f:I \to O$, where I and O are finite sets. The general scheme for the implementation of such a function is given in Fig. 3.1.

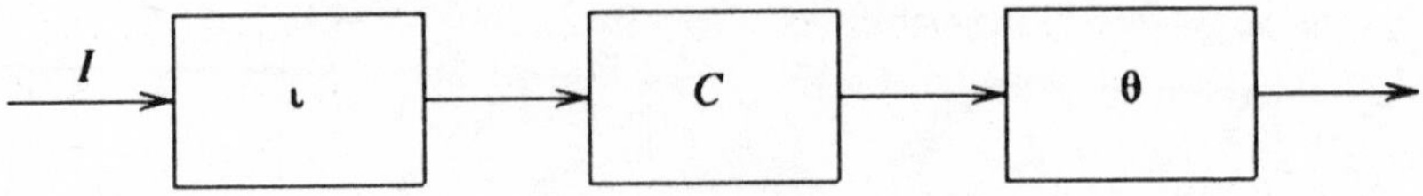

Fig. 3.1

Here, C is a logic circuit with n input lines and m output lines. An input i is received by the encoder ι, which translates it to voltages on the input lines. The circuitry in C is clocked and voltages are placed on C's output lines and are translated by θ into some output o.

We may usefully make this explanation more formal by considering the inputs and outputs of C as vectors. Thus an input to C would be a vector $\mathbf{v} = (v_1, ..., v_n)$ and an output would be a vector $\mathbf{w} = (w_1, ..., w_m)$, where each coordinate is either 0 or 1 and v_i is 0 (respectively 1) if the ith input line is low (respectively, high) and w_j is 0 (respectively 1) if the jth output line is low (respectively, high).

The set of n length vectors whose coordinates are either 0 or 1 is the n-fold Cartesian product, $\mathbf{B} \times \cdots \times \mathbf{B}$ (n times), where $\mathbf{B} = \{0, 1\}$, and which we shall write $\mathbf{B}^n$. Thus, we may regard ι and θ as determining functions $\iota I: \to \mathbf{B}^n$ and $\theta:\mathbf{B}^m \to O$, and C as determining a function $f_C:\mathbf{B}^n \to \mathbf{B}^m$.

An input i to the system is translated by ι to $\iota(i)$. C turns this into $f_C(\iota(i))$ and θ translates this into $\theta[f_C(\iota(i))]$. For the system to implement f correctly, we need

$$\theta[f_C(\iota(i))] = f(i), \ \textit{all}\ i \in I \qquad [3.1]$$

We may achieve such a system by following the recipe below. First, construct *injective* functions:

$$\iota:I \to \mathbf{B}^n \quad \omega:O \to \mathbf{B}^m$$

From ω, we may construct a function θ by defining $\theta(\mathbf{v}) = o$ if $\omega(o) = \mathbf{v}$ - the fact that ω is injective means that the o is unique - and letting $\theta(\mathbf{v})$ be any element of O if there is no o such that $\omega(o) = \mathbf{v}$. We now define:

$$f_C(\mathbf{v}) = \begin{cases} \omega(f(i)) & \text{if } \iota(i) = \mathbf{v} \\ \textit{anything} & \textit{otherwise} \end{cases} \qquad [3.2]$$

It is easy to check that ι, f_C and θ satisfy [3.1].

f_C may now be implemented using gate logic. We note that it determines m Boolean functions, $f_C^1,...,f_C^m$, where for each j, $f_C^j:\mathbf{B}^n \to \mathbf{B}$ is defined

$$f_C^j(\mathbf{v}) = w_j \text{ if } f_C(\mathbf{v}) = (w_1,...,w_m) \qquad [3.3]$$

Thus, given f_C as in [3.1], we may use [3.3] to construct m truth tables or Karnaugh maps to derive expressions for the f_C^j in disjunctive normal form (sum of min-terms) which may then be translated into logic circuitry in the usual way.

We note that:

(a) any function between finite sets may be implemented in this manner; and

(b) any such system determines a function between two finite sets.

3.3 IMPLEMENTATION OF MEALY AUTOMATA

If we now turn to Mealy machines with more than one state, then we see that half the work has been done already, since it is mostly a question of implementing the two functions δ and β and we know how to do this.

The main difference is the presence of S. States persist between steps of a machine; they need to be 'stored'. We therefore encode states as binary vectors and store these in an array of binary storage cells (for example, D-type flip-flops).

At each step of the machine, the contents of these cells are made available as inputs to the circuitry implementing the δ and β functions, together with encodings of the I input. Outputs from the δ circuitry reset the contents of the storage cells and outputs from the β box are decoded to elements of O. The resulting system is pictured in Fig. 3.2.

Before describing the construction formally, we give an example.

3.3.1 Example

We take the example of the simple parser of Chapter 2, which we shall call M_{parse}. For convenience, we reprint its flow table in Table 3.1. We encode each state, input and output as a binary sequence of an appropriate length. Substituting, the encoding for that which it encodes gives us a table

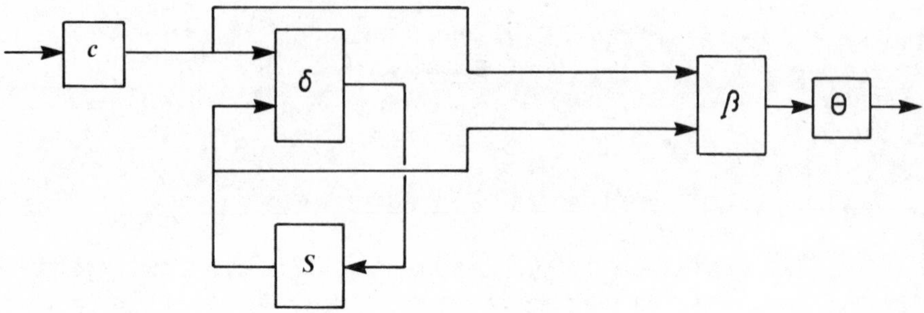

Fig. 3.2

Table 3.1. M_{parse}

	a	+	;	a	+	;
1	2	1	1	!	?	?
2	1	1	1	?	!	!

of the appropriate sort.

For this example, we construct the following encoding:

$$\alpha(1) = 0 \quad \iota(a) = 01 \quad \omega(!) = 0$$

$$\alpha(2) = 1 \quad \iota(+) = 10 \quad \omega(?) = 1$$

$$\iota(;) = 11$$

and replace each element in Table 3.1 by its encoding to give the Table 3.2. This gives us a new machine, which we shall call M_{code}.

Table 3.2. M_{code}

	01	10	11	01	10	11
0	1	0	0	0	1	1
1	0	0	0	1	0	0

This table determines two functions, which we shall call f_{code} and g_{code}, which implement δ_{parse} and β_{parse} respectively. f_{code} satisfies $f_{code}(b_1, b_2, b_3) = \delta_{code}(b_1, b_2 b_3)$.

g_{code} satisfies $g_{code}(b_1, b_2, b_3) = \beta_{code}(b_1, b_2 b_3)$

Table 3.3 gives the values of f_{code} and g_{code}.

Table 3.3. Table for f_{code} and g_{code}

y	$x1$	$x2$	$f_{code}(y, x1, x2)$	$g_{code}(y, x1, x2)$
0	0	1	1	0
0	1	0	0	1
0	1	1	0	1
1	0	1	0	1
1	1	0	0	0
1	1	1	0	0

Now, these truth tables are incomplete. f_{code} and g_{code} are not defined for certain values of $(y, x1, x2)$ – namely $(0, 0, 0)$ and $(1, 0, 0)$. Such values are known as *don't care conditions*, because we may fill them in any way we like. One way of completing Table 3.3 is given in Table 3.4. This gives two new functions $f_{circ} : \mathbf{B}^3 \to \mathbf{B}$ and $g_{circ} : \mathbf{B}^3 \to \mathbf{B}$.

Table 3.4. Truth table for f_{circ} and g_{circ}

y	$x1$	$x2$	$f_{circ}(y, x1, x2)$	$g_{circ}(y, x1, x2)$
0	0	0	1	0
0	0	1	1	0
0	1	0	0	1
0	1	1	0	1
1	0	0	0	1
1	0	1	0	1
1	1	0	0	0
1	1	1	0	0

From Table 3.4, we may derive the disjunctive normal form for the two functions:

$$f_{circ}(y, x_1, x_2) = \overline{y}.\overline{x}_1$$

$$g_{circ}(y, x_1, x_2) = \overline{y}.x_1 + y.\overline{x}_1$$

From these, the circuitry may be constructed, as given in Fig. 3.3.

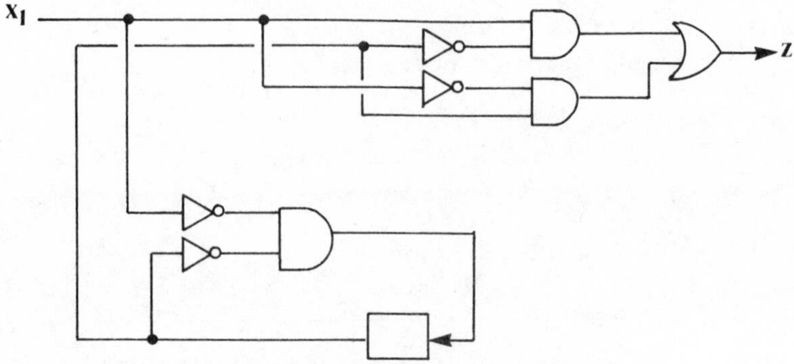

Fig. 3.3. Implementation of the parser

3.3.2 The General Construction

Now let us explain the general construction. Let M be a Mealy machine. The first thing to do is to construct encodings of the elements of S, I and O into the appropriate set $\mathbf{B}^k$, that is, we construct *injective* functions:

$$\alpha{:}S \to \mathbf{B}^l, \text{ where } 2^{l-1} < |S| \leq 2^l$$

$$\iota{:}I \to \mathbf{B}^m, \text{ where } 2^{m-1} < |I| \leq 2^m$$

$$\omega{:}O \to \mathbf{B}^n, \text{ where } 2^{n-1} < |O| \leq 2^n$$

We have chosen l, m and n to be as small as possible.

Now replace each element of the flow table by its encoding. This gives a new machine, which we shall denote by $M_{(\alpha,\iota,\omega)}$. Thus, $S_{(\alpha,\iota,\omega)} = \alpha(S)$, $I_{(\alpha,\iota,\omega)} = \iota(I)$ $O_{(\alpha,\iota,\omega)} = \omega(O)$ and the transition and output functions are given by:

$$\delta_{(\alpha,\iota,\omega)}(\alpha(s),\iota(i)) = \alpha(\delta(s,i))$$

$$\beta_{(\alpha,\iota,\omega)}(\alpha(s),\iota(i)) = \omega(\beta(s,i))$$

This squares with the informal idea of replacing each element by its encoding. For example, consider row s and column i. The entry in the next-state table will be $\delta(s,i)$. In the encoded machine, the row will be labelled by $\alpha(s)$ and the column by $\iota(i)$ and the entry will be $\alpha(\delta(s,i))$. Thus, $\delta_{(\alpha,\iota,\omega)}(\alpha(s),\iota(i)) = \alpha(\delta(s,i))$.

Note that since the three functions are injective, both $\delta_{(\alpha,\iota,\omega)}$ and $\beta_{(\alpha,\iota,\omega)}$ are well defined.

Next, observe that $\delta_{(\alpha,\iota,\omega)}{:}\alpha(S) \times \iota(I) \to \alpha(S)$ and that $\beta_{(\alpha,\iota,\omega)}{:}\alpha(S) \times \iota(I) \to \omega(O)$. We may extend them to functions $\delta_{circ}{:}\mathbf{B}^l \times \mathbf{B}^m \to \mathbf{B}^l$ and $\beta_{circ}{:}\mathbf{B}^l \times \mathbf{B}^m \to \mathbf{B}^n$, that is δ_{circ}, β_{circ} are any two functions such that whenever $\mathbf{u} = \alpha(s)$ and $\mathbf{v} = \iota(i)$ then $\delta_{(\alpha,\iota,\omega)}(\mathbf{u},\mathbf{v}) = \delta_{circ}(\mathbf{u},\mathbf{v})$ and $\beta_{(\alpha,\iota,\omega)}(\mathbf{u},\mathbf{v}) = \beta_{circ}(\mathbf{u},\mathbf{v})$.

Thus we have a new machine M_{circ}, where $S_{circ} = \mathbf{B}^l$ $I_{circ} = \mathbf{B}^m$ and $O_{circ} = \mathbf{B}^n$.

From M_{circ}, we obtain two functions, $f_{circ}:\mathbf{B}^{l+m} \to \mathbf{B}^l$ and $g_{circ}:\mathbf{B}^{l+m} \to \mathbf{B}^n$, defined by:

$$f_{circ}((u_1, ..., u_l, v_1, ..., v_m)) = \delta_{circ}((u_1, ..., u_l), (v_1, ..., v_m))$$

and

$$g_{circ}((u_1, ..., u_l, v_1, ..., v_m)) = \beta_{circ}((u_1, ..., u_l), (v_1, ..., v_m)).$$

From these we obtain $(l + n)$ functions $f^j_{circ}:\mathbf{B}^{l+m} \to \mathbf{B}$ and $g^j_{circ}:\mathbf{B}^{l+m} \to \mathbf{B}$ such that if:

$$f_{circ}((u_1, ..., u_l, v_1, ..., v_m)) = (w_1, ..., w_l)$$

then

$$f^j_{circ}((u_1, ..., u_l, v_1, ..., v_m)) = w_j$$

and if

$$g_{circ}((u_1, ..., u_l, v_1, ..., v_m)) = (w_1, ..., w_n)$$

then

$$g^j_{circ}((u_1, ..., u_l, v_1, ..., v_m)) = w_j.$$

These may be considered as Boolean functions for which gate logic may be derived in the usual manner.

3.3.3 Logic Circuitry as an Automaton

We have seen that any Mealy automaton may be implemented with a circuit of the type described in the previous section. We shall show that any such circuit may also be considered as a Mealy automaton.

Figure 3.4 illustrates the general circuit (we have omitted coders and decoders). The arrow labelled 'input' represents m input wires whose values we shall represent as binary vectors, $(x_1, ..., x_m)$, where x_j describes the logic value on the jth wire. The box S represents a set of l binary

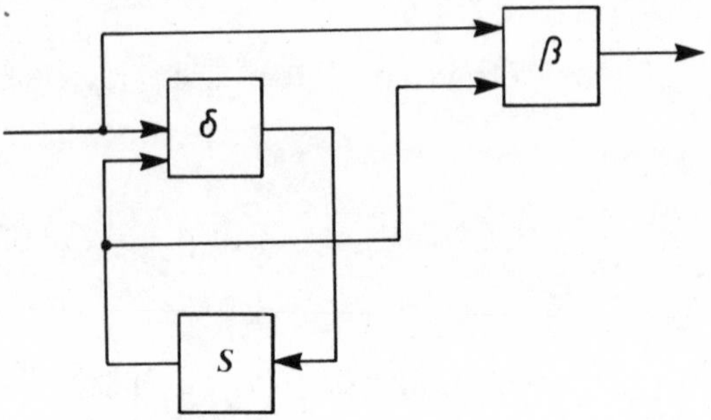

Fig. 3.4

storage cells, whose contents we shall represent as binary vectors, $(y_1, ..., y_l)$, where y_j describes the contents of the jth cell. The box labelled δ consists of a system of logic gates with inputs from the input wires and wires from S. The gates are arranged so that there are no loops, that is, there is no route through the network of gates in δ starting and ending at any particular gate. The arrow from δ to S represents a set of at most l wires carrying output from δ which resets the contents of S. In a similar way, the β box contains an arrangement of gates without loops whose inputs come from S and from the input wires. The arrow labelled *output* represents a set of n output wires.

Since there are no loops in δ, the voltage on each of these wires will be a Boolean function of the $l + m$ values $(y_1, ..., y_l, x_1, ..., x_m)$. We may therefore think of δ as an implementation of l functions.

$$f_1(y_1, ..., y_l, x_1, ..., x_m)$$

$$\cdots$$

$$f_j(y_1, ..., y_l, x_1, ..., x_m)$$

$$\cdots$$

$$f_m(y_1, ..., y_l, x_1, ..., x_m)$$

If the contents of S are $(y_1, ..., y_l)$ and inputs to the circuit are given by the vector $(x_1, ..., x_m)$, then after one clock pulse, the contents of S will be $(Y_1, ..., Y_l)$, where for each j, $1 \leq j \leq l$,

$$Y_j = f_j(y_1, ..., y_l, x_1, ..., x_m)$$

If we interpret vectors $(y_1, ..., y_l)$ as states and vectors $(x_1, ..., x_m)$ as inputs, then δ (as the choice of notation suggests) may be interpreted as defining a state transition function, given by:

$$\delta((y_1, ..., y_l), (x_1, ..., x_m)) = (Y_1, ..., Y_l) \qquad [3.4]$$

Likewise, β may be described by a set of n Boolean functions:

$$g_1(y_1, ..., y_l, x_1, ..., x_m)$$

$$...$$

$$g_j(y_1, ..., y_l, x_1, ..., x_m)$$

$$...$$

$$g_n(y_1, ..., y_l, x_1, ..., x_m)$$

Again, if the contents of S are $(y_1, ..., y_l)$ and inputs to the circuit are given by the vector $(x_1, ..., x_m)$, then after one clock pulse, the values appearing on the output wires may be regarded as a vector $(z_1, ..., z_n)$, where for each j, $1 \leq j \leq n$,

$$z_j = g_j(y_1, ..., y_l, x_1, ..., x_m)$$

Again, interpreting vectors $(y_1, ..., y_l)$ as states and vectors $(x_1, ..., x_m)$ as inputs, we may regard β as defining an output function, given by:

$$\beta((y_1, ..., y_l), (x_1, ..., x_m)) = (z_1, ..., z_n) \qquad [3.5]$$

We thus have all five ingredients of a Mealy machine. If C is the circuit, we denote this machine by *Mealy*(C).

Note that in the construction of 3.3.2, the circuit C obtained satisfies *Mealy*$(C) = M_{circ}$.

Let us illustrate what we have just seen by an example. The circuit is given in Fig. 3.5. The Boolean functions are given by:

$$F_1(y_1, y_2, x_1, x_2) = x_1 + y_2$$

$$F_2(y_1, y_2, x_1, x_2) = x_1.x_2$$

$$G_1(y_1, y_2, x_1, x_2) = y_1$$

$$G_2(y_1, y_2, x_1, x_2) = x_1.y_2$$

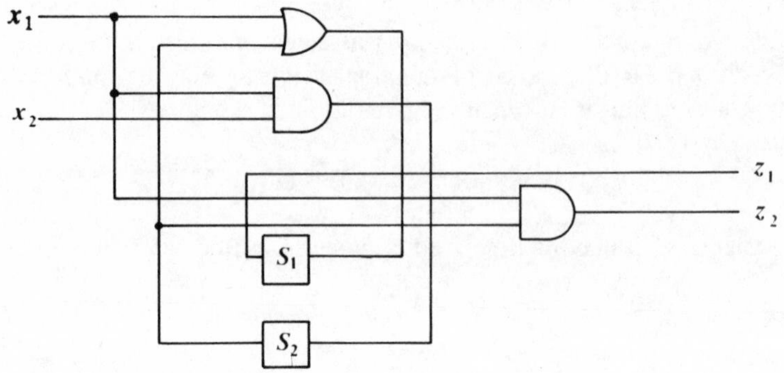

Fig. 3.5. Example of a simple circuit

From these, and the definitions of the next state and output functions in [3.1] and [3.2], we may construct a flow table for the circuit. For example:

$$\delta((0,\mathit{1}),(0,\mathit{0})) = (0 + 1, \mathit{0}.0) = (1,\mathit{0})$$

$$\beta((0,\mathit{1}),(0,\mathit{0})) = (0, \mathit{0}.1) = (0,\mathit{0})$$

The flow table is given in full in Table 3.5.

Table 3.5. The flow table of the circuit of Fig. 3.2

	00	01	10	11	00	01	10	11
00	00	00	10	11	00	00	00	00
01	10	10	10	11	00	00	01	01
10	00	00	10	11	10	10	10	10
11	10	10	10	11	10	10	11	11

3.4 SOFTWARE IMPLEMENTATION

From the point of view of software, automata provide an abstract view of control flow in a program and it is relatively easy to see how automata may be implemented using compare and branch instructions.

One problem does confront us. The circuit diagrams of the previous sections are considered to be composed of 'ideal' elements, whose meaning is fully specified – by truth tables, for example. This allowed us to make the translations between circuitry and automata and will allow us to prove formally that the circuit does implement the abstract machine. It is not always the case – indeed, it is seldom the case – that a programming language possesses a semantics in this way.

To get round this, we shall discuss implementation in a 'toy' language for which we shall provide a formal semantics.

3.5 AUTRAN

AUTRAN stands for 'Automata Translation'. We give part of the formal syntax in a BNF style. '<*CR*>' stands for carriage return.

< *program* > ::= < *input-list* ><*CR*>< *output-list* ><*CR*>
< *start* ><*CR*>< *body* >

< *input-list* > ::= **INPUT** < *list-of-inputs* >

< *list-of-inputs* > ::= < *input* > | < *input* >,< *list-of-inputs* >

< *output-list* > ::= **OUTPUT** < *list-of-outputs* >

< *list-of-outputs* > ::= < *output* > | < *output* >,< *list-of-outputs* >

< *start* > ::= **START** < *line-no* >

< *body* > ::= < *statement* >|< *statement* ><*CR*>< *body* >

< *statement* > ::= < *line-no* > **CASE READ OF** <*CR*>< *cases* >

< *cases* > ::= < *case* >|< *case* ><*CR*>< *cases* >

< *case* > ::= < *input* > : < *output* > **GOTO** < *line-no* >

We shall not specify any particular form for inputs or outputs – use ALGOL identifiers if you like. Line numbers are what you think they are. There is no need to order them, but no two statements must begin with the same line number. Also, in a statement, every input must appear exactly once as the heading of a case.

Now let us give the language a formal semantics. Consider a program P. This will have the form:

$$Inputs <CR> Outputs <CR> S_1 <CR> \cdots S_r$$

Let I denote the set of inputs listed in *Input* and let O denote the set of outputs listed in *Output*. Let S be the set of line numbers.

Now, consider some element $s \in S$. This will be the line number of a unique statement S_k. Let $i \in I$, then there is a case belonging to S_k of the form:

$$i : o \text{ GOTO } s'$$

Define:

$$\delta(s,i) = s' \quad \beta(s,i) = o$$

The program P thus determines a Mealy automaton $M(P) = (S,I,O,\delta,\beta)$. If s_o is the line number mentioned in the start statement, then it is supposed that the program will start execution from that state and so we can finally ascribe a meaning to it. The meaning of P is the function:

$$f_P : I^* \to O^*$$

satisfying:

$$f_P(x) = \delta^*(s_o, x)$$

Given a Mealy automaton, it should be easy to see how to implement it in AUTRAN. As an example, we will implement Great Aunt Eugenia. Here is the program:

```
INPUT gin, video-nasty, ghetto-blaster
OUTPUT wake, snore, harangue, refulse, drink,
        cackle, snipe, collapse
START 10
10 CASE READ OF
ghetto-blaster : wake GOTO 20
video-nasty : snore GOTO 10
gin : snore GOTO 10
20 CASE READ OF
ghetto-blaster : harangue GOTO 30
video-nasty : refuse GOTO 20
gin : drink GOTO 40
```

30 **CASE READ OF**

ghetto-blaster : *harangue* **GOTO** 30

video-nasty : *cackle* **GOTO** 20

gin : *drink* **GOTO** 50

40 **CASE READ OF**

ghetto-blaster : *snipe* **GOTO** 50

video-nasty : *cackle* **GOTO** 40

gin : *collapse* **GOTO** 10

50 **CASE READ OF**

ghetto-blaster : *snipe* **GOTO** 50

video-nasty : *cackle* **GOTO** 40

gin : *collapse* **GOTO** 10

3.6 FUNCTIONAL APPROACHES

AUTRAN is an imperative language in the old style.* A more modern approach would be to regard an automaton as something acting on infinite lists. Roughly speaking, we can imagine it as something which takes an infinite list of inputs and delivers an infinite list of outputs. In any finite time, it will only have processed a finite amount of the input list, but as it goes on working, it will produce better and better approximations to the final answer. This is not unlike the way in which we can produce better and better approximations to the value of π without actually ever finding the precise value of the number.†

Functional languages which can employ lazy evaluation for the processing of partially defined, infinite objects are ideal for this kind of application.

---

* One might add, in the *very* old style. It has hardly a feature that has not been objected to in the literature.

† This idea of partially computed values of an element is an important aspect of the Scott-Strachey approach to programming language semantics. See Stoy (1979).

EXERCISES

1 Great Aunt Eugenia is not immortal (despite the fact that the description of her suggests the contrary) and the family, rather ghoulishly, perhaps, would like to construct a robot simulacrum of her. Design logic circuitry that would simulate the old lady.

2 Do the same for the robot described in the exercises to Chapter 2.

3 Devise implementation techniques for Moore automata.

4 In the constructions of this chapter, we have stipulated that all the encoding functions must be injective. Suppose $f : \to O$ is not injective. How could you implement f with I encoded by a set $\mathbf{V}$ of vectors and $|\mathbf{V}| < |I|$?

5 Repeat **4** in for the implementation of Mealy automaton.

6 Devise a general method for implementing AUTRAN programs in digital circuitry.

The next few exercises extend AUTRAN to give a new language, TURTRAN.

(a) There is no *<output -list>* and *input* is globally replaced by *symbol*.

(b) There are two new basic symbols **INCR** and **DECR**.

(c) *<case>* is now translated to
<symbol>:*<symbol>*/*<mod>* **GOTO** *<line−no>* and there is a rule, *<mod>* ::= **INCR** | **DECR**.

Intuitively, there is a sequence of memory locations, each capable of storing one symbol, and numbered $0, 1, 2, ...$ There is also an address pointer, which initially points to location 0. The execution of a program, is as follows. The program selects the case s:s'/m **GOTO** n, where s is the contents of the location l at which the address counter is currently pointing.

If there is no such case (and we permit this), then the program halts.

The location is rewritten with s' and the address pointer reset to $l + 1$ (if $m = INCR$) or $l - 1$ (if $m = DECR$). If $l = 0$ and $m =$ **DECR**, then the program halts.

7 Give a formal syntax for TURTRAN.

8 Give a formal semantics for TURTRAN in terms of Turing machines.

9 Show that any Turing machine may be 'implemented' in TURTRAN.

10 Conclude (following Turing's thesis), that TURTRAN is as powerful, computationally, as (say) FORTRAN.

Chapter 4

Implementation and Realisation

It is comparison that makes men miserable.

FRENCH PROVERB

4.1 INTRODUCTION

In Chapter 3, we described two of the ways to implement a Mealy machine. However, we did not give any formal justification for the claim that our implementations were truly implementations. Indeed, we have not said what we mean by the term.

Evidently, to say that A implements B is to assert that a relationship of some sort exists between A and B. What sort of relationship should this be ?

Let us think back to Chapter 3. The case of AUTRAN is fairly simple because we used Mealy automata to give a semantics to the language. To each AUTRAN program, P, we associated a machine $Mealy(P)$, which provides P with part of its meaning (we also have to make the start state explicit). If P is a program that implements a machine M, and if the line number of P are the states of M, then we would expect M and $Mealy(P)$ to be the same.

Here, incidentally, is our first relationship between two machines, equality.*

4.1.1 Definition

We shall say that M_1 is equal to M_2, and write $M_1 = M_2$† if and only if they have the same states, inputs, outputs and next-state and output functions, that is:

* Actually, this definition is more or less forced on us; it derives from the definition of equality between 5-tuples – corresponding coordinates are equal – and of equality between sets and functions.

† Recall the convention 2.1.3. For example, S_2 is the state set of M_2.

$$S_1 = S_2 \quad I_1 = I_2 \quad O_1 = O_2$$

and for all $s \in S_1$, $i \in I_1$,

$$\delta_1(s,i) = \delta_2(s,i) \text{ and } \beta_1(s,i) = \beta_2(s,i)$$

It seems reasonable to suppose that any given machine implements itself. However, equality is too restrictive a relationship to serve as a definition of 'implements'. How could we apply it to implementation by circuits, for instance. Let us return to example 3.3.1 of Chapter 3.

We began with a digital circuit of a certain type, C, and showed that it could be regarded as a Mealy machine, $Mealy(C)$. We also showed that from a given Mealy machine we could construct a class of circuits. Let $Circ(M)$ denote a typical member of this class. We assert that $Circ(M)$ implements M, that some kind of relationship exists between them.

The relationship cannot be between M and $Circ(M)$ directly, because they are two different kinds of object. However, we *can* relate M to $Mealy(Circ(M))$, because the two are both Mealy machines.

In order that this relationship has significance for the circuit $Circ(M)$, we shall make the following assumption: the dynamic behaviour of a given circuit C of the type described in Chapter 3 is accurately reflected by the dynamic behaviour of $Mealy(C)$, they have 'the same' input/output behaviour.

The assumption is to do with the real behaviour of gates and flip-flops and its justification is outside the scope of this book.

Now, in general $Mealy(Circ(M))$ will not be equal to M. For example, the input set of the former will always be of the form $\mathbf{B}^n$, for some n. If $|I|$ is not a power of two, then $Mealy(Circ(M))$ will have more inputs than M.

Suppose, however, that $|S|$, $|I|$ and $|O|$ are all powers of two. This means that we can construct our encodings α, ι and ω as *bijections* and in this case, we can find a very strong structural relationship between the two machines. They are identical except for the names of states, inputs and outputs. In this case, the machines are said to be isomorphic§. (cf. 4.4).

§ The word derives from two Greek words: *isos*, meaning 'equal' and *morphē*, meaning 'form'.

4.2 ISOMORPHISMS

4.2.1 Definition

Let M_1, M_2 be machines. An input/output isomorphism between M_1 and M_2 is a triple $\phi = (\alpha,\iota,\theta)$, where α, ι and θ are bijective functions:

$$\alpha:S_1 \to S_2 \quad \iota:I_1 \to I_2 \quad \theta:O_2 \to O_1$$

such that for all $s \in S_1$, $i \in I_1$,

$$\alpha(\delta_1(s,i)) = \delta_2(\alpha(s),\iota(i))$$

$$\beta_1(s,i) = \theta[\beta_2(\alpha(s),\iota(i))]$$

We write $\phi:M_1 \approx M_2$ to indicate that ϕ is an input/output isomorphism from M_1 to M_2. If such an input/output isomorphism exists, then we shall say that M_1, M_2 are input/output isomorphic, and we write $M_1 \approx M_2$.

From now on, we shall abbreviate 'input/output isomorphism' to plain *isomorphism* unless necessary.‡

We shall use a convention similar to that of 2.2.3 regarding the components of a subscripted object, that they inherit the subscript (or whatever). Thus if $\phi_3:M_1 \approx M'$, then $\phi_3 = (\alpha_3,\iota_3,\theta_3)$ and, for instance, $\alpha_3:S_1 \to S'$ and $\theta_3:O' \to O_1$.

4.2.2 Example

Let M_{parse} be the machine whose flow table is given in Table 3.1, and M_{code}, be the machine whose flow table is given in Table 3.2. There is an isomorphism ϕ_{code} between these two machines, where:

$$\alpha_{code}(1) = 0 \quad \alpha_{code}(2) = 1$$

$$\iota_{code}(a) = 01 \quad \iota_{code}(+) = 10 \quad \iota_{code}(;) = 11$$

$$\theta_{code}(0) = ! \quad \theta_{code}(1) = ?$$

Note that if $\phi:M_1 \to M_2$, then α and ι map from components of M_1 to components of M_2, but that θ maps in the reverse direction. We can think of ι and θ as representing encoding and decoding boxes, translating

‡ We use the prefix 'input/output' to distinguish this form of isomorphism from a more conventional type. See the notes at the end of the chapter.

from I_1 to I_2 and from O_2 to O_1, as pictured in Fig. 4.1.

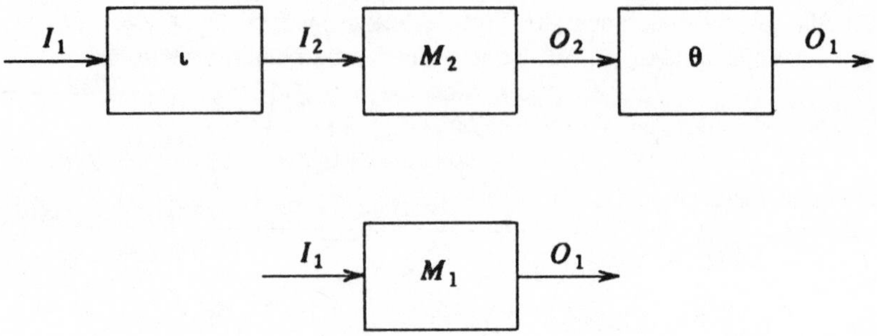

Fig. 4.1

Let us compare the behaviours of these two machines, M_1 and the composite, which we shall call ι-M_2-θ.

Let us therefore suppose that M_1 is in state s_1 and that ι-M_2-θ is in state s_2. Now suppose that an input $i \in I_1$ is presented to both systems, then:

(a) M_1 goes to a new state $\delta_1(s_1, i)$ and produces an output $\beta_1(s_1, i)$;

(b) ι-M_2-θ will receive the input which will be encoded by ι to give an input $\iota(i)$ to M_2. M_2 will change state to $\delta_2(s_2, \iota(i))$ and produce an output $\beta_2(s_2, \iota(i))$ which is fed into the decoder θ to give, finally, the output $\theta[\beta_2(s_2, \iota(i))]$.

Now, if you look at definition 4.2.1, you will see that if $\alpha(s_1) = s_2$, then the two outputs, $\beta_1(s_1, i)$ and $\theta[\beta_2(s_2, \iota(i))]$ are *equal*. We may express this by saying that outputs are equal from corresponding states.

That is not all. Suppose $\delta_1(s_1, i) = s_1'$ and $\delta_2(s_2, \iota(i)) = s_2'$; recall that these are the new states of the system after input i has been applied. Then we may show (in 4.2.4) that if $\alpha(s_1) = s_2$, then $\alpha(s_1') = s_2'$. So we may apply the argument again, to show that a second input will give the same output in both machines and α of the new state of M_1 will be the new state of M_2.

Thus, informally, if we start M_1 and ι-M_2-θ in corresponding states and give them the same input sequence, then

(a) they will produce the same output sequence;

(b) they will end up in corresponding states.

Let us make these remarks more precise. First of all, we shall need some notation. If x is an input string, then ι will transform it, symbol by symbol. Given $\iota : I \to O$, we may construct a function $\iota^* : I^* \to O^*$ as the following definition shows.

4.2.3 Definition

Suppose A and B are sets and f be a function $f:A \to B$. We define a function $f^*:A^* \to B^*$ as follows. First, $f^*(\varepsilon) = \varepsilon$. Secondly, if $x = a_1...a_n$, then let $f^*(x) = f(a_1)...f(a_n)$.

For example, if A, the set of alphanumeric characters and f is a function $f:A \to A$ which sends each letter to the letter preceding it in cyclic order, then $f^*(FXReid) = EWQdhc$.

We may now describe the behaviour of ι-M_2-θ, from state s with input x. This input will be encoded as $\iota^*(x)$ and M_2 will produce an output $\beta_2^*(s,\iota^*(x))$ (Section 2.2.6). This will be decoded by θ to give $\theta^*[\beta_2^*(s,\iota^*(x))]$.

Also, note that this input will drive M_2 to state $\delta^*(s,\iota^*(x))$.

Let us therefore define:

$$\delta_{\iota-\theta}^*(s,x) = \delta^*(s,\iota^*(x)) \qquad [4.1]$$

$$\beta_{\iota-\theta}^*(s,x) = \theta^*[\beta^*(s,\iota^*(x))] \qquad [4.2]$$

We may now explain in what way M_1 and ι-M_2-θ have the same behaviour.

4.2.4 Proposition

Suppose $\phi:M_1 \approx M_2$, then for all $s \in S_1$ and for all $x \in I_1^*$:

$$\beta_1^*(s,x) = \beta_{\iota-\theta}^*(\alpha(s),x) \qquad [4.3]$$

Proof

We argue by induction on $lnth(x)$. If $lnth(x) = 0$, then $x = \varepsilon$ and so $\beta_1^*(s,\varepsilon) = \varepsilon$, by 2.2.6. But also:

$$\theta^*[\beta_2^*(\alpha(s),\iota^*(\varepsilon))] = \theta^*(\beta_2^*(\alpha(s),\varepsilon)) \text{ (by 4.2.3)}$$
$$= \theta^*(\varepsilon) = \varepsilon \text{ (by 2.2.6 and 4.2.3)}$$

Thus, [4.3] holds when $lnth(x) = 0$.

Now suppose [4.3] holds whenever $lnth(x) = n$, and suppose $x = a.y$, with $a \in I$ and $y \in I_1^*$ and $lnth(y) = n$, that is, $lnth(x) = n + 1$.

By definition of β_1^*, definition 2.2.6:

$$\beta_1{}^*(s,x) = \beta_1(s,a).\beta_1{}^*(\delta_1(s,a),y) \qquad [4.4]$$

By definition of ι^*, $\iota^*(a.y) = \iota(a).\iota^*(y)$ and so, using the definition of $\beta_2{}^*$, Section 2.2.6:

$$\begin{aligned}\theta^*[\beta_2{}^*(\alpha(s),\iota^*(x))]\\ &= \theta^*[\beta_2(\alpha(s),\iota(a)).\beta_2{}^*(\delta_2(\alpha(s),\iota(a)),\iota^*(y))]\\ &= \theta[\beta_2(\alpha(s),\iota(a))].\theta^*[\beta_2{}^*(\delta_2(\alpha(s),\iota(a)),\iota^*(y))] \qquad [4.5]\end{aligned}$$

But ϕ is an isomorphism, and so, by Section 4.2.1, $\alpha(\delta_1(s,a)) = \delta_2(\alpha(s),\iota(a))$ and so:

$$\theta^*[\beta_2{}^*(\delta_2(\alpha(s),\iota(a)),\iota^*(y))] = \theta^*[\beta_2{}^*(\alpha(\delta_1(s,a)),\iota^*(y))] \qquad [4.6]$$

But now the right hand side is of the form $\theta^*[\beta_2{}^*(\alpha(s'),\iota^*(y))]$, where $s' = \delta_1(s,a))$ Since $lnth(y) = n$, we may use induction and conclude that:

$$\theta^*[\beta_2{}^*(\alpha(s'),\iota^*(y))] = \beta_1{}^*(s',y) \qquad [4.7]$$

and that hence by [4.6] and [4.7]:

$$\theta^*[\beta_2{}^*(\delta_2(\alpha(s),\iota(a)),\iota^*(y))] = \beta_1{}^*(\delta_1(s,a),y)) \qquad [4.8]$$

Again, ϕ is an isomorphism, and so, by Section 4.2.1,

$$\beta_1(s,a) = \theta[\beta_2(\alpha(s),\iota(a))]. \qquad [4.9]$$

Putting [4.8] and [4.9] together gives:

$$\begin{aligned}\theta[\beta_2(\alpha(s),\iota(a))].\theta^*[\beta_2{}^*(\delta_2(\alpha(s),\iota(a)),\iota^*(y))] \qquad [4.10]\\ = \beta_1(s,a).\beta_1{}^*(\delta_1(s,a),y))\end{aligned}$$

Thus:

$$\begin{aligned}\beta_1{}^*(s,x) &= \beta_1(s,a).\beta_1{}^*(\delta_1(s,a),y) \text{ (by [4.4])}\\ &= \theta[\beta_2(\alpha(s),\iota(a))].\theta^*[\beta_2{}^*(\delta_2(\alpha(s),\iota(a)),\iota^*(y))] \text{ (by [4.10])}\\ &= \theta^*[\beta_2{}^*(\alpha(s),\iota^*(x))] \text{ (by [4.5])}\\ &= \beta_{\iota-\theta}{}^*(\alpha(s),x) \text{ (by [4.2])}\end{aligned}$$

proving [4.3].

We conclude this section with a few remarks about isomorphisms in general.

4.2.5 Remark

1 Let M be a machine, and let $\alpha : S \to S$, $\iota : I \to I$, and $\theta : O \to O$ be identity functions, that is, for all $s \in S$, $i \in I$ and $o \in O$:

$$\alpha(s) = s \quad \iota(i) = i \quad \theta(o) = o$$

Let $Id_M = (\alpha,\iota,\theta)$ then Id_M is an isomorphism, $Id_M : M \approx M$, called the *identity isomorphism* for M.
2 Let $\phi = (\alpha,\iota,\theta)$ be an isomorphism, $\phi : M_1 \approx M_2$, then $\phi^{-1} = (\alpha^{-1},\iota^{-1},\theta^{-1})$ is an isomorphism, $\phi : M_2 \approx M_1$ called the *inverse* of ϕ.

The following result indicates that isomorphism is an abstract type of equality.

4.2.6 Remark

Let M, M_1, M_2, M_3 be any machines. Then:
(a) $M \approx M$;
(b) $M_1 \approx M_2 \Rightarrow M_2 \approx M_1$;
(c) $M_1 \approx M_2$ & $M_2 \approx M_3 \Rightarrow M_1 \approx M_3$;
In other words, if **M** is any set of machines, then $\approx$ is an equivalence relation on **M**.*

Proof

(a) and (b) follow directly from 1 and 2, of 4.2.5; (c) will wait until we have discussed composition in the next section.

* It is tempting to say that '$\approx$ is an equivalence relation on the set of all machines', but this would be wrong. Clearly, given *any* finite set S, we may form a machine having S as its set of states. If there were a set of all machines, then we could legitimately construct a set of all finite sets. We could then legitimately construct its power set. We could then construct a set **U** as follows. If X is an element of the powerset, then **U** contains the union of all sets in X. But then, **U** would be the set of all sets, but, as a consequence of *Russell's paradox*, there is no such thing.

4.3 HOMOMORPHISMS

Now let us return to example 4.2.2. Our actual implementation of M_{parse} was not by M_{code} but by the circuit defining a machine, M_{circ}. M_{parse} is not isomorphic to M_{circ}. If it were, then S_{circ} and S_{parse} would have the same number of elements, which they do not.

However, we may make two remarks:

1 There is a relationship between the two which may be described in terms of coder/decoder functions as in the case of isomorphic machines.

2 The definition of $M_{\iota-\theta}$ and the proof of proposition 4.2.4 made no reference at all to the bijectivity of the functions α, ι and θ.

Thus, we may *generalize* the notion of isomorphism to deal with the example and behavioural relationships are preserved. These observations inspire the following.

4.3.1 Definition

Let M_1 , M_2 be machines; then the triple $\phi = (\alpha,\iota,\theta)$ will be said to be an input/output homomorphism of M_1 into M_2 if and only if $\alpha{:}S_1 \rightarrow S_2$, $\iota{:}I_1 \rightarrow I_2$ and $\theta{:}O_2 \rightarrow O_1$ are functions such that for all $s \in S_1$ and for all $i \in I_1$:

$$\delta_2(\alpha(s),\iota(i)) = \alpha(\delta_1(s,i))$$

$$\theta[\beta_2(\alpha(s),\iota(i))] = \beta_1(s,i)$$

As with isomorphisms, we shall leave out the prefix 'input/output'.

If ϕ is a homomorphism of M_1 into M_2, then write $\phi{:}M_1 \rightarrow M_2$. If such a homomorphism exists, then we shall say that M_2 *implements* M_1.

If α is injective, then we call ϕ a *state behaviour assignment*. If such a state behaviour assignment exists, then M_2 is said to be a *realization* of M_1. We shall write $M_1 \leq M_2$ to denote this.

Finally, if C is a circuit, then we shall say that C implements or realizes M if and only if $Mealy(C)$ implements or realizes M.

4.3.2 Example

We illustrate definition 4.3.1 with an example. Consider the two machines described in Tables 4.2 and 4.3.

The morphism $\phi = (\alpha,\iota,\theta)$ is given by:

$$\alpha(s1) = \alpha(s2) = t2 \quad \alpha(s3) = t3$$

Table 4.2. M1

	i1	*i2*	*i1*	*i2*
s1	*s2*	*s1*	*p1*	*p2*
s2	*s1*	*s2*	*p1*	*p2*
s3	*s3*	*s3*	*p2*	*p1*

Table 4.3. M2

	j1	*j2*	*j1*	*j2*
t1	*t3*	*t1*	*o2*	*o1*
t2	*t2*	*t2*	*o3*	*o2*
t3	*t3*	*t3*	*o1*	*o3*

$$\iota(i\,1) = j\,2 \quad \iota(i\,2) = j\,1$$

$$\theta(o\,1) = \theta(o\,2) = p\,1 \quad \theta(o\,3) = p\,2$$

We may check that ϕ is a homomorphism. Computing:

$$\alpha(\delta 1(s\,1, i1)) = \alpha(s\,2) = t\,2 = \delta 2(t\,2, j2) = \delta 2(\alpha(s\,1), \iota(i\,1))$$

$$\alpha(\delta 1(s\,2, i1)) = \alpha(s\,1) = t\,2 = \delta 2(t\,2, j2) = \delta 2(\alpha(s\,2), \iota(i\,1))$$

$$\alpha(\delta 1(s\,3, i1)) = \alpha(s\,3) = t\,3 = \delta 2(t\,3, j2) = \delta 2(\alpha(s\,3), \iota(i\,1))$$

$$\alpha(\delta 1(s\,1, i2)) = \alpha(s\,1) = t\,2 = \delta 2(t\,2, j1) = \delta 2(\alpha(s\,1), \iota(i\,2))$$

$$\alpha(\delta 1(s\,2, i2)) = \alpha(s\,2) = t\,2 = \delta 2(t\,2, j1) = \delta 2(\alpha(s\,2), \iota(i\,2))$$

$$\alpha(\delta 1(s\,3, i2)) = \alpha(s\,3) = t\,3 = \delta 2(t\,3, j1) = \delta 2(\alpha(s\,3), \iota(i\,2))$$

This shows that α has the right properties. Now we check θ:

$$\beta_1(s\,1, i1) = p\,1 = \theta(o\,2) = \theta(\beta_2(t\,2, j2)) = \theta(\beta_1(\alpha(s\,1), \iota(i\,1)))$$

$$\beta_1(s\,2, i1) = p\,1 = \theta(o\,2) = \theta(\beta_2(t\,2, j2)) = \theta(\beta_1(\alpha(s\,2), \iota(i\,1)))$$

$$\beta_1(s\,3, i1) = p\,2 = \theta(o\,3) = \theta(\beta_2(t\,3, j2)) = \theta(\beta_1(\alpha(s\,3), \iota(i\,1)))$$

$$\beta_1(s\,1, i2) = p\,2 = \theta(o\,3) = \theta(\beta_2(t\,2, j1)) = \theta(\beta_1(\alpha(s\,1), \iota(i\,2)))$$

$$\beta_1(s\,2, i2) = p\,2 = \theta(o\,3) = \theta(\beta_2(t\,2, j1)) = \theta(\beta_1(\alpha(s\,2), \iota(i\,2)))$$

$$\beta_1(s\,3, i2) = p\,1 = \theta(o\,1) = \theta(\beta_2(t\,3, j1)) = \theta(\beta_1(\alpha(s\,3), \iota(i\,2)))$$

The following is immediate from the definitions.

4.3.3 Remark

Suppose M_1, M_2 are machines and suppose $\phi = (\alpha,\iota,\theta)$ where $\alpha:S_1 \rightarrow S_2$, $\iota:I_1 \rightarrow I_2$ and $\theta:O_2 \rightarrow O_1$, then:

1 ϕ is an isomorphism $\Rightarrow$ ϕ is a state behaviour assignment.

2 ϕ is a state behaviour assignment $\Rightarrow$ ϕ is a homomorphism.

3 M_2 realises $M_1 \Rightarrow M_2$ implements M_1.

As we have already observed, the proof of 4.2.4 makes no reference to the fact that all three functions are bijections. We may therefore define for any homomorphism, $\phi:M_1 \rightarrow M_2$:

$$\beta_{\iota-\theta}^*(s,x) = \theta^*[\beta^*(s,\iota^*(x))]$$

and the proof of 4.2.4 gives the following.

4.3.4 Proposition

Suppose $\phi:M_1 \rightarrow M_2$, then for all $s \in S_1$ and for all $x \in I_1^*$:

$$\beta_1^*(s,x) = \beta_{\iota-\theta}^*(\alpha(s),x)$$

We conclude this section by looking at ways in which homomorphisms may be combined to give new homomorphisms.

4.3.5 Definition

Suppose M_1,M_2,M_3 are machines and that $\phi_1 = (\alpha_1,\iota_1,\theta_1):M_1 \rightarrow M_2$ and $\phi_2 = (\alpha_2,\iota_2,\theta_2):M_2 \rightarrow M_3$. Define $\phi_2.\phi_1 = (\alpha_2.\alpha_1,\iota_2.\iota_1,\theta_1.\theta_2)$. $\phi_2.\phi_1$ is called the *composite* of ϕ_1 and ϕ_2.

Of course, we must show that the composite of two homomorphisms is *itself* a homomorphism.

4.3.6 Lemma

Suppose M_1,M_2,M_3 are machines and that $\phi_1:M_1 \rightarrow M_2$ and $\phi_2:M_2 \rightarrow M_3$ then $\phi_2.\phi_1:M_1 \rightarrow M_3$ is a homomorphism.

Proof

It is simply a matter of checking that the two conditions of definition 4.3.1 hold. Let $\phi_2.\phi_1 = (\alpha,\iota,\theta)$, then computing:

$$\begin{aligned}\alpha(\delta_1(s,i)) &= \alpha_2[\alpha_1(\delta_1(s,i))]\\ &= \alpha_2[\delta_2(\alpha_1(s),\iota_1(i))]\\ &= \delta_3[\alpha_2(\alpha_1(s)),\iota_2(\iota_1(i))]\\ &= \delta_3[\alpha(s),\iota(i)]\end{aligned}$$

so that α behaves properly. For θ, we compute:

$$\begin{aligned}\theta[\beta_3(\alpha(s),\iota(i))] &= \theta_1[\theta_2(\beta_3[\alpha_2(\alpha_1(s)),\iota_2(\iota_1(i))])]\\ &= \theta_1[\beta_2(\alpha_1(s),\iota_1(i))]\\ &= \beta_1(s,i)\end{aligned}$$

This completes the proof.

For special kinds of morphism, we have the following, which depends on the fact that the composition of two functions of a particular type – injective, bijective and so on – is also of that type.

4.3.7 Lemma

Suppose M_1,M_2,M_3 are machines and that $\phi_1{:}M_1 \rightarrow M_2$ and $\phi_2{:}M_2 \rightarrow M_3$ then:

1 ϕ_2 and ϕ_1 are isomorphisms $\Rightarrow$ $\phi_2.\phi_1$ is an isomorphism.

2 ϕ_2 and ϕ_1 are state behaviour assignments $\Rightarrow$ $\phi_2.\phi_1$ is a state behaviour assignment.

Note that 4.2.6 (c) is now a direct consequence of 4.3.7 (2)

We conclude this section with a number of simple observations about homomorphisms. First, we need a definition.

4.3.8 Definition

Let ϕ_1,ϕ_2 be homomorphisms. We say that ϕ_1 and ϕ_2 are *equal*, and write $\phi_1 = \phi_2$ if and only if there exists M_1, M_2 such that $\phi_{1:M_1} \rightarrow M_2$, $\phi_{2:M_1} \rightarrow M_2$ and $\alpha_1 = \alpha_2$, $\iota_1 = \iota_2$ and $\theta_1 = \theta_2$.

4.3.9 Lemma

Suppose $\phi_1:M_1 \to M_2$, $\phi_2:M_2 \to M_3$ and $\phi_3:M_3 \to M_4$ then $(\phi_3.\phi_2).\phi_1 = \phi_3.(\phi_2.\phi_1)$.

Proof

Exercise **4**.

4.3.10 Lemma

Suppose $\phi_1:M_1 \to M_2$, then $Id_{M_2}.\phi = \phi$ and $\phi.Id_{M_1} = \phi$.

Proof

Exercise **5**.

4.3.11 Lemma

Suppose $\phi:M_1 \approx M_2$, then $\phi^{-1}.\phi = I_{M_1}$ and $\phi.\phi^{-1} = I_{M_2}$.

4.4 IMPLEMENTATION BY CIRCUITRY REVISITED

Let us return to the discussion of Section 3.2. We suppose M is a machine and define injective functions $\alpha:S \to \mathbf{B}^l$, $\iota:I \to \mathbf{B}^m$ and $\omega:O \to \mathbf{B}^n$. These determine a machine M_{code}, where $S_{code} = \alpha(S)$, $I_{code} = \iota(I)$, $O_{code} = \omega(O)$ and δ_{code}, β_{code} are given by:

$$\delta_{code}(\alpha(s),\iota(i)) = \alpha(\delta(s,i)) \qquad [4.11]$$

$$\beta_{code}(\alpha(s),\iota(i)) = \omega(\beta(s,i)) \qquad [4.12]$$

Both these functions are well-defined since α, ι and ω are injective. This latter fact also allows us to construct a function $\theta_{code}:\omega(O) \to O$ such that $\theta(\omega(o)) = o$ for all $o \in O$. Define $\alpha_{code}:S \to \alpha(S)$ by $\alpha_{code}(s) = \alpha(s)$ and define $\iota_{code}:I \to \iota(I)$ by $\iota_{code}(i) = \iota(i)$. By construction, the three functions, α_{code}, ι_{code} and θ_{code}, are bijective. From [4.11], we obtain:

$$\delta_{code}(\alpha_{code}(s),\iota_{code}(i)) = \alpha_{code}(\delta(s,i)) \qquad [4.13]$$

and from [4.12]:

$$\theta_{code}(\beta_{code}(\alpha_{code}(s),\iota_{code}(i))) = \theta_{code}(\omega_{code}(\beta(s,i))) = \beta(s,i) \quad [4.14]$$

4.4.1 Proposition

From [4.13] and [4.14], $\phi_{code}:M \approx M_{code}$.
The next step in implementation was to extend δ_{code} and β_{code} by adding values for the don't care conditions. This involves constructing a machine M_{circ}, where $S_{circ} = \mathbf{B}^l$, $I_{circ} = \mathbf{B}^m$ and $O_{circ} = \mathbf{B}^n$ and δ_{circ} and β_{circ} are any two functions such that for all $s \in S$ and $i \in I$:

$$\delta_{circ}(\alpha(s),\iota(i)) = \delta_{code}(\alpha(s),\iota(i)) \quad [4.15]$$

$$\beta_{circ}(\alpha(s),\iota(i)) = \beta_{code}(\alpha(s),\iota(i)) \quad [4.16]$$

We now define $\alpha_{circ}:S_{code} \rightarrow S_{circ}$, $\iota_{circ}:I_{code} \rightarrow I_{circ}$ and $\theta_{circ}:S_{circ} \rightarrow S_{code}$, by $\alpha_{circ}(\mathbf{v}) = \mathbf{v}$, $\iota_{circ}(\mathbf{v}) = \mathbf{v}$ and

$$\theta_{circ}(\mathbf{v}) = \begin{cases} \mathbf{v} & \text{if } \mathbf{v} \in O_{code} \\ \textit{anything} & \textit{otherwise} \end{cases}$$

then by [4.15] and [4.16], $\phi_{circ}:M_{code} \rightarrow M_{circ}$. Since α_{circ} is injective, it follows that $M_{code} \leq M_{circ}$.

4.4.2 Proposition

Hence, by 4.4.1 and 4.3.7, we obtain: $M \leq M_{circ}$.
However, from M_{circ}, we construct our circuit $Circ(M)$. Its construction ensures that $Mealy(Circ(M)) = M_{circ}$.

4.4.3 Corollary

Thus, finally $Circ(M)$ implements M.

4.5 A CATEGORY OF MACHINES

The reader may have observed, in contemplation of machines and homomorphisms, a similarity (in notation if in nothing else) to sets and functions. In both cases, one has a class of objects (sets, machines) and those things that connect them together and allow a means of comparison.

This duality pervades mathematics. In group theory, there are groups and homomorphisms, in topology there are topological spaces and continuous maps, in linear algebra there are vector spaces and linear maps. In each case, we have a class* of *objects*; and a class of *morphisms* such that:

(a) To each morphism, ϕ, is associated a *source*, $\partial_0(\phi)$ and a *target*, $\partial_1(\phi)$. If $\partial_0(\phi) = A$ and $\partial_1(\phi) = B$ then write $\phi:A \to B$.

(b) To each object, A, there is associated an *identity morphism* Id_A with $\partial_0(Id_A) = A$ and $\partial_1(Id_A) = A$.

(c) If ϕ and ψ are morphisms and $\partial_1(\phi) = \partial_0(\psi)$ then there exists a composite morphism, $\psi.\phi$, which satisfies:

$$\partial_0(\psi.\phi) = \partial_0(\phi)$$

$$\partial_1(\psi.\phi) = \partial_1(\psi)$$

(d) If ϕ, ψ and χ are morphisms and either of $\phi.(\psi.\chi))$ or $(\phi.\psi).\chi$ is defined, then so is the other and they are equal.

(e) If $\phi:A \to B$, then $Id_B.\phi = \phi$ and $\phi.Id_A = \phi$.

A system satisfying these properties is called a *category*.

4.5.1 Proposition

Mealy machines form a category, with input/output homomorphisms as morphisms.

Proof

We check the clauses of the definition. (i) If $\phi:M_1 \Rightarrow M_2$, then we define $\partial_0 = M_1$ and $\partial_1 = M_2$. (ii) We define Id_m as in 1 in Section 4.2.5. (iii) Composition of homomorphisms is given in Section 4.3.5. (iv) See Section 4.3.9. (v) See Section 4.3.10.

EXERCISES

1 Let M be a machine and let $\alpha:S \to S'$, $\iota:I \to I'$ and $\theta:O' \to O$ be bijections. Show that there exists a machine M' such that $(\alpha,\iota,\theta):M \approx M'$.

* Classes are similar to sets but there are differences. For example, one has not the freedom of forming subclasses that one has in forming subsets. This means that when forming the class of all sets, one avoids Russell's paradox.

2 Prove remark 4.2.5.

3 Prove for machines M, M_1, M_2, M_3 that $M \leq M$, and if $M_1 \leq M_2$ and $M_2 \leq M_3$ then $M_1 \leq M_3$.

4 Prove 4.3.9.

5 Prove 4.3.10.

6 Prove 4.3.11.

7 Suppose $\phi:M \to M'$. Show that for all $s \in S$ and $x \in I^*$,

$$\alpha(\delta^*(s,x)) = \delta_{\iota-\theta}^*(\alpha(s),x)$$

8 Devise definitions of homomorphism for Moore machines and state machines. Construct analogues of the results of this chapter and prove them.

9 Consider the machine M_{phys} described in Table 4.3 below, describing the 'physiological Aunt' who was introduced in Chapter 1.

Table 4.3. The Physiological Aunt

	gin	ghetto-b	video	gin	ghetto-b	video
asleep	asleep	sober	asleep	a	b	c
sober	drunk	sober	sober	d	e	f
drunk	asleep	drunk	drunk	g	h	i

Show that there exists a homomorphism $\phi:M_{Eugenia} \to M_{phys}$, such that ι is the identity and α maps according to Table 1.3.

10 Suppose $\phi_1:M_1 \to M_2$ and $\phi_2:M_2 \to M_1$ such that $\phi_1.\phi_2 = Id_{M_2}$. Show that ϕ_1 and ϕ_2 are isomorphisms and that $\phi_2.\phi_1 = Id_{M_1}$.

11 Suppose $\phi:M_1 \to M_2$. Using exercise **10** and 4.3.11, show that ϕ is an isomorphism if and only if there exists ϕ' such that $\phi'.\phi = Id_{M_1}$. What is ϕ'

NOTES

Hartmanis & Stearns (1966) give the more *natural* definition of homomorphism.

Definition A

Let M_1, M_2 be machines, then a homomorphism from M_1 to M_2 is a triple $\phi = (\sigma,\iota,\omega)$, where σ, ι and ω are functions $\sigma:S_1 \to S_2$ $\iota:I_1 \to I_2$ and $\omega:O_1 \to O_2$ such that for all $s \in S_1$, $i \in I_1$:

$$\sigma(\delta_1(s,i)) = \delta_2(\sigma(s),\iota(i))$$

$$\omega(\beta_1(s,i)) = \beta_2(\sigma(s),\iota(i))$$

where ω is now pointed in the right direction. The Hartmanis & Stearns definition is natural because Mealy machines may be viewed as being what are called 'many sorted algebras' and there is a general notion of homomorphism which agrees with definition A. This is why we qualified our notion with the prefix 'input/output'.

Hartmanis & Stearns also has a notion of an *assignment*.

Definition B

Let M_1, M_2 be machines, then an assignment from M_1 to M_2 is a triple $\phi = (\alpha,\iota,\zeta)$, where α is a function $\alpha:S_1 \to \underline{P}(S_2) - \{\emptyset\}$ and ι and ζ are functions $\iota:I_1 \to I_2$ and $\zeta:O_2 \to O_1$ such that for all $s \in S_1$, $s' \in S_2$ and $i \in I_1$:

$$\{\delta_2(s',\iota(i)) \mid s' \in \alpha(s)\} \subseteq \alpha(\delta_1(s,i))$$

if $s' \in \alpha(s)$, then:

$$\beta_1(s,i) = \zeta[\beta_2(s',\iota(i))]$$

Note that ζ is pointing the 'wrong way'.

Hartmanis & Stearns then defined M_2 to realize M_1 if there existed an assignment from M_1 to M_2. Later, they defined M_2 to *realize the state behaviour* of M_1 if there existed an assignment from M_1 to M_2 in which α is an injective function. As this is the kind of assignment they use in serial and parallel decomposition, we have concentrated upon it and called it a state behaviour assignment. We have also chosen to make our notion of homomorphism (distinguished by the prefix 'input/output') a generalization of the state behaviour assignment, partly because this makes things more uniform and partly because it has a simpler *concrete* explanation.

The concept of category is of growing interest to computer scientists because, among other things, it provides them with a natural way of describing data types and constructions on data types.

Chapter 5

Behavioural Equivalence, SP Partitions and Reduced Machines

A landlady may be reduced to her lowest terms by a sequence of propositions.

STEPHEN LEACOCK
Boarding House Geometry

5.1 INTRODUCTION

The central issue of this chapter is the following: given two machines M_1 and M_2, what does it mean to say that they can both do the same job, that they are interchangeable, and what may we infer about them if this is the case ?

This is a very important aspect of certain theories of systems. The idea of similarity of behaviour is central to the calculus of communicating systems, which we examine in Chapter 12, for example.

Again, we are talking about relationships between machines, but in contrast to the discussion in the previous chapter, we are comparing not their *structure*, but their *behaviour*. They do the same job if they are capable of the same input/output behaviour.

What does this mean ? Consider a state $s_1 \in S_1$. From this state, M_1 has input/output behaviour described by the function $\beta_1{}^*(s_1,-):I_1{}^* \rightarrow O_1{}^*$, which maps $x \in I_1{}^*$ to $\beta_1{}^*(s_1,x)$.

If M_2 is to be capable of the same input/output behaviour, then we must be able to find a state $s_2 \in S_2$ such that $\beta_2{}^*(s_2,x) = \beta_1{}^*(s_1,x)$.

Also, since M_1 is to able to do whatever M_2 can do, the argument must work the other way round; for every $s_2 \in S_2$, there must exist an $s_1 \in S_1$ such that if $x \in I_2{}^*$ then $\beta_2{}^*(s_2,x) = \beta_1{}^*(s_1,x)$.

Now let us try to make this a little more precise. First, we have a means of associating elements of S_1 with elements of S_2. Formally, this is a *relation* $R \subseteq S_1 \times S_2$. Furthermore, if $s_1 \in S_1$, then there must be at least one $s_2 \in S_2$ related to s_1. Similarly, if $s_2 \in S_2$, then there must be at least one $s_1 \in S_1$ related to s_2.

This means that the *domain* of R, defined to be the set $Domain(R) = \{s_1 \in S_1 | s_1 \; R \; s_2, \textit{ some } s_2 \in S_2\}$, must be the whole of

S_1. Likewise, the *range* of R, defined to be the set $Range(R) = \{s_2 \in S_2 | s_1 R s_2, \text{ some } s_1 \in S_1\}$ must be the whole of S_2.

Secondly, we note that $x \in I_1^*$ if and only if $x \in I_2^*$. Otherwise one machine could accept an input that the other could not. In particular, $I_1 = I_2$.

We encapsulate these observations in a definition.

5.1.1 Definition

Let M_1, M_2 be machines then M_1 and M_2 will be said to be *behaviourally equivalent* if and only if $I_1 = I_2$ and $O_1 = O_2$ and there exists a relation $R \subseteq S_1 \times S_2$, which we shall call a *behavioural equivalence* between M_1 and M_2 satisfying:

(a) $Domain(R) = S_1$ and $Range(R) = S_2$.

(b) If $s_1 R s_2$, then for all $x \in I_1^*$, $\beta_1^*(s_1,x) = \beta_2^*(s_2,x)$.

We write $M_1 \equiv M_2$ to indicate that M_1 and M_2 are behaviourally equivalent.

5.1.2 Remark

$\equiv$ is reflexive, symmetrical and transitive.

Proof

Exercise **4**.

It is reasonable to ask what is the connection between a behavioural relationship like behavioural equivalence and structural relationships like isomorphism or realization. For example, what sort of structural properties imply the existence of a behavioural equivalence ?

If we are to search for such a property among the results we already possess, then we must restrict ourselves to the previous chapter, since it is there that we began our studies of the relationships between machines. The one result that seems relevant is proposition 4.3.4, which relates the behaviour of machines related by a homomorphism. If $\phi: M_1 \to M_2$ then:

$$\beta_1^*(s,x) = \theta^*[\beta_2^*(\alpha(s),\iota^*(x))] \qquad [5.1]$$

This looks a bit like (b) of 5.1.1. It will look a lot more like it if we constrain ι and θ to be inclusion functions, that is, satisfying $\iota(i) = i$ and $\theta(o) = o$, for all $i \in I_1$ and $o \in O_1$. (Actually, this will make ι and θ identity functions, since $I_1 = I_2$ and $O_1 = O_2$). [5.1] then becomes:

$$\beta_1^*(s,x) = \beta_2^*(\alpha(s),x)$$

It only remains to uncover a relation in all this and such a relation is easy enough to find. Define $s_1 \; R \; s_2$ if and only if $\alpha(s_1) = s_2$, then it is certainly the case that if $s_1 \; R \; s_2$, then $\beta_1^*(s_1,x) = \beta_2^*(s_2,x)$ and it is also true that $Domain(R) = S_1$, since α is a function. In order that R be a behavioural equivalence, it suffices to insist that α is onto. This will entail that $Range(R) = \alpha(S_1) = S_2$.

5.1.3 Definition

Suppose $\phi: M_1 \rightarrow M_2$, then ϕ is a *reduction homomorphism* or just a *reduction* if and only if:

(a) α is onto;

(b) $I_1 = I_2$ and ι is the identity function;

(c) $O_1 = O_2$ and θ is the identity function.

We note that to check that ϕ is a reduction, we need to know that ι and θ are identity functions and that α is onto. The two conditions that make ϕ a homomorphism reduce to:

$$\alpha(\delta_1(s,i)) = \delta_2(\alpha(s),i)$$

$$\beta_1(s,i) = \beta_2(\alpha(s),i)$$

It is generally these two equations we shall use when proving or using the fact that a given triple is a reduction.

5.1.4 Example

We consider two machines M_1 and M_2, described in Tables 5.1 and 5.2, and a triple ϕ, where the function α is defined in Table 5.3 and ι and θ are identity functions.

Table 5.1. The machine M_1

	1	2	1	2
$s1$	$s2$	$s3$	b	a
$s2$	$s1$	$s3$	b	a
$s3$	$s2$	$s4$	a	b
$s4$	$s1$	$s4$	a	b

We may verify that ϕ is a homomorphism. For the function α:

Table 5.2. The machine M_2

	1	2	1	2
$t1$	$t1$	$t2$	b	a
$t2$	$t1$	$t3$	a	b
$t3$	$t1$	$t3$	a	b

Table 5.3. The function α

s	$\alpha(s)$
$s1$	$t1$
$s2$	$t1$
$s3$	$t2$
$s4$	$t3$

$$\alpha(\delta_1(s1,1)) = \alpha(s2) = \delta_1(t1,1) = \delta_1(\alpha(s1),\iota(1))$$
$$\alpha(\delta_1(s1,2)) = \alpha(s3) = \delta_1(t1,2) = \delta_1(\alpha(s1),\iota(2))$$
$$\alpha(\delta_1(s2,1)) = \alpha(s1) = \delta_1(t1,1) = \delta_1(\alpha(s2),\iota(1))$$
$$\alpha(\delta_1(s2,2)) = \alpha(s3) = \delta_1(t1,2) = \delta_1(\alpha(s2),\iota(2))$$
$$\alpha(\delta_1(s3,1)) = \alpha(s2) = \delta_1(t2,1) = \delta_1(\alpha(s3),\iota(1))$$
$$\alpha(\delta_1(s3,2)) = \alpha(s4) = \delta_1(t2,2) = \delta_1(\alpha(s3),\iota(2))$$
$$\alpha(\delta_1(s4,1)) = \alpha(s1) = \delta_1(t3,1) = \delta_1(\alpha(s4),\iota(1))$$
$$\alpha(\delta_1(s4,2)) = \alpha(s4) = \delta_1(t3,2) = \delta_1(\alpha(s4),\iota(2))$$

and for the function θ:

$$\theta[\beta_2(\alpha(s1),\iota(1))] = b = \beta_1(s1,1) \text{ and } \theta[\beta_2(\alpha(s1),\iota(2))] = a = \beta_1(s1,2)$$
$$\theta[\beta_2(\alpha(s2),\iota(1))] = b = \beta_1(s2,1) \text{ and } \theta[\beta_2(\alpha(s2),\iota(2))] = a = \beta_1(s2,2)$$
$$\theta[\beta_2(\alpha(s3),\iota(1))] = a = \beta_1(s3,1) \text{ and } \theta[\beta_2(\alpha(s3),\iota(2))] = b = \beta_1(s3,2)$$
$$\theta[\beta_2(\alpha(s4),\iota(1))] = a = \beta_1(s4,1) \text{ and } \theta[\beta_2(\alpha(s4),\iota(2))] = b = \beta_1(s4,2)$$

For the rest, α is onto and ι and θ are identity mappings. Thus, ϕ is a reduction.

To sum up the above discussion:

5.1.5 Proposition

Suppose there exists $\phi : M_1 \to M_2$, a reduction, then $M_1 \equiv M_2$.

Proof

As we have explained, the relation given by: $s_1 \, R \, s_2$ if and only if $\alpha(s_1) = s_2$ is a behavioural equivalence.

5.2 SP PARTITIONS

In general, the converse of 5.1.5 does not hold. Indeed, if it did, then it would be the case that $M_1 \equiv M_2$ implies $M_1 \approx M_2$ (see exercises **6** and **7**). This certainly is not always true. For instance, in example 5.1.4, we defined two machines M_1 and M_2 and a homomorphism $\phi : M_1 \to M_2$ which turned out to be a reduction. Thus, $M_1 \equiv M_2$, but the machines are not isomorphic. If they were, there would be a bijection from S_1 to S_2. But there cannot be such a bijection since $|S_1| \neq |S_2|$.

So what is the truth of the matter ? We shall discover this after a closer look at reductions.

Suppose $\phi : M_1 \to M_2$ is a reduction. The key fact is the following:

> α is a surjection and hence determines a partition* of S_1, whose blocks are in a one-to-one correspondence with the elements of S_2. We could therefore construct a copy of M_2 using the blocks of this partition as states.

To be more detailed, to every $s' \in S_2$, there is a set $\alpha^{-1}(s')$, the set of all states of S_1 that map to s' under α. These sets form a partition – let's call it π – of S_1. We can construct a machine isomorphic to M_2, by replacing each s' in S_2 by $\alpha^{-1}(s')$. This gives a machine $M' = (\pi, I_1, O_1, \delta', \beta')$, where:

$$\delta_2(s, i) = s' \Rightarrow \delta'(\alpha^{-1}(s), i) = \alpha^{-1}(s'). \qquad [5.2]$$

$$\beta'(\alpha^{-1}(s'), i) = \beta_2(s', i) \qquad [5.3]$$

* See A.1.15.

5.2.1 Example

Going back to example 5.1.4, we can see that $\alpha^{-1}(t1) = \{s1, s2\}$, $\alpha^{-1}(t2) = \{s3\}$ and $\alpha^{-1}(t3) = \{s4\}$. Thus the new machine would have a flow table as given in Table 5.4.

Table 5.4. The machine M'

	1	2	1	2
$\{s1,s2\}$	$\{s1,s2\}$	$\{s3\}$	b	a
$\{s3\}$	$\{s1,s2\}$	$\{s4\}$	a	b
$\{s4\}$	$\{s1,s2\}$	$\{s4\}$	a	b

So, if $\phi: M_1 \to M_2$ is a reduction, then we may construct an isomorphic copy of M_2 using subsets of S_1. This is all very well, but surely we may make isomorphic copies of M_2 using anything we like, including subsets of S_2. So there must be more to it than that:

There is. Let us examine M' more carefully. Suppose $X, X' \in \pi$, $i \in I_1$ and $o \in O_1$ and suppose that:

$$\delta'(X, i) = X' \text{ and } \beta'(X, i) = o$$

By definition of π and by [5.2] and [5.3], we must have $s_2, s_2' \in S_2$ such that:

$$X = \alpha^{-1}(s_2),\ X' = \alpha^{-1}(s_2'),\ \delta_2(s_2, i) = s_2' \text{ and } \beta_2(s_2, i) = o \qquad [5.4]$$

Now, suppose $s_1 \in X$ and let $s_1' = \delta_1(s_1, i)$. Since $X = \alpha^{-1}(s_2)$, it follows that $\alpha(s_1) = s_2$. Thus:

$$\delta_2(s_2, i) = \delta_2(\alpha(s_1), \iota(i)) \text{ and } \theta[\beta_2(\alpha(s_1), \iota(i))] = \beta_2(s_2, i) \qquad [5.5]$$

Now we use the fact that ϕ is a homomorphism to deduce that:

$$\delta_2(\alpha(s_1), \iota(i)) = \alpha(\delta_1(s_1, i)) \text{ and } \theta[\beta_2(\alpha(s_1), \iota(i))] = \beta_1(s_1, i) \qquad [5.6]$$

Thus, by [5.4], [5.5] and [5.6]:

$$\alpha(\delta_1(s_1, i)) = s_2' \text{ and } \beta_1(s_1, i) = o \qquad [5.7]$$

Since $X' = \alpha^{-1}(s_2')$, it follows that $\delta_1(s_1, i) \in X'$.

We can see, therefore, that π is not any old partition of S_1. It has the two properties:

$$\delta'(X, i) = X' \ \& \ s_1 \in X, \Rightarrow \delta_1(s_1, i) \in X' \qquad [5.8]$$

$$\beta'(X, i) = o \ \& \ s_1 \in X \Rightarrow \beta_1(s_1, i) = o. \qquad [5.9]$$

We can simplify these statements by the following definition.

5.2.2 Definition

Let M be a machine and let $X \subseteq S$ and $i \in I$. Define:
(a) $\delta(X, i) = \{\delta(s, i) \mid s \in X\}$
(b) $\beta(X, i) = \{\beta(s, i) \mid s \in X\}$
We may now express [5.8] and [5.9] in the following form.

5.2.3 Lemma

With the above notation, for all $X, X' \in \pi$, $i \in I_1$ and $o \in O_1$:
(a) $\delta'(X, i) = X' \Rightarrow \delta_1(X, i) \subseteq X'$
(b) $\beta'(X, i) = o \Rightarrow \beta_1(X, i) = \{o\}$
Thus:
(c) For all $X \in \pi$ and $i \in I_1$, there exists $X' \in \pi$ and $o \in O_1$ such that $\delta_1(X, i) \subseteq X'$ and $\beta_1(X, i) = \{o\}$.
With (c), we have properties of M_1 that make no reference to M' or M_2 or ϕ; they are purely internal. Because there is a reduction of M_1, such a partition of S_1 exists. Before we do anything else, let us name these properties.

5.2.4 Definition

Let M be a machine and let π be a partition of S, then π will be said to be *admissible* or possess the *substitution property* if and only if for every $X \in \pi$ and $i \in I$ there exists $Y \in \pi$ such that:

$$\delta(X, i) \subseteq Y.$$

We shall abbreviate 'substitution property' to SP, from now on, and refer to partitions with the SP as *SP partitions*.

5.2.5 Example

Let us see how this works in practice by looking at the partition defined in 5.2.1. which we shall call π_1. We note that:

$$\delta_1(\{s1, s2\}, 1) = \{s1, s2\} \subseteq \{s1, s2\} \in \pi_1$$

and

$$\delta_1(\{s1, s2\}, 2) = \{s3\} \subseteq \{s3\} \in \pi_1$$

We do not need to check the other blocks of π_1 because they are singletons. In general, if $X \in \pi$ and π is a partition and $X = \{s\}$ for some s, then for any $i \in I$, there exists $Y \in \pi$ such that $\delta(s, i) \in Y$. Hence $\delta(X, i) = \{\delta(s, i)\} \subseteq Y$.

Thus, π_1 has the SP property.

5.2.6 Definition

Let M be a machine and let π be a partition of S, then π will be said to *output consistent* if and only if for every $X \in \pi$ and every $i \in I$ and $s_1, s_2 \in X$:

$$\beta(s_1, i) = \beta(s_2, i)$$

5.2.7 Example

Returning to our example π_1, we show that it is output consistent. Again, it is simply a matter of calculation. For the block $\{s1, s2\}$, we have:

$$\beta_1(s1, 1) = b = \beta_1(s2, 1) \text{ and } \beta_1(s1, 2) = a = \beta_1(s2, 2)$$

As in 5.2.5, we have no need to check the other blocks of π_1.

Thus π_1 is output consistent. We may now rephrase 5.2.3, as below.

5.2.8 Proposition

Let $\phi: M_1 \to M_2$ be a reduction and define $Ker(\phi)$, the *kernel* of ϕ, to be the partition $\{\alpha^{-1}(s) \mid s \in S_2\}$, then $Ker(\phi)$ is SP and output consistent.

Let us now return to the machine M'. Remember that we made it from M_2 by replacing each $s \in S_2$ by $\alpha^{-1}(s)$. Thus if $\delta_2(s_2, i) = s_2'$, then $\delta'(\alpha^{-1}(s_2), i) = \alpha^{-1}(s_2')$.

As we shall see, δ' and β' may be defined directly from $Ker(\phi)$.

For example, suppose $X \in Ker(\phi)$ and $i \in I$.

Let $\delta_1(X, i) \subseteq X'$ and suppose $\delta'(X, i) = X''$. By 5.2.3(a), $\delta_1(X, i) \subseteq X''$. But this means that $\delta_1(X, i) \subseteq X' \cap X''$, and since

$\delta_1(X,i) \neq \emptyset$, it follows that $X' \cap X'' \neq \emptyset$. Since both belong to a partition, we must have $X' = X''$. Thus:

$$\delta_1(X,i) \subseteq X' \Rightarrow \delta'(X,i) = X' \quad [5.10]$$

Likewise, suppose $\beta_1(X,i) = \{o\}$ and $\beta'(X,i) = \{o'\}$. Then $\beta_1(X,i) = \{o'\}$ by 5.2.3(b) and so $o' = o$. Thus:

$$\beta_1(X,i) = \{o\} \Rightarrow \beta'(X,i) = o \quad [5.11]$$

From 5.2.3 and [5.10] and [5.11], we have the following.

5.2.9 Lemma

With the above notation, for all $X, X' \in Ker(\phi)$, $i \in I_1$ and $o \in O_1$:
(a) $\delta'(X,i) = X' \Leftrightarrow \delta_1(X,i) \subseteq X'$
(b) $\beta'(X,i) = o \Leftrightarrow \beta_1(X,i) = \{o\}$

Thus, the machine M' may be constructed entirely from the partition $Ker(\phi)$. Not only that, but the construction may be made for *any* partition which is SP and output consistent, as we now define.

5.2.10 Definition

Let M be a machine and let π be a partition of S which is both SP and output consistent, then the *quotient machine* of M by π, written M/π, is the machine $(\pi, I, O, \delta_\pi, \beta_\pi)$, where:
(a) $\delta_\pi(X,i) = Y$ if and only if $\delta(X,i) \subseteq Y$
(b) $\beta_\pi(X,i) = o$ if and only if $\beta(X,i) = \{o\}$

5.2.11 Example

Consider the following partition π_{exam} on the machine M_1 of example 5.1.4. We let $\pi_{exam} = \{\{s1,s2\},\{s3,s4\}\}$. We check:

$$\delta_1(\{s1,s2\},1) = \{s1,s2\} \subseteq \{s1,s2\} \in \pi_{exam}$$

$$\delta_1(\{s1,s2\},2) = \{s3\} \subseteq \{s3,s4\} \in \pi_{exam}$$

$$\delta_1(\{s3,s4\},1) = \{s1,s2\} \subseteq \{s1,s2\} \in \pi_{exam}$$

$$\delta_1(\{s3,s4\},2) = \{s4\} \subseteq \{s3,s4\} \in \pi_{exam}$$

Thus, π_{exam} has the SP property.

Returning to our example π_{exam}, we show that it is output consistent. Again, it is simply a matter of calculation. For the block $\{s1, s2\}$, we have

$$\beta_1(s1, 1) = b = \beta_1(s2, 1) \text{ and } \beta_1(s1, 2) = a = \beta_1(s2, 2)$$

and for the block $\{s3, s4\}$, we have:

$$\beta_1(s3, 1) = a = \beta_1(s4, 1) \text{ and } \beta_1(s3, 2) = b = \beta_1(s4, 2)$$

Thus π_{exam} is output consistent.

Thus, we may construct M_1/π_{exam}. For example, since:

$$\delta_1(\{s1, s2\}, 1) = \{s1, s2\} \subseteq \{s1, s2\} \in \pi_{exam}$$

$$\delta_1(\{s1, s2\}, 2) = \{s3\} \subseteq \{s3, s4\} \in \pi_{exam}$$

then we would define:

$$\delta_{\pi_{exam}}(\{s1, s2\}, 1) = \{s1, s2\} \text{ and } \delta_{\pi_{exam}}(\{s1, s2\}, 2) = \{s3, s4\}$$

and since:

$$\beta_1(s1, 1) = b = \beta_1(s2, 1) \text{ and } \beta_1(s1, 2) = a = \beta_1(s2, 2)$$

we would define:

$$\beta_{\pi_{exam}}(s1, 1) = b \text{ and } \beta_{\pi_{exam}}(s1, 2) = a$$

The full flow table for M_1/π_{exam} is given in Table 5.5.

Table 5.5. The machine M_1/π_{exam}

	1	2	1	2
$\{s1, s2\}$	$\{s1, s2\}$	$\{s3, s4\}$	b	a
$\{s3, s4\}$	$\{s1, s2\}$	$\{s3, s4\}$	a	b

Let us return to our discussion. We have now shown that given a reduction $\phi: M_1 \rightarrow M_2$, we may construct an isomorphic copy of M_2, which we called M', by *substituting* elements of S_2 by blocks of a partition of M_1. This partition turned out to have the *substitution* property. We have also shown how to construct a quotient machine, $M_1/Ker(\phi)$ and

5.2.9 entails that $M' = M_1/Ker(\phi)$. But, M' was constructed in such a way as to ensure that it is an isomorphic copy of M_2. We should not, therefore, be surprised by the following.

5.2.12 Proposition

Let $\phi: M_1 \rightarrow M_2$ be a reduction then $M_2 \approx M_1/Ker(\phi)$.

Proof

We construct an isomorphism.

Let $\phi' = (\alpha', \iota', \theta')$, where ι' and θ' are both identities (this is possible, since $I_1 = I_2$ and $O_1 = O_2$ by 5.1.3 (b) and (c)) and $\alpha'(s) = \alpha^{-1}(s)$. We note that all three functions are bijective. To complete the proof, we must show that:

$$\delta_{Ker(\phi)}(\alpha'(s), i) = \alpha'(\delta_2(s, i)) \qquad [5.12]$$

and

$$\beta_{Ker(\phi)}(\alpha'(s), i) = \beta_2(s, i) \qquad [5.13]$$

In order to prove [5.12], by definition of α', we must show that:

$$\delta_{Ker(\phi)}(\alpha^{-1}(s), i) = \alpha^{-1}(\delta_2(s, i)) \qquad [5.14]$$

which, by definition of $\delta_{Ker(\phi)}$ is the case if and only if:

$$\delta_1(\alpha^{-1}(s), i) \subseteq \alpha^{-1}(\delta_2(s, i)) \qquad [5.15]$$

To prove [5.15], let $s' \in \alpha^{-1}(s)$; we must show that $\delta_1(s', i) \in \alpha^{-1}(\delta_2(s, i))$, that is:

$$\alpha(\delta_1(s'), i) = \delta_2(s, i) \qquad [5.16]$$

But, since $s' \in \alpha^{-1}(s)$, we have $s = \alpha(s')$ and so [5.16] is equivalent to $\alpha(\delta_1(s'), i) = \delta_2(\alpha(s'), i)$, which is true because ϕ is a reduction.

Finally, we show [5.13]. Suppose $\beta_2(s, i) = o$ and let $s' \in \alpha^{-1}(s)$. In view of definition 5.2.10(b), it suffices to prove that $\beta_1(s', i) = o$. But, since ϕ is a reduction, $\beta_1(s', i) = \beta_2(\alpha(s'), i) = \beta_2(s, i)$ and we are done.

Now let us continue. We know that if we have a reduction $\phi: M_1 \rightarrow M_2$, then we can construct an SP partition of M_2, $Ker(\phi)$, which is output consistent. However, the construction 5.2.10 may be made with any partition π of a machine M if the partition is SP and output consistent. The following proposition gives the relationship between M and M/π.

5.2.13 Proposition

Suppose π is a partition of a machine M which is both SP and output consistent, then there is a reduction $\phi_\pi : M \to M/\pi$, onto the quotient machine M/π such that $\alpha_\pi(s) = X \Leftrightarrow s \in X$ and ι_π and θ_π are identity functions.

We shall refer to ϕ_π as the *natural reduction* of M onto M/π.

Proof

Define ϕ_π as in the statement of the proposition. We need only show that ϕ_π is a homomorphism since it clearly satisfies all other conditions for being a reduction.

Let $s \in S$ and let $i \in I$. Because ι_π and θ_π are identity maps, it suffices to show that:

$$\alpha_\pi(\delta(s,i)) = \delta_\pi(\alpha_\pi(s),i)$$
$$\beta(s,i) = \beta_\pi(\alpha_\pi(s),i)$$

First, $s \in \alpha_\pi(s)$ and so $\delta(s,i) \in \delta(\alpha_\pi(s),i)$. But, by definition of δ_π, we must have $\delta(\alpha_\pi(s),i) \subseteq \delta_\pi(\alpha_\pi(s),i)$ and so $\delta(s,i) \in \delta_\pi(\alpha_\pi(s),i)$. Since $s \in X$ if and only if $\alpha_\pi(s) = X$, for $X \in \pi$, it follows that $\alpha_\pi(\delta(s,i)) = \delta_\pi(\alpha_\pi(s),i)$.

As far as output is concerned, by definition of β_π, if $s \in X \in \pi$ then $\beta_\pi(X,i) = \beta(s,i)$, and the equation follows from the fact that by definition $s \in \alpha_\pi(s)$.

This concludes the proof.

5.3 BEHAVIOURAL EQUIVALENCE REVISITED

Now that we have related the existence of reductions to something internal to machines, we may resume our study of the question 'when do we have $M_1 \equiv M_2$?' Suppose $M_1 \equiv M_2$ with behavioural equivalence R.

We shall first look at the case when the machines are what we call *reduced*.

5.3.1 Definition

Let M be a machine, then we shall say that M is reduced if and only if for all $s, s' \in S$, if $s \neq s'$, then for some $x \in I^*$, $\beta^*(s,x) \neq \beta^*(s',x)$.

If M is reduced, then every distinct pair of states have distinct input/output behaviour.

Now, if M_2 is reduced, the the behavioural equivalence R will be a *function* from S_1 to S_2. To see that, note first that $Dom(R) = S_1$, by 5.1.1(a), which is one property that a function from S_1 must have. The second is that for every $s \in S_1$ and $s_1, s_2 \in S_2$, if $s\ R\ s_1$ and $s\ R\ s_2$, then $s_1 = s_2$.

But, if $s\ R\ s_1$, then for all x, $\beta_2^*(s_1,x) = \beta_1^*(s,x)$, by 5.1.1(b) and if $s\ R\ s_2$, then for all x, $\beta_1^*(s,x) = \beta_2^*(s_2,x)$, also by 5.1.1(b).

Thus, if $s\ R\ s_1$ and $s\ R\ s_2$, then for all x, $\beta_2^*(s_1,x) = \beta_1^*(s,x) = \beta_2^*(s_2,x)$ and so for all x, $\beta_2^*(s_1,x) = \beta_2^*(s_2,x)$, which is impossible for $s_1 \neq s_2$, by definition 5.3.1, and so $s_1 = s_2$.

Define $\alpha: S_1 \rightarrow S_2$, by $\alpha(s) = s'$ if and only if $s\ R\ s'$ and let $\iota: I_1 \rightarrow I_2$ and $\theta: O_2 \rightarrow O_1$ be identity functions.

Note also that since $Range(R) = S_2$, then α is onto. And not only is α an onto function, but it also satisfies

$$\beta_2^*(\alpha(s),x) = \beta_1^*(s,x) \qquad [5.17]$$

for all x. This is because $s\ R\ \alpha(s)$ by definition and R is a behavioural equivalence and so 5.1.1(b) holds.

Therefore $\phi = (\alpha, \iota, \theta)$ is almost a reduction. All that we would need to prove in addition is that for all $s \in S_1$ and $i \in I_1$:

$$\alpha(\delta_1(s,i)) = \delta_2(\alpha(s),i))$$

Let us do so. Let $s_1 = \alpha(\delta_1(s,i))$ and $s_2 = \delta_2(\alpha(s),i))$. We need to show that $s_1 = s_2$.

Since M_2 is reduced, it will suffice to show that for all x, $\beta_2^*(s_1,x) = \beta_2^*(s_2,x)$.

This will follow, if we can show that for any $i \in I_2$:

$$\beta_2(\alpha(s),i).\beta_2^*(s_1,x) = \beta_2(\alpha(s),i).\beta_2^*(s_2,x) \qquad [5.18]$$

for then we may cancel out $\beta_2(\alpha(s),i)$ from both sides. In fact, we shall show that both sides are equal to $\beta_2^*(\alpha(s),ix)$. Calculating:

$$\beta_2^*(\alpha(s),ix) = \beta_2(\alpha(s),i).\beta_2^*(\delta_2(\alpha(s),i),x) \text{ (by 2.2.6)}$$

$$= \beta_2(\alpha(s), i).\beta_2^*(s_2, x) \text{ (by definition of } s_2)$$

and

$$\beta_2^*(\alpha(s), ix) = \beta_1^*(s, ix) \text{ (by 5.17)}$$
$$= \beta_1(s, i).\beta_1^*(\delta_1(s, i), x) \text{ (by 2.2.6)}$$
$$= \beta_2(\alpha(s), i).\beta_2^*(\alpha(\delta_1(s, i)), x) \text{ (by 5.17)}$$
$$= \beta_2(\alpha(s), i).\beta_2^*(s_1, x) \text{ (by definition of } s_1)$$

We have therefore shown the following.

5.3.2 Lemma

Suppose $M_1 \equiv M_2$ and M_2 is reduced, then there exists a reduction $\phi: M_1 \to M_2$.

It may easily be shown (see exercise 6) that if there exist reductions $\phi_1: M_1 \to M_2$ and $\phi_2: M_2 \to M_1$, then $M_1 \approx M_2$. We thus have the following.

5.3.3 Corollary

Suppose $M_1 \equiv M_2$ and M_1, M_2 are reduced, then $M_1 \approx M_2$.

Proof

By 5.3.2, there exists a reduction $\phi_1: M_1 \to M_2$. Since $M_2 \equiv M_1$, by 5.1.2, we may also apply 5.3.2 to conclude the existence of a reduction $\phi_2: M_2 \to M_1$.

Now we turn to the case where M_2 is not reduced. The idea here is to collapse each set of states, all of whose members have the same input/output behaviour, down to a single point, giving a new machine which should be reduced. We begin by defining a relation which identifies states with the same input/output behaviour.

5.3.4 Definition

Let M be any machine and let $s_1, s_2 \in S$, then $s_1 \equiv s_2$ if and only if, for all $x \in I^*$:

$$\beta^*(s_1, x) = \beta^*(s_2, x) \qquad [5.19]$$

5.3.5 Lemma

$\equiv$ is an equivalence relation.

Proof

We have to show that $\equiv$ satisfies the three laws that an equivalence relation must satisfy.

1 Certainly, for any $s \in S$, $\beta^*(s,x) = \beta^*(s,x)$, so $s \equiv s$ and so $\equiv$ is reflexive.

2 If $s_1 \equiv s_2$, then for all x, $\beta^*(s_1,x) = \beta^*(s_2,x)$ holds and so for all x, $\beta^*(s_2,x) = \beta^*(s_1,x)$ holds and thus $s_2 \equiv s_1$. Thus, $\equiv$ is symmetric.

3 Finally, suppose $s_1 \equiv s_2$ and $s_2 \equiv s_3$ then for all x, $\beta^*(s_1,x) = \beta^*(s_2,x)$ and $\beta^*(s_2,x) = \beta^*(s_3,x)$ holds and so for all x, $\beta^*(s_1,x) = \beta^*(s_3,x)$ holds and thus $s_1 \equiv s_3$. Thus, $\equiv$ is transitive.

This concludes the proof.

Since $\equiv$ is an equivalence relation, it determines a partition (see A.2.9). Let us call this partition ρ_M (ρ for 'reduce'). The next lemma indicates that ρ_M is a partition of the kind we are looking for.

5.3.6 Lemma

ρ_M is SP and output consistent.

Proof

Let $X \in \rho_M$ and let $s \in X$. If $i \in I$, then there is a block $Y \in \rho_M$ such that $\delta(s,i) \in Y$. We shall show that $\delta(X,i) \subseteq Y$. ρ_M will satisfy 5.2.4, since this works for any $X \in \rho_M$ and therefore ρ_M will be proved to be SP.

We want to show that if s' is any other element of X, then $\delta(s',i)$ is in the same block as $\delta(s,i)$. In other words, we want to show that if $s \equiv s'$, then $\delta(s,i) \equiv \delta(s',i)$. So, let $s' \in X$.

Now, from definition [5.19] if x is any element of I^*, then:

$$\beta^*(s,i.x) = \beta^*(s',i.x) \qquad [5.20]$$

But by definition of β^*, 2.2.6:

$$\beta^*(s,i.x) = \beta(s,i).\beta^*(\delta(s,i),x) \qquad [5.21]$$

and similarly:

$$\beta^*(s', i.x) = \beta(s', i).\beta^*(\delta(s', i), x) \qquad [5.22]$$

Substituting [5.21] and [5.22] into [5.20], we get:

$$\beta(s, i).\beta^*(\delta(s, i), x) = \beta(s', i).\beta^*(\delta(s', i), x) \qquad [5.23]$$

But from [5.9], with i substituted for x, since $s \equiv s'$, we must have:

$$\beta(s, i) = \beta^*(s, i) = \beta^*(s', i) = \beta(s', i)$$

and so cancelling $\beta(s, i)$ from both sides of equation [5.23], we obtain, finally, that for all $x \in I^*$:

$$\beta^*(\delta(s, i), x) = \beta^*(\delta(s', i), x)$$

and hence $\delta(s, i) \equiv \delta(s', i)$ as required.

Next, we must show that ρ_M is output consistent. Suppose $X \in \rho_M$ and let $s, s' \in X$, then $s \equiv s'$ and so if i is any input, we have again:

$$\beta(s, i) = \beta^*(s, i) = \beta^*(s', i) = \beta(s', i)$$

and so ρ_M has the required property.

This concludes the proof.

From proposition 5.2.13 and the preceding lemma, we obtain the following.

5.3.7 Corollary

There exists a reduction $\phi : M \to M/\rho_M$.

Our motive for constructing M/ρ_M was to find a reduced machine related to M. We have succeeded in this because of the following.

5.3.8 Proposition

M/ρ_M is reduced.

Proof

Let $X_1, X_2 \in \rho_M$ and suppose that for all x,

$$\beta_{\rho_M}{}^*(X_1, x) = \beta_{\rho_M}{}^*(X_2, x). \qquad [5.24]$$

We must show that $X_1 = X_2$.

Since X_1 and X_2 are equivalence classes, it suffices to show that $s_1 \equiv s_2$ for some $s_1 \in X_1$ and $s_2 \in X_2$, for then $s_1, s_2 \in X_1 \cap X_2$, which is impossible if the two sets are distinct.

So let $s_1 \in X_1$ and $s_2 \in X_2$. We must have $\alpha(s_1) = X_1$ and $\alpha(s_2) = X_2$, where ϕ is the natural reduction of M onto M/ρ_M of 5.2.13.

Since ϕ is a reduction, we have that for all x,

$$\beta_{\rho_M}(X_1, x) = \beta_{\rho_M}(\alpha(s_1), x) = \beta(s_1, x)$$

and

$$\beta_{\rho_M}(X_2, x) = \beta_{\rho_M}(\alpha(s_2), x) = \beta(s_2, x)$$

from whence, by application of [5.24], we deduce that for all x, $\beta(s_1, x) = \beta(s_2, x)$ and hence that $s_1 \equiv s_2$, which is what we wanted to show.

5.3.9 Proposition

Let M_1, M_2 be machines, then $M_1 \equiv M_2$ implies that $M_1/\rho_{M_1} \approx M_2/\rho_{M_2}$.

Proof

By 5.3.7, there exists reductions, $\phi_1{:}M_1 \to M_1/\rho_1$ and $\phi_2{:}M_2 \to M_2/\rho_2$. Thus, by 5.1.5, $M_1/\rho_1 \equiv M_1 \equiv M_2 \equiv M_2/\rho_2$. Hence, $M_1/\rho_1 \equiv M_2/\rho_2$, by 5.1.2. But, M_1/ρ_1 and M_2/ρ_2 are both reduced. Hence $M_1/\rho_1 \approx M_2/\rho_2$, by 5.3.3.

From this, we finally arrive at our result.

5.3.10 Theorem

Let M_1, M_2 be machines, then $M_1 \equiv M_2$ if and only if there exists M and reductions $\phi_1{:}M_1 \to M$ and $\phi_2{:}M_2 \to M$.

Proof

First, suppose that we have reductions $\phi_1:M_1 \to M$ and $\phi_2:M_2 \to M$, then $M_1 \equiv M \equiv M_2$ by 5.1.5 and so $M_1 \equiv M_2$ by 5.1.2.

Next, suppose $M_1 \equiv M_2$. Let $M = M_2/\rho_{M_2}$, then there exists a reduction $\phi_2:M_2 \to M$, by 5.3.7. We show that there exists a reduction $\phi_1:M_1 \to M$.

Let $M_1' = M_1/\rho_{M_1}$. By 5.3.7, there exists a reduction $\phi_1':M_1 \to M_1'$. By 5.3.9, there exists an isomorphism $\phi:M_1' \approx M$. Define $\phi_1 = \phi_1'.\phi$, then $\phi_1:M_1 \to M$ is the composite of a reduction and an isomorphism and hence a reduction (see exercise **8**).

In fact, we may say even more. M/ρ_M is in a sense the smallest machine possible which does the same as M.

5.3.11 Proposition

Let M be a machine and suppose ρ_M is the partition described above. Suppose there is a reduction $\phi:M \to M'$ then there is a reduction $\phi':M' \to M/\rho_M$.

M/ρ_M is called the *reduced* machine of M.*

Proof

$M \equiv M'$, by 5.1.5 and so we have a reduction $\phi:M' \to M'/\rho_{M'}$, by 5.3.7 and an isomorphism $\phi'':M'/\rho_{M'} \approx M/\rho_M$. $\phi''.\phi$ is now the required reduction.

Returning to our example, it is in fact the case that the partition π_{exam} that we defined is ρ_M for M_1. According to the proposition, there ought to be a reduction from M_2, defined in Table 5.2, to M_1/π, defined in Table 5.5. Indeed there is. The map α of this reduction is:

$$\alpha(t1) = \{s1, s2\} \quad \alpha(t2) = \{s3, s4\} \quad \alpha(t3) = \{s3, s4\}$$

Proposition 5.3.11 shows that we can find a 'unique' smallest machine that will do the same things as a given machine M. Of course this machine may be isomorphic to M, that is, M is as efficient as it could be.

* Strictly speaking, we should call it *a* reduced machine of M since any other machine isomorphic to it would be as useful.

However, constructing the relation $\equiv$ does not look too easy. How can we find out whether $\beta^*(s,x) = \beta^*(s',x)$ for *every* string x ? We cannot try every one of them – there are an infinite number – so how can we tell ?

We shall find the answer to that later, when we look in greater detail at SP partitions in Chapter 9. Briefly, partitions may be ordered and there will be a unique 'largest' output consistent SP partition. This, in virtue of proposition 5.3.11, will be ρ_M.

EXERCISES

1 Let M be any machine. Show that the partitions $\perp = \{\{s\} \mid s \in S\}$ and $\top = \{S\}$ are SP. Prove that if $\beta(s,i) \neq \beta(s',i)$ for all i and all $s \neq s'$, then $\rho_M = \perp$.

2 Consider the Mealy machine describing Great Aunt Eugenia (Table 1.1 of Chapter 1). Which of the following are (i) partitions (ii) SP partitions of her state space ?
(a) $\{\{A\},\{I,U\},\{G,M\}\}$
(b) $\{\{A\},\{I,G,M\},\{U,G\}\}$
(c) $\{\{A\},\{I,G\},\{U,M\}\}$
What can you say about her reduced machine ?

3 Do the same for the robot whose flow table is given in exercise 4 of Chapter 2 with the following sets:
(a) $\{\{S1,S3,S5\},\{S2,S4,S6\}\}$
(b) $\{\{S6,S5\},\{S4,S3\},\{S2,S1\}\}$
(c) $\{\{S1,S4\},\{S2,S5\},\{S3,S6\}\}$

4 Prove remark 5.1.2.

5 Show that if $\phi_1{:}M_1 \to M_2$ and $\phi_2{:}M_2 \to M_1$ are reductions, then $M_1 \approx M_2$

6 Let $\sim$ be a relation on machines such that:
(a) If $M_1 \sim M_2$ then $M_2 \sim M_1$
(b) If $M_1 \sim M_2$ then there exists a reduction $\phi{:}M_1 \to M_2$.
Prove that if $M_1 \sim M_2$, then $M_1 \approx M_2$.

7 Let $\phi_1{:}M_1 \to M_2$ be an isomorphism and $\phi_2{:}M_2 \to M_3$ be a reduction. Prove that $\phi_2.\phi_1{:}M_1 \to M_3$ is a reduction

8 Let M_1, M_2 be machines such that $I_1 = I_2$ and $O_1 = O_2$. Let $R \subseteq S_1 \times S_2$ satisfy $Dom(R) = S_1$ and $Range(R) = S_2$. Show that if:

$$s_1 \; R \; s_2 \Rightarrow \delta_1(s_1,i) \; R \; \delta_2(s_2,i) \text{ and } \beta_1(s_1,i) = \beta_2(s_2,i)$$

then R is a behavioural equivalence. The reader might like to compare this relation with the strong congruence relation defined in Chapter 12.

NOTES

This material is mostly taken from Hartmanis & Stearns (1966) parts 1.2 and 2.5. We have put more emphasis on the relationship between reductions and homomorphisms than they. Also, Hartmanis & Stearns speak only of equivalence. We have added the prefix 'behavioural' partly to distinguish it from other equivalences and partly to suggest the connection with observational equivalence discussed in Chapter 12.

Hartmanis & Stearns do not bring in SP partitions straightaway and relate them to reduced machines only after discussing them in terms of serial and parallel decomposition – which we cover in Chapters 7 and 8.

However, 5.2.8, 5.2.12 and 5.2.13 are analogous with the relationship between 'congruences' and 'onto homomorphisms' which are found generally in algebra and is generally introduced before any consideration of decomposition.

Chapter 6

Parallel and Serial Composition of Automata

Composition is not a profession – it's a mania, a kind of gentle madness.

ARTHUR HONEGGER

6.1 INTRODUCTION

We have seen how to define automata, how to implement them and compare them and how to reduce the sizes of their state spaces. In this chapter, we shall be looking at ways of combining machines to make other machines.

Composition must be an important part of any serious theory of systems. It is rarely sensible or safe to design a large system as a single unit. Rather, such systems should be built up out of smaller and more tractable components.

We shall examine two forms of composition. In the first, the two component machines M_1 and M_2 are simply run synchronously in parallel. The new machine will take a pair of inputs, one from I_1 and one from I_2. These are processed by the two components in the normal way, and the outputs are produced together as a pair. This *parallel* composite of two machines M_1 and M_2 will be written $M_1 \mid\mid M_2$.

In the second, outputs from M_1 are used as inputs to M_2, possibly after passing through an encoder. Thus one 'step' of the new machine consists of M_1 performing one step, the output from M_1 being modified to make it suitable for input to M_2 and, finally, the modified output being used by M_2. This *serial* composite of two machines M_1 and M_2 will be written $M_1 \ominus M_2$ or $M_1 \ominus_\kappa M_2$.

While it is fairly easy to see *informally* how such composites work, we must remember that we are talking about them being machines, that is, ordered quintuples of sets and functions. We must therefore *define* $M_1 \ominus M_2$ and $M_1 \mid\mid M_2$ as ordered quintuples.

6.2 PARALLEL COMPOSITION

We may picture the parallel composite of two machines M_1 and M_2 as in Fig. 6.1.

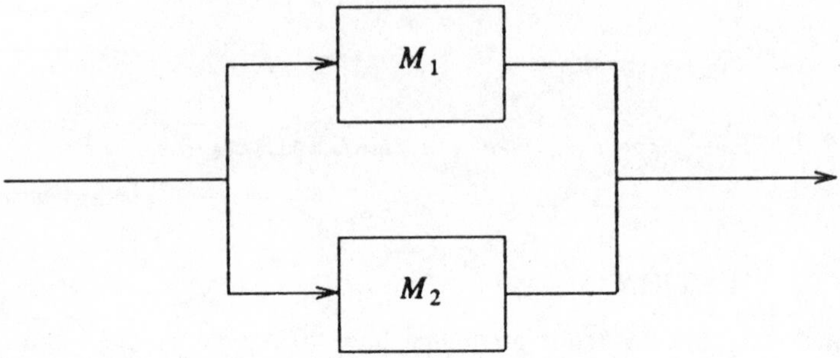

Fig. 6.1. Parallel Composition

As we explained, an input to this pair will be a pair of inputs, one from I_1 and one from I_2, clocked in simultaneously. So, what does the composite do ? Let us suppose that M_1 is in state s_1 and that M_2 is in state s_2. Let us suppose that $i_1 \in I_1$ and $i_2 \in I_2$ are presented as inputs. What will happen ?

Well, i_1 will be input to M_1, which will change state to $\delta_1(s_1, i_1)$ and output $\beta_1(s_1, i_1)$. Similarly, i_2 will be input to M_2, which will change state to $\delta_2(s_2, i_2)$ and output $\beta_2(s_2, i_2)$.

So, what comes out of the composite machine is a *pair* of outputs, $\beta_1(s_1, i_1)$ and $\beta_2(s_2, i_2)$ and what *changes internally* is a *pair* of states, s_1 into $\delta_1(s_1, i_1)$ and s_2 into $\delta_2(s_2, i_2)$.

So, informally, inputs are pairs of inputs, one from each machine, outputs are pairs of outputs, one from each machine and states are pairs of states, one from each machine. But what should they be, formally ?

Well, we could try as the set of inputs, all sets $\{i_1, i_2\}$ with $i_1 \in I_1$ and $i_2 \in I_2$, but this presents difficulties. What if $\{i_1, i_2\} \subseteq I_1 \cap I_2$? How do we know which input is to go to which machine ?*

No, somehow or other we must be able to indicate the destination of the individual inputs and the simplest way of doing this is to *order* them and to make it a rule that the first input of the pair goes to M_1 and that the second goes to M_2.

* I hope I didn't hear anybody say, 'Look at the subscripts'.

Inputs to the composite machine $M_1 \,||\, M_2$ are therefore to be *ordered pairs* and hence the set of all inputs to $M_1 \,||\, M_2$ will be the Cartesian product of the two input sets, that is:

$$I_{M_1 \,||\, M_2} = I_1 \times I_2$$

Exactly the same argument goes for outputs and states: they must be ordered pairs, so that we know to which machine they apply. So:

$$O_{M_1 \,||\, M_2} = O_1 \times O_2$$

$$S_{M_1 \,||\, M_2} = S_1 \times S_2$$

We can now work out what the state transition and output functions ought to be. In the case discussed above, the input was (i_1, i_2) and the state was (s_1, s_2). After one step, the states of the two machines were $\delta_1(s_1, i_1)$ and $\delta_2(s_2, i_2)$, so the state of the composite is $(\delta_1(s_1, i_1), \delta_2(s_2, i_2))$.

Thus we have:

$$\delta_{M_1 \,||\, M_2}((s_1, s_2), (i_1, i_2)) = (\delta_1(s_1, i_1), \delta_2(s_2, i_2)).$$

A similar argument gives us the output function:

$$\beta_{M_1 \,||\, M_2}((s_1, s_2), (i_1, i_2)) = (\beta_1(s_1, i_1), \beta_2(s_2, i_2)).$$

Putting these all together, we may now formally define parallel composition.

6.2.1 Definition

Let M_1 and M_2 be machines, then their parallel composite, written $M_1 \,||\, M_2$ is defined to be the machine M, where:

(a) $I = I_1 \times I_2$
(b) $O = O_1 \times O_2$
(c) $S = S_1 \times S_2$
(d) $\delta((s_1, s_2), (i_1, i_2)) = (\delta_1(s_1, i_1), \delta_2(s_2, i_2))$
(e) $\beta((s_1, s_2), (i_1, i_2)) = (\beta_1(s_1, i_1), \beta_2(s_2, i_2))$.

6.2.2 Example

Consider the machine M_{cell} defined by the flow table of Table 6.1.

Table 6.1

	0	1	R	0	1	R
0	0	1	0	0	0	0
1	0	1	1	1	1	1

M_{cell} is a single binary storage cell. It has two states, depending on its contents, and three inputs, 0 and 1, which overwrite the previous contents and output it, and R, which acts as a non-destructive read. The parallel composite of M_{cell} with itself will be a storage device capable of holding two bits which may be overwritten or read independently.

Let $M_1 = M_2 = M_{cell}$, and define $M_{2\text{-}cell}$ as $M_1 \mid\mid M_2$. Applying definition 6.2.1, we have, for example:

$$\delta_{2\text{-}cell}((1,\mathit{0}),(R,\mathit{1})) = (\delta_1(1,R),\delta_2(0,\mathit{1})) = (1,\mathit{1})$$

$$\beta_{2\text{-}cell}((0,\mathit{0}),(R,\mathit{1})) = (\beta_1(0,R),\beta_2(0,\mathit{1})) = (0,\mathit{0})$$

The full next-state and output tables are given in Tables 6.2 and 6.3.

Table 6.2. $M_{2\text{-}cell}$: state transitions

	(0,0)	(0,1)	(0,R)	(1,0)	(1,1)	(1,R)	(R,0)	(R,1)	(R,R)
(0,0)	(0,0)	(0,1)	(0,0)	(1,0)	(1,1)	(1,0)	(0,0)	(0,1)	(0,0)
(0,1)	(0,0)	(0,1)	(0,1)	(1,0)	(1,1)	(1,1)	(0,0)	(0,1)	(0,1)
(1,0)	(0,0)	(0,1)	(0,0)	(1,0)	(1,1)	(1,0)	(1,0)	(1,1)	(1,0)
(1,1)	(0,0)	(0,1)	(0,1)	(1,0)	(1,1)	(1,1)	(1,0)	(1,1)	(1,1)

Table 6.3. $M_{2\text{-}cell}$: output

	(0,0)	(0,1)	(0,R)	(1,0)	(1,1)	(1,R)	(R,0)	(R,1)	(R,R)
(0,0)	(0,0)	(0,0)	(0,0)	(0,0)	(0,0)	(0,0)	(0,0)	(0,0)	(0,0)
(0,1)	(0,1)	(0,1)	(0,1)	(0,1)	(0,1)	(0,1)	(0,1)	(0,1)	(0,1)
(1,0)	(1,0)	(1,0)	(1,0)	(1,0)	(1,0)	(1,0)	(1,0)	(1,0)	(1,0)
(1,1)	(1,1)	(1,1)	(1,1)	(1,1)	(1,1)	(1,1)	(1,1)	(1,1)	(1,1)

6.3 SERIAL DECOMPOSITION

In the serial composition of two machines M_1 and M_2, the output of M_1 will be used as input to M_2. This is quite straightforward if every output of M_1 is also an input of M_2, that is, if $O_1 \subseteq I_2$. But otherwise, if $o \in O_1$ but $o \notin I_2$, then M_2 will not know what to do with it.

In such cases, we would interface the two machines by a coding device, as pictured in Fig. 6.2.

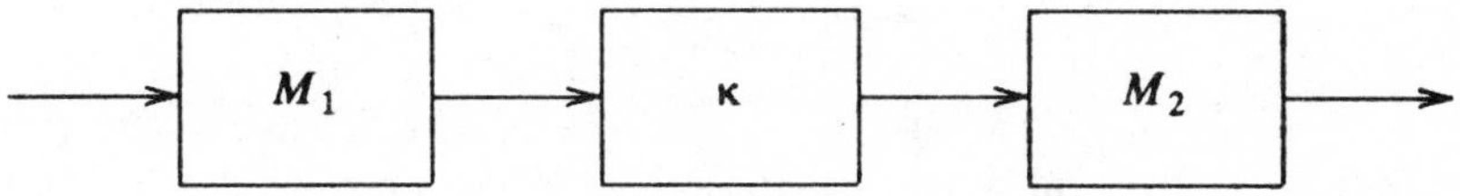

Fig. 6.2. Serial composition

Evidently, κ may be represented by a function:

$$\kappa{:}O_1 \to I_2$$

We shall write the parallel composition of M_1 and M_2 with mediating function κ as $M_1 \ominus_\kappa M_2$. If κ happens to be an inclusion function, that is, $\kappa(o) = o$ for all $o \in O_1$, then we shall just write $M_1 \ominus M_2$.

As in the case of parallel composition, we will arrive at a formal definition of $M_1 \ominus_\kappa M_2$ by looking at one step of its operation.

Let us suppose that M_1 is in state s_1 and that M_2 is in state s_2. Let us suppose that $i \in I_1$ is presented as an input to M_1. First M_1 will change state to $\delta_1(s_1, i)$ and will output $\beta_1(s_1, i)$. This will be passed to the encoder, to emerge as $\kappa(\beta_1(s_1, i))$ and this will be input to M_2.

M_2 will treat $\kappa(\beta_1(s_1, i))$ as it would any input. It changes state to $\delta_2[s_2, \kappa(\beta_1(s_1, i))]$ and outputs $\beta_2[s_2, \kappa(\beta_1(s_1, i))]$.

These formulae are beginning to look a little horrible, but all that they do is express precisely the intuitive behaviour of the machine.

Again, we must work out what $M_1 \ominus_\kappa M_2$ is as a quintuple. Inputs and outputs are easy. We have:

$$I_{M_1 \ominus_\kappa M_2} = I_1$$

$$O_{M_1 \ominus_\kappa M_2} = O_2$$

Again, what is changing internally in the composite is a pair of states. Using exactly the same argument as in the parallel case, we take the Cartesian product of S_1 and S_2 as the state set of the composite, that is:

$$S_{M_1 \ominus_\kappa M_2} = S_1 \times S_2$$

In one step of the composite's operation, M_1 changes from s_1 to state $\delta_1(s_1, i)$ and M_2 changes state from s_2 to $\delta_2[s_2, \kappa(\beta_1(s_1, i))]$. Thus, the state transition function is defined as:

$$\delta_{M_1 \ominus_\kappa M_2}((s_1, s_2), i) = (\delta_1(s_1, i), \delta_2[s_2, \kappa(\beta_1(s_1, i))])$$

We have worked out the output already, for a single step, it is $\beta_2[s_2, \kappa(\beta_1(s_1, i))]$, and so the output function is given by:

$$\beta_{M_1 \ominus_\kappa M_2}((s_1, s_2), i) = \beta_2[s_2, \kappa(\beta_1(s_1, i))]$$

Putting these all together, we obtain our second definition. The reader is advised not to learn (d) and (e) off by heart. Try to remember how they were *derived* and reconstruct the definition, as we have done here.

6.3.1 Definition

Let M_1 and M_2 be machines, and let κ be a function, $\kappa: O_1 \to I_2$, then their serial composite with respect to κ, written $M_1 \ominus_\kappa M_2$, is defined to be the machine M, where:

(a) $I = I_1$
(b) $O = O_2$
(c) $S = S_2 \times S_2$
(d) $\delta((s_1, s_2), i) = (\delta_1(s_1, i), \delta_2[s_2, \kappa(\beta_1(s_1, i))])$
(e) $\beta((s_1, s_2), i) = \beta_2[s_2, \kappa(\beta_1(s_1, i))]$

In the composition, we refer to M_1 as the *head* machine and M_2 as the *tail* machine.

6.3.2 Note

In 2.2.4, we asked whether the output function β of is defined completely by a flow table. We can now reveal the answer; 'no'. The problem is that β may be defined $\beta: S \times I \to O$, but that the set of outputs appearing in the flow table is $O' \subset O$. This problem would go away if β were required to be surjective, but that would lead to complications.

Suppose that κ is the identity and that M_1 has a single output o. Also assume that for all $s \in S_2$, $\delta_2(s,o) = s$ and that $\beta_2(s,o) = o'$. It is clear that the only output that $M_1 \ominus M_2$ may ever make is o'. If O_2 contains any other element different from o', then $\beta_{\ominus}$ is not surjective and so, in the revised notion of automata, $M_1 \ominus M_2$ would not be an automaton.

The same remarks may be made for parallel composition.

Of course, we could get round this by revising our definition of $O_{\ominus}$ but the definition would be clumsy. (Try it for yourself.)

6.3.3 Example

In 1.3, we presented a Mealy machine description of a three-frame pipeline and promised to explain how to define an n-frame pipeline later. Of course, we can use set theory language to do this. For example, define P_n to be the machine $(\{0,1\}^n, \{0,1\}, \{0,1\}, \delta_n, \beta_n)$, where:

$$\delta_n((b_1,...,b_n),b) = (b, b_1,..., b_{n-1})$$

and

$$\beta_n((b_1,...,b_n),b) = b_n$$

But there is another way, which reflects the structure of the pipeline and that is simple to define:

$$Pipe_1 = P_1 \quad Pipe_n = Pipe_1 \ominus Pipe_{n-1}$$

Since the composite of two machines is also a machine, we may form composites of composites. We illustrate in the next example.

6.3.4 Example

We shall take the two frame buffer defined in example 6.2.2 and compose it with a second machine to produce a device with serial input and parallel output. For notational convenience, we will drop parentheses from the states, inputs and outputs of $M_{2\text{-}cell}$. The new machine is given in Table 6.4.

M_{front} has four inputs: 0 and 1 change the content of the buffer so that an input i_0 in state $i_1 i_2$ produces a new state $i_0 i_1$; L is an instruction to load the contents of the buffer into $M_{2\text{-}cell}$; R is an instruction to non-destructively read the contents of $M_{2\text{-}cell}$. Indeed, all instructions, other

Table 6.4. M_{front}

	0	1	L	R	0	1	L	R
00	00	10	00	00	RR	RR	00	RR
01	00	10	01	01	RR	RR	01	RR
10	01	11	10	10	RR	RR	10	RR
11	01	11	11	11	RR	RR	11	RR

than L will cause the non-destructive reading of $M_{2\text{-}cell}$, but R does not change the contents of M_{front}.

Let $M = M_{front} \ominus M_{2\text{-}cell}$. Again, we apply the appropriate formulae to calculate δ and β. For example:

$$\delta((01,\mathit{10}),L) = (\delta_{front}(01,L),\delta_{2\text{-}cell}[10,\beta_{front}(01,L)])$$
$$= (\delta_{front}(01,L),\delta_{2\text{-}cell}(10,\mathit{01})) = (01,\mathit{01})$$
$$\beta((01,\mathit{00}),\mathit{1}) = \beta_{2\text{-}cell}(00,\beta_{front}(01,\mathit{1}))$$
$$= \beta_{2\text{-}cell}(00,RR) = 00$$

This new machine M is pictured in Fig. 6.3, and its flow table is given in Table 6.5.

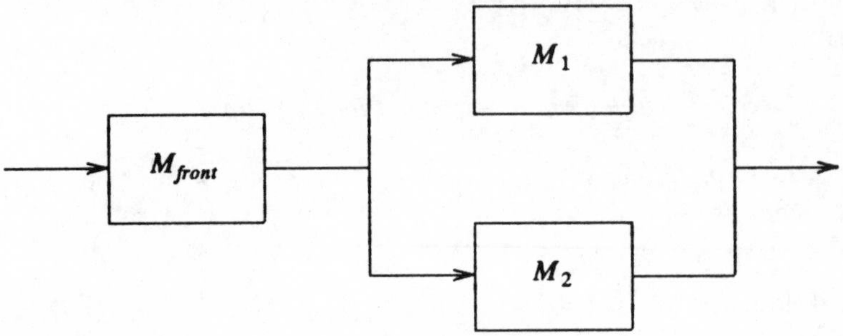

Fig. 6.3

6.4 PROPERTIES OF THE COMPOSITION OPERATORS

As we have remarked, the two composition operators rather resemble + and × in that with them you can take two objects and construct a third. The arithmetic operators satisfy certain important relations. For example:

Table 6.5

	0	1	L	R	0	1	L	R
(00,00)	(00,00)	(10,00)	(00,00)	(00,00)	00	00	00	00
(00,01)	(00,01)	(10,01)	(00,00)	(00,01)	01	01	01	01
(00,10)	(00,10)	(10,10)	(00,00)	(00,10)	10	10	10	10
(00,11)	(00,10)	(10,10)	(00,00)	(00,10)	11	11	11	11
(01,00)	(00,00)	(10,00)	(01,01)	(01,00)	00	00	00	00
(01,01)	(00,01)	(10,01)	(01,01)	(01,01)	01	01	01	01
(01,10)	(00,10)	(10,10)	(01,01)	(01,10)	10	10	10	10
(01,11)	(00,11)	(10,11)	(01,01)	(01,11)	11	11	11	11
(10,00)	(01,00)	(11,00)	(10,10)	(10,00)	00	00	00	00
(10,01)	(01,01)	(11,01)	(10,10)	(10,01)	01	01	01	01
(10,10)	(01,10)	(11,10)	(10,10)	(10,10)	10	10	10	10
(10,11)	(01,11)	(11,11)	(10,10)	(10,11)	11	11	11	11
(11,00)	(01,00)	(11,00)	(11,11)	(11,00)	00	00	00	00
(11,01)	(01,01)	(11,01)	(11,11)	(11,01)	01	01	01	01
(11,10)	(01,10)	(11,10)	(11,11)	(11,10)	10	10	10	10
(11,11)	(01,11)	(11,11)	(11,11)	(11,11)	11	11	11	11

$$x + (y + z) = (x + y) + z$$

or

$$x + y = y + x$$

for any numbers x, y, z. Is the same sort of thing true for automata ?

Pictorially, one might think so. For example, suppose M_1, M_2 and M_3 are machines and $\kappa_1 : O_1 \to I_2$ and $\kappa_2 : O_2 \to I_3$. We may form a machine $M' = M_1 \ominus_{\kappa_1} M_2$, and since $O' = O_2$, κ_2 may be regarded as a function $\kappa_2 : O' \to I_3$. We may therefore form a machine $M' \ominus_{\kappa_2} M_3$. Similarly, we may construct $M'' = M_2 \ominus_{\kappa_2} M_3$, and since $O_1 = I''$, we may construct $M_1 \ominus_{\kappa_1} M''$. Writing these out in full, we have two machines:

$$M_1 \ominus_{\kappa_1} M'' = M_1 \ominus_{\kappa_1} (M_2 \ominus_{\kappa_2} M_3)$$

$$M' \ominus_{\kappa_2} M_3 = (M_1 \ominus_{\kappa_1} M_2) \ominus_{\kappa_2} M_3$$

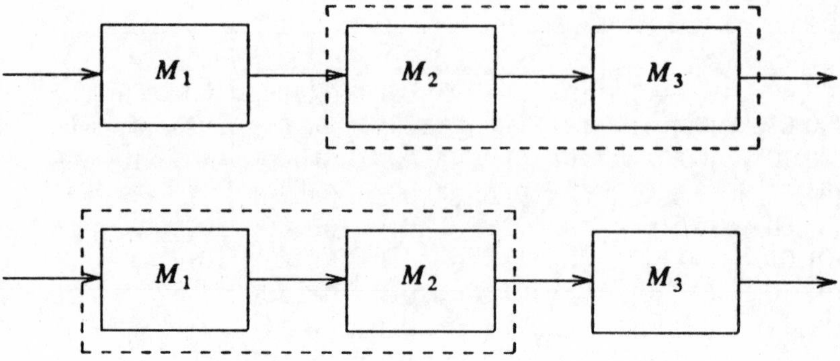

Fig. 6.4

These are pictured in Fig. 6.4. Common sense would suggest that they are the same. Is it the case that:

$$M_1 \ominus_{\kappa_1} (M_2 \ominus_{\kappa_2} M_3) = (M_1 \ominus_{\kappa_1} M_2) \ominus_{\kappa_2} M_3 \; ?$$

Well, we can check this, because we know from Chapter 4 what '=' means. Write M_{LHS} for the machine on the left hand side of the 'equation' and M_{RHS} for the other. We would need to have:

$$I_{LHS} = I_{RHS} \text{ and } O_{LHS} = O_{RHS}$$

and indeed, both these hold, since, for example:

$$I_{LHS} = I_1 = I_{M'} = I_{RHS}$$

$$O_{LHS} = O_{M''} = O_3 = O_{RHS}$$

However:

$$S_{LHS} = S_1 \times (S_2 \times S_3)$$

$$S_{RHS} = (S_1 \times S_2) \times S_3$$

and these two sets are not equal. It must be admitted that it is sometimes convenient to pretend that they are, but this will not work in the second case to be considered. Given M_1 and M_2, is it true that:

$$M_1 \mid\mid M_2 = M_2 \mid\mid M_1 \; ?$$

Again, writing M_{LHS} for the machine on the left hand side and so on, we need to check that, for example, $I_1 \times I_2 = I_2 \times I_1$, which is not the case unless $I_1 = I_2$.

So, if these various machines are not equal, how are they related ? From a structural point of view, they differ only in the names of states: the state $(s_1,(s_2,s_3))$ of $M_1 \ominus_{\kappa_1} (M_2 \ominus_{\kappa_2} M_3)$ corresponds to the state $((s_1,s_2),s_3)$ of $(M_1 \ominus_{\kappa_1} M_2) \ominus_{\kappa_2} M_3$. Intuitively, if I start $M_1 \ominus_{\kappa_1} (M_2 \ominus_{\kappa_2} M_3)$ off in state $(s_1,(s_2,s_3))$, it should behave in the same way as $(M_1 \ominus_{\kappa_1} M_2) \ominus_{\kappa_2} M_3$ started off in state $((s_1,s_2),s_3)$.

The following proposition tells the whole story. The machines in question are not equal but they are isomorphic.

6.4.1 Proposition

Suppose M_1, M_2 and M_3 are machines and that $\kappa_1:O_1 \rightarrow I_2$ and $\kappa_2:O_2 \rightarrow I_3$, then:

(a) $M_1 \ominus_{\kappa_1} (M_2 \ominus_{\kappa_2} M_3) \approx (M_1 \ominus_{\kappa_1} M_2) \ominus_{\kappa_2} M_3$.

(b) $M_1 \mid\mid (M_2 \mid\mid M_3) \approx (M_1 \mid\mid M_2) \mid\mid M_3$.

(c) $M_1 \mid\mid M_2 \approx M_2 \mid\mid M_1$.

Proof

The trick in each case is to find suitable bijections between the corresponding sets of the machines and to show that they have the required properties. We shall give the bijections for all three, but only demonstrate that they constitute an isomorphism in case 1 (the hardest case). The rest is left as an exercise.

1 Define functions α, ι, θ by:

$$\alpha(s_1,(s_2,s_3)) = ((s_1,s_2),s_3)$$

$$\iota(i) = i \quad \theta(o) = o$$

Define $M' = M_2 \ominus_{\kappa_2} M_3$ and $M_{LHS} = M_1 \ominus_{\kappa_1} M'$. Define $M'' = M_1 \ominus_{\kappa_1} M_2$ and $M_{LHS} = M'' \ominus_{\kappa_2} M_3$.

We must show that (α,ι,θ) is an isomorphism, that is, that the functions α, ι and θ are bijections (which they obviously are) and that for $s \in S_{LHS}$ and $i \in I_{LHS}$:

$$\alpha(\delta_{LHS}(s,i)) = \delta_{RHS}(\alpha(s),\iota(i))$$

$$\beta_{LHS}(s,i) = \theta(\beta_{RHS}(\alpha(s),\iota(i)))$$

To prove this, we simply apply the definitions.

Suppose $s = (s_1(s_2,s_3))$, then by definition, $\alpha(s) = ((s_1,s_2),s_3)$ and $\iota(i) = i$.

Calculating:

$$\begin{aligned}
\alpha(\delta_{LHS}(s,i)) &= \alpha(<\delta_1(s_1,i),\delta'[(s_2,s_3),\kappa_1(\beta_1(s_1,i))]>) \text{ (by 6.3.1(d))}\\
&= \alpha(<\delta_1(s_1,i),<\delta_2[s_2,\kappa_1(\beta_1(s_1,i))],\\
&\quad \delta_3[s_3,\kappa_2(\beta_2[s_2,\kappa_1(\beta_1(s_1,i))])]>>) \text{ (by 6.3.1(d))}\\
&= \ll\delta_1(s_1,i),\delta_2[s_2,\kappa_1(\beta_1(s_1,i))]>,\\
&\quad \delta_3[s_3,\kappa_2(\beta_2[s_2,\kappa_1(\beta_1(s_1,i))])]> \text{ (by definition of } \alpha)\\
&= <\delta''((s_1,s_2),i),\delta_3[s_3,\kappa_2(\beta''[(s_1,s_2),i)])]> \text{ (by 6.3.1(d))}\\
&= \delta_{RHS}[((s_1,s_2),s_3),i]\\
&= \delta_{RHS}(\alpha(s),\iota(i))
\end{aligned}$$

Similarly:

$$\begin{aligned}
\beta_{LHS}(s,i) &= \beta'[(s_2,s_3),\kappa_1(\beta_1(s_1,i))]\\
&= \beta_3[s_3,\kappa_2(\beta_2[s_2,\kappa_1(\beta_1(s_1,i))])]\\
&= \beta_3[s_3,\kappa_2(\beta''((s_1,s_2),i)]\\
&= \beta_{RHS}[((s_1,s_2),s_3),i] = \beta_{RHS}(\alpha(s),\iota(i))\\
&= \theta[\beta_{RHS}(\alpha(s),\iota(i))]
\end{aligned}$$

2 Define functions α, ι, θ by: $\alpha(s_1,(s_2,s_3)) = ((s_1,s_2),s_3)$, $\iota(i_1,(i_2,i_3)) = ((i_1,i_2),i_3)$, and $\theta((o_1,o_2),o_3) = (o_1,(o_2,o_3))$.

3 Define functions α, ι, θ by: $\alpha(s_1,s_2) = (s_2,s_1)$, $\iota(i_1,i_2) = (i_2,i_1)$, and $\theta(o_2,o_1) = (o_1,o_2)$.

This concludes the proof.

Since for any two machines, $M \leq M'$ if $M \approx M'$, we have the following corollary.

6.4.2 Corollary

Suppose M_1, M_2 and M_3 are machines and that $\kappa_1:O_1 \to I_2$ and $\kappa_2:O_2 \to I_3$, then:

(a) $M_1 \ominus_{\kappa_1} (M_2 \ominus_{\kappa_2} M_3) \leq (M_1 \ominus_{\kappa_1} M_2) \ominus_{\kappa_2} M_3$.
(b) $(M_1 \ominus_{\kappa_1} M_2) \ominus_{\kappa_2} M_3 \leq M_1 \ominus_{\kappa_1} (M_2 \ominus_{\kappa_2} M_3)$.
(c) $M_1 \mid\mid (M_2 \mid\mid M_3) \leq (M_1 \mid\mid M_2) \mid\mid M_3$.
(d) $(M_1 \mid\mid M_2) \mid\mid M_3 \leq M_1 \mid\mid (M_2 \mid\mid M_3)$.
(e) $M_1 \mid\mid M_2 \leq M_2 \mid\mid M_1$.

It is also of interest to examine the relationship between composition and realization. For example, if I know that I can implement a machine M_1 by a machine M_1' and that I can implement a machine M_2 by a machine M_2', then can I conclude, say, that $M_1 \mid\mid M_2$ can be implemented by $M_1' \mid\mid M_2'$? The answer is yes, as the following proposition explains:

6.4.3 Proposition

Let M_1, M_1', M_2, M_2' be machines and let $(\alpha_1,\iota_1,\theta_1)$ (respectively, $(\alpha_2,\iota_2,\theta_2)$) be a state behaviour assignment of M_1 into M_1' (respectively, M_2 into M_2'), so that $M_1 \leq M_1'$ and $M_2 \leq M_2'$. Then:

(a) If $\kappa{:}O_1 \rightarrow I_2$ and $\kappa'{:}O_1' \rightarrow I_2'$, such that $\iota_2(\kappa(\theta_1(o))) = \kappa'(o)$ for every $o \in O_1'$, then $M_1 \ominus_\kappa M_2 \leq M_1' \ominus_{\kappa'} M_2'$.
(b) $M_1 \mid\mid M_2 \leq M_1' \mid\mid M_2'$.

Proof

In both cases, we must construct state behaviour assignments between the composites. As in the preceding proposition, we shall only prove that the first triple actually *is* a state behaviour assignment, the second is left as an exercise.

1 Define $(\alpha_\ominus,\iota_\ominus,\theta_\ominus)$ by:

$$\alpha_\ominus(s_1,s_2) = (\alpha_1(s_1),\alpha_2(s_2))$$

$$\iota_\ominus(i) = \iota_1(i)$$

$$\theta_\ominus(o) = \theta_2(o)$$

where $s_1 \in S_1$, $s_2 \in S_2$, $i \in I_1$, $o' \in O_2'$.

Let $M = M_1 \ominus_\kappa M_2$ and $M' = M_1' \ominus_{\kappa'} M_2'$. We must show that:

$$\alpha_\ominus(\delta(s,i)) = \delta'(\alpha_\ominus(s),\iota_\ominus(i))$$

$$\beta(s,i) = \theta_\ominus[\beta'(\alpha_\ominus(s),\iota_\ominus(i))]$$

This is largely a question of applying the definitions. By definition of serial composition, Section 6.3.1:

$$\delta((s_1, s_2), i) = <\delta_1(s_1, i), \delta_2[s_2, \kappa(\beta_1(s_1, i))]>$$

and so:

$$\alpha_{\oplus}(\delta((s_1, s_2), i)) = <\alpha_1(\delta_1(s_1, i)), \alpha_2(\delta_2[s_2, \kappa(\beta_1(s_1, i))])> \quad [6.1]$$

and using the fact that α_1 and α_2 are part of state behaviour assignments, we obtain:

$$\alpha_{\oplus}(\delta((s_1, s_2), i)) = <\delta_1'(\alpha_1(s_1), \iota_1(i)), \delta_2'(\alpha_2(s_2), \iota_2[\kappa(\beta_1(s_1, i))])> \quad [6.2]$$

But, $\beta_1(s_1, i) = \theta_1[\beta_1'(\alpha_1(s_1), \iota_1(i))]$ and so:

$$\iota_2[\kappa(\beta_1(s_1, i))] = \iota_2[\kappa(\theta_1(\beta_1'[\alpha_1(s_1), \iota_1(i)]))] \quad [6.3]$$

and by hypothesis, for every $o \in O_1'$, $\iota_2[\kappa(\theta_1(o))] = \kappa'(o)$ and so from [6.3]:

$$\iota_2[\kappa(\beta_1(s_1, i))] = \kappa'[\beta_1'(\alpha_1(s_1), \iota_1(i))] \quad [6.4]$$

Substituting [6.4] into [6.2], gives:

$$\alpha_{\oplus}(\delta((s_1, s_2), i)) = <\delta_1'(\alpha_1(s_1), \iota_1(i)), \delta_2'(\alpha_2(s_2), \kappa'[\beta_1'(\alpha_1(s_1), \iota_1(i))])> \quad [6.5]$$

But the right hand side of [6.5] equals $\delta'(\alpha_{\oplus}(s_1, s_2), \iota_{\oplus}(i))$ by the definition of serial composition (6.3.1) and we are done.

For the second equation, we have:

$$\begin{aligned}
\beta((s_1, s_2), i) &= \beta_2[s_2, \kappa(\beta_1(s_1, i))] \text{ (by 6.3.1)} \\
&= \theta_2[\beta_2'(\alpha_2(s_2), \iota_2[\kappa(\beta_1(s_1, i))])] \text{ (by 4.3.1)} \\
&= \theta_2[\beta_2'(\alpha_2(s_2), \iota_2[\kappa(\theta_1[\beta_1'(\alpha_2(s_1), \iota_1(i))])])] \text{ (by 4.3.1)} \\
&= \theta_2[\beta_2'(\alpha_2(s_2), \kappa'[\beta_1'(\alpha_1(s_1), \iota_1(i))])] \text{ (by property of } \kappa') \\
&= \theta_2[\beta'((\alpha_1(s_1), \alpha_2(s_2)), \iota_1(i))] \text{ (by 6.3.1)} \\
&= \theta_{\oplus}[\beta'(\alpha_{\oplus}(s_1, s_2)), \iota_{\oplus}(i))]
\end{aligned}$$

as required.

2 In the second part, define $(\alpha_{||},\iota_{||},\theta_{||})$ by:

$$\alpha_{||}(s_1,s_2) = (\alpha_1(s_1),\alpha_2(s_2))$$

$$\iota_{||}(i_1,i_2) = (\iota_1(i_1),\iota_2(i_2))$$

$$\theta_{||}(o_1,o_2) = (\theta_1(o_1),\theta_2(o_2))$$

This concludes the proof.

EXERCISES

1 Can it ever be the case that
(a) $(M_1 \,||\, M_2) \ominus_\kappa M_3 \approx (M_1 \ominus_{\kappa_1} M_3) \,||\, (M_2 \ominus_{\kappa_2} M_3)$
(b) $(M_1 \ominus_\kappa M_2) \,||\, M_3 \approx (M_1 \,||\, M_3) \ominus_{\kappa'} (M_2 \,||\, M_3)$
for M_i and κ, κ_i, κ' ?

2 Complete the proof of proposition 6.4.1.

3 Complete the proof of proposition 6.4.3.

4 Prove that for the machines defined in 6.3.3, $P_n \approx Pipe_n$, for all n.

5 Suppose $\phi_1:M_1 \to M'_1$ and $\phi_2:M_2 \to M'_2$. Define $\alpha:S_1 \times S_2 \to S'_1 \times S'_2$ by $\alpha((s_1,s_2) = (\alpha_1(s_1),\alpha_2(s_2))$, $\iota:I_1 \times I_2 \to I'_1 \times I'_2$ by $\iota((i_1,i_2) = (\iota_1(i_1),\iota_2(i_2))$ and $\omega:O'_1 \times O'_2 \to O_1 \times O_2$ by $\omega((o_1,o_2) = (\omega_1(o_1),\omega_2(o_2))$. Let $\phi_1 \,||\, \phi_2 = (\alpha,\iota,\omega)$. Show that $\phi_1 \,||\, \phi_2:M_1 \,||\, M_2 \to M'_1 \,||\, M'_2$.

6 Prove that $\phi_1 \,||\, \phi_2$ is an isomorphism if and only if ϕ_1 and ϕ_2 are isomorphisms. Prove that $\phi_1 \,||\, \phi_2$ is a reduction if and only if ϕ_1 and ϕ_2 are reductions. (Hint: the arguments are largely set-theoretical).

7 Suppose that ϕ_1 is the natural reduction of M_1 onto M_1/ρ_{M_1} and that ϕ_2 is the natural reduction of M_2 onto M_2/ρ_{M_2}. Deduce that $\phi_1 \,||\, \phi_2:M_1 \,||\, M_2 \to (M_1/\rho_{M_1}) \,||\, (M_2/\rho_{M_2})$ is a reduction.

8 Let $\equiv$ be the relation on $S_1 \times S_2$ defined in 5.3.4. Show that $Ker(\phi_1 \,||\, \phi_2) = \equiv$ and hence deduce that:

$$(M_1 \,||\, M_2)/\rho_{M_1 \,||\, M_2} \approx (M_1/\rho_{M_1}) \,||\, (M_2/\rho_{M_2})$$

NOTES

Heartmanis & Stearns (1966) define serial composition in 2.2 and parallel composition in 2.3. We have reversed the order because we find it easier to deal with parallel decomposition before serial decomposition.

We have concocted the material of section 6.4 so that we can deal later with decompositions into more than two machines. For example, proposition 6.4.3 and the fact that $\leq$ is reflexive and transitive, allows us to deduce that if $M \leq M_1 \ominus M'$ and $M' \leq M_2 \ominus M_3$ then $M \leq M_1 \ominus (M_2 \ominus M_3)$.

The more advanced structure theory of automata tends to work with state machines. These may be considered as Mealy automata in which for each $s \in S$ and $i \in I$, $\beta(s,i) = (s,i)$. The notions of serial and parallel composition may be easily modified to suit state machines.

Holcombe (1982) gives other types of composition, of which the most important is the *wreath product*. If M_1, M_2 are machines, then their wreath product $M_1 \; o \; M_2$ is the machine M where:

(a) $S = S_1 \times S_2$.

(b) $I = I_1 \times [S_1 \rightarrow I_2]$. $[S_1 \rightarrow I_2]$ is the set of all functions from S_1 to I_2.

(c) $O = O_1 \times O_2$.

(d) $\delta((s_1, s_2), (i, f)) = [\delta_1(s_1, i), \delta_2(s_2, f(s_1))]$.

(e) $\beta((s_1, s_2), (i, f)) = [\beta_1(s_1, i), \beta_2(s_2, f(s_1))]$.

Wreath product actually generalizes both serial and parallel composition. To see this, suppose $\kappa : O_1 \rightarrow I_2$, then for each $i \in I_1$, we may define a function f_i by $f_i(s) = \kappa(\beta_1(s, i))$ and then $\delta_{\ominus}((s_1, s_2), i) = [\delta_1(s_1, i), \delta_2(s_2, f_i(s_1))]$.

Similarly, if we define $f_i(s) = i$, then $\delta_{||}((s_1, s_2), (i, i')) = [\delta_1(s_1, i), \delta_2(s_2, f_{i'}(s_1))]$.

Thus, for some f, $M_1 \; o \; M_2$ behaves like a serial composite and for others, it behaves like a parallel composite. Indeed, we may show that $M_1 \ominus M_2 \leq M_1 \; o \; M_2$ and $M_1 \; || \; M_2 \leq M_1 \; o \; M_2$.

Wreath product is interesting because of the related decomposition theory. See Holcombe (1982).

Chapter 7

The Parallel Decomposition Theorem

Flashes of blue light terrified his fellow workers as he pulled things to bits. 'No man,' he said, 'can do his job thoroughly until he has mastered what lies behind the machinery of it.' By tea-time he had melted down his earphones on a small stove. But it was only when he began to take the switchboards to pieces that the controller asked him to go.

J. B. MORTON ('Beachcomber')
The Adventures of Charles Suet

7.1 INTRODUCTION

We have seen how to put machines together. Now let us see how to take them apart. In this and the following chapter, we shall be looking at conditions under which a Mealy automaton may be realized by a parallel (serial) composition of two machines, or, more briefly, has a parallel (serial) decomposition.

7.1.1 Definition

Suppose M is a machine. M will be said to have a parallel decomposition if and only if there exist machines M_1 and M_2 such that $M \leq M_1 \mid\mid M_2$.

The decomposition will be said to be *non-trivial* if $|S_1| < |S|$ and $|S_2| < |S|$, that is, the state sets of the composites are strictly smaller than that of M.

Our aim is to find *necessary* and *sufficient* conditions for decomposability. That is to say, we shall find conditions which hold if and only if a machine has a parallel decomposition. How should we go about this ?

Our strategy will be as follows. First, we will take some arbitrary machine and suppose that it has a parallel decomposition. It will follow that various things must be true about the machine, things which are consequences of the definitions of composition and realization. We look for properties that might allow us to go in the opposite direction, properties that assert the existence of things from which we might *build* a parallel decomposition of the machine. This will give us necessary conditions for decomposability which will hopefully also be sufficient.

The main result is stated in theorem 7.3.3.

7.2 NECESSARY CONDITIONS

Let us suppose that M has a parallel decomposition $M \leq M_1 \mid\mid M_2$. For notational simplicity, define $M_{\mid\mid} = M_1 \mid\mid M_2$.

There are two pieces of information to chew on here. Firstly, M and $M_{\mid\mid}$ are structurally related, via some state behaviour assignment $\phi: M \to M_{\mid\mid}$. Secondly, there is a certain regularity about the state behaviour of $M_{\mid\mid}$ which derives from the fact that it is a parallel composite. Let us look at the first clue first. We recall from 4.3.1 that a state behaviour assignment is a triple $\phi = (\alpha, \iota, \theta)$, where α is an injective function:

$$\alpha: S \to S_{\mid\mid} = S_1 \times S_2$$

and ι and θ are functions:

$$\iota: I \to I_{\mid\mid} = I_1 \times I_2$$

$$\theta: O_{\mid\mid} = O_1 \times O_2 \to O$$

satisfying the two rules:

$$\delta_{\mid\mid}(\alpha(s), \iota(i)) = \alpha(\delta(s, i)) \qquad [7.1]$$

$$\theta[\beta_{\mid\mid}(\alpha(s), \iota(i))] = \beta(s, i)$$

Let us look at this in more detail. We may picture the state space of $M_{\mid\mid}$ as an 'egg-box', as shown in Fig. 7.1. Here, rows correspond to elements of S_1 and columns to elements of S_2. In the intersection of row $s_{1,j}$ and column $s_{2,k}$ is the pair $(s_{1,j}, s_{2,k})$.

We may now use the fact that α is injective to conclude that the state space of M is a perfect copy of a subset of the state space of $M_{\mid\mid}$. By that, we mean that there is a one to one correspondence between the elements of S and those of $\alpha(S) \subseteq S_{\mid\mid}$, so that we may impose the 'egg-box' structure of $S_{\mid\mid}$ onto S as shown in Fig. 7.2.

Here, the row $S_{1,j}$ corresponds to the row $s_{1,j}$ in $S_{\mid\mid}$, so:

$$S_{1,j} = \{s \in S \mid \alpha(s) = (s_{1,j}, s') \text{ some } s'\} \qquad [7.2]$$

Likewise, the column $S_{2,k}$ corresponds to the column $s_{2,k}$ and so:

	$S_{2,1}$	$S_{2,2}$	
$S_{1,1}$	$(s_{1,1}, s_{2,1})$	$(s_{11}, s_{2,2})$	
$S_{1,2}$	$(s_{1,2}, s_{2,1})$	$(s_{1,2}\, s_{2,2})$	
$S_{1,3}$	$(s_{1,3}, s_{2,1})$	$(s_{1,3}, s_{2,2})$	

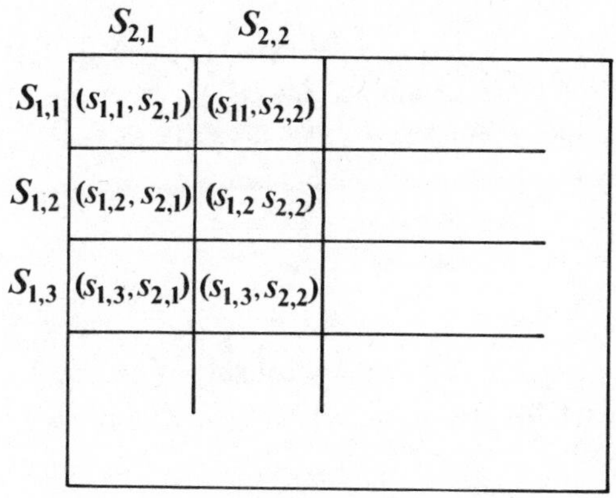

Fig. 7.1

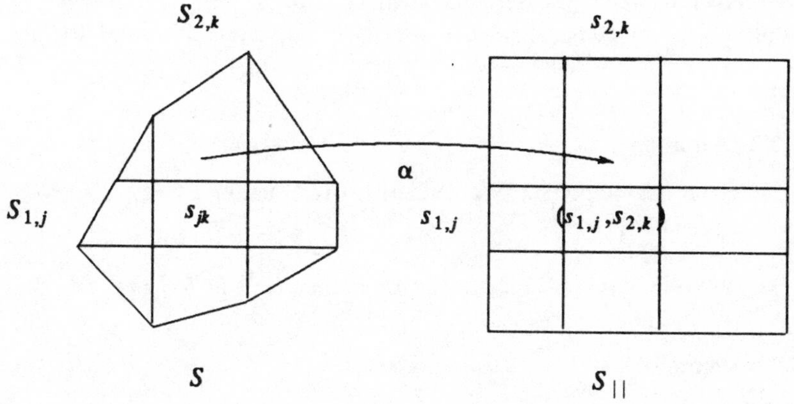

Fig. 7.2

$$S_{2,k} = \{ s \in S \mid \alpha(s) = (s', s_{2,k})\ some\ s' \}$$

We have found our first connection between structure in M_{11} and structure in M. There is something promising about it, because of the relationship between rows and columns in S and states of M_1 and M_2. (We shall see later that we may construct the state spaces of component machines from sets such as $S_{1,j}$.) Let us note down in formal jargon what we have found.

7.2.1 Remark

Let $\pi_1 = \{S_{1,j} | s_{1,j} \in S_1\}$ and $\pi_2 = \{S_{2,k} | s_{2,k} \in S_2\}$, then π_1 and π_2 are both partitions of S. Furthermore, for each j,k either $S_{1,j} \cap S_{2,k} = \varnothing$ or there is a unique $s \in S$ such that $S_{1,j} \cap S_{2,k} = \{s\}$ and for this s, $\alpha(s) = (s_{1,j}, s_{2,k})$.

Proof

Exercise 1.

We may express this more succinctly if we define $\pi_1.\pi_2$ to be the partition obtained by taking all the intersections $X \cap Y$ and keeping the non-empty ones.*

$$\pi_1.\pi_2 = \{X \cap Y \mid X \in \pi_1 \text{ and } Y \in \pi_2 \text{ and } X \cap Y \neq \varnothing\}$$

From the above remark, we see that $\pi_1.\pi_2$ is the partition in which each block contains precisely one element. This is one of two *trivial* partitions. (It is no coincidence that we have also used the word trivial to describe decompositions, as we shall see.)

7.2.2 Definition

Let X be a non-empty set. We define the trivial partitions of X:

(a) $\perp_X = \{\{x\} \mid x \in X\}$.

(b) $\top_X = \{X\}$.

We may now reformulate part of remark 7.2.1 as follows.

7.2.3 Lemma

The π_i are partitions satisfying $\pi_1.\pi_2 = \perp_S$. We shall sometimes speak of partitions with this property as being *orthogonal*.

Next, let us look at state transitions in both machines. If $i \in I$, then $\iota(i)$ is an input to $M_{||}$ and is hence a pair (i_1, i_2). We can picture the effect of this pair of inputs in terms of the egg-box diagram shown in Fig. 7.3. Here, it is assumed that $\delta_{||}((s_{1,j}, s_{2,k}), (i_1, i_2)) = (s_{1,l}, s_{2,m})$. Applying i_1 as an input would cause any state in row $s_{1,j}$ to change to some state of row $s_{1,l}$.

* As we shall see in Chapter 9, $\pi_1.\pi_2$ is the greatest lower bound of the two with respect to an ordering on partitions according to their coarseness.

$$\delta_{||}((s_{1,j},-),(i_1,-)) = (s_{1,l},-)$$

Likewise, if i_2 is applied as an input, then every state in column $s_{2,k}$ changes to some state from column $s_{2,m}$.

$$\delta_{||}((-,s_{2,k}),(-,i_2)) = (-,s_{2,m})$$

The *combined* effect of the inputs i_1 and i_2 is to take the machine from the state in the intersection of the old row and column, $(s_{1,j},s_{2,k})$, to the state in the intersection of the new row and the new column, $(s_{1,l},s_{2,m})$.

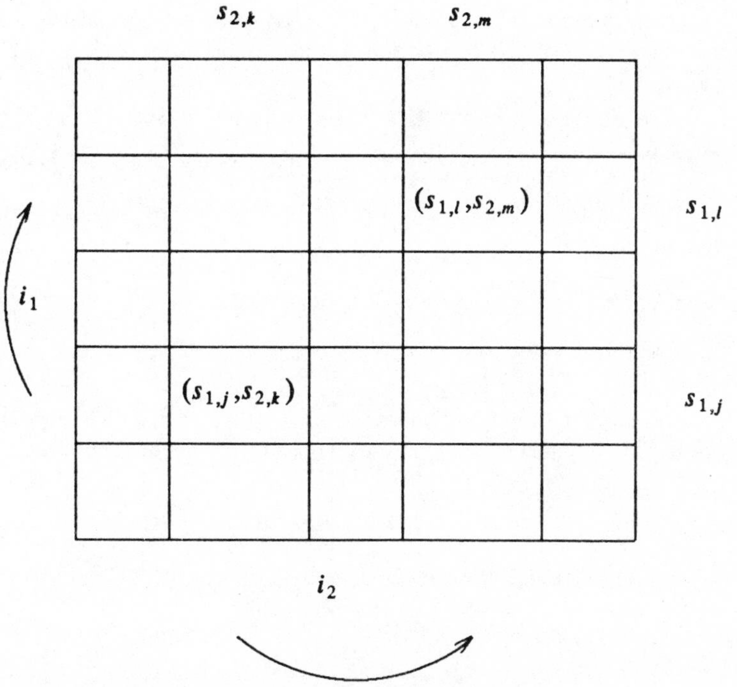

Fig. 7.3

Now, condition [7.1] entails that *exactly the same thing* happens to the egg-box structure we have found in S; i carries row $S_{1,j}$ into $S_{1,l}$ and also carries column $S_{2,k}$ into column $S_{2,m}$. We shall state and prove this formally in a little while, but first we shall remark that what we have done is discover *pictorially* the way in which the structure of $M_{||}$ is reflected in that of M. From the pictures, the reader might be able to see how we may make partial copies of M_1 and M_2 out of M and the partitions π_1 and

π_2. The reader might even recognize what special properties the partitions possess. For those who do not, let us put them out of their misery.

7.2.4 Lemma

Suppose $\iota(i) = (i_1, i_2)$, then, with the above notation:

(a) If $S_{1,j} \neq \varnothing$, then $\delta(S_{1,j}, i) \subseteq S_{1,l} \Leftrightarrow \delta_1(s_{1,j}, i_1) = s_{1,l}$.

(b) If $S_{2,k} \neq \varnothing$, then $\delta(S_{2,k}, i) \subseteq S_{2,m} \Leftrightarrow \delta_2(s_{2,k}, i_2) = s_{2,m}$.

In particular, π_1 and π_2 are both SP partitions.

Proof

That the π_i are SP is an immediate consequence of (a) and (b) and the definition (5.2.4) of SP partition. (a) and (b) are very similar; we shall prove (a).

First, we show the '$\Leftarrow$' part. Suppose that $\delta_1(s_{1,j}, i_1) = s_{1,l}$. We need to show that if $s \in S_{1,j}$, then $\delta(s, i) \in S_{1,l}$. If we look at equation [7.2], we see that this is equivalent to showing that if $\alpha(s)$ is of the form $(s_{1,j}, s')$, then $\alpha(\delta(s, i))$ is of the form $(s_{1,l}, s'')$. But, by definition of state behaviour assignments, we have:

$$\begin{aligned}\alpha(\delta(s, i)) &= \delta_{||}(\alpha(s), \iota(i)) \\ &= \delta_{||}((s_{1,j}, s'), (i_1, i_2))\end{aligned} \qquad [7.3]$$

And now we can appeal to the definition of parallel composition (Section 6.2.1), which tells us how to work out $\delta_{||}$ given δ_1 and δ_2.

$$\delta_{||}((s_{1,j}, s'), (i_1, i_2)) = (\delta_1(s_{1,j}, i_1), \delta_2(s', i_2)) \qquad [7.4]$$

Putting [7.3] and [7.4] together, we get:

$$\begin{aligned}\alpha(\delta(s, i)) &= (\delta_1(s_{1,j}, i_1), \delta_2(s', i_2)) \\ &= (s_{1,l}, s'')\end{aligned} \qquad [7.5]$$

which is what we wanted. (The last equality was obtained from [7.5] by using the hypothesis that $\delta_1(s_{1,j}, i_1) = s_{1,l}$, and we have set $s'' = \delta_2(s', i_2)$).

We have shown one direction of the argument. Now let us show the other. We suppose that $\delta(S_{1,j}, i) \subseteq S_{1,l}$ and prove that $\delta_1(s_{1,j}, i_1) = s_{1,l}$.

We may restate this, using equation [7.2]. We are assuming that if $\alpha(s) = (s_{1,j}, s')$, some s', then $\alpha(\delta(s, i)) = (s_{1,l}, s'')$, some s''. From this we wish to deduce that $\delta_1(s_{1,j}, i_1) = s_{1,l}$.

Now, we may again start plugging in definitions. Because α is part of a state behaviour assignment, we have:

$$(s_{1,l}, s'') = \alpha(\delta(s, i)) \text{ (by hypothesis)}$$
$$= \delta_{||}(\alpha(s), \iota(i)) \text{ (by [7.1])}$$
$$= \delta_{||}((s_{1,j}, s'), (i_1, i_2)) \text{ (by hypothesis)}$$
$$= (\delta_1(s_{1,j}, i_1), \delta_2(s', i_2)) \text{ (by [7.4])}$$

Thus $(s_{1,l}, s'') = (\delta_1(s_{1,j}, i_1), \delta_2(s', i_2))$ and the result follows from a comparison of coordinates.

So far, we have discovered that if M has a parallel decomposition, then it has SP partitions π_i with $\pi_1.\pi_2 = \perp_S$. This is a precise way of representing our pictorial intuition which sees S as a copy of part of the egg-box $S_1 \times S_2$ and which has an identical transition structure in terms of the way in which columns and rows are transformed into each other under inputs.

Finally in this section, we examine non-triviality of the decomposition.

We may begin by noting that the egg-box S must have more than one row and more than one column. If, for example, it had only one row, then every state would belong to a different column and as each column corresponds to a *distinct* element of S_2, it would follow that $|S| \leq |S_2|$, which would contradict non-triviality of the decomposition. The argument for columns goes similarly.

These requirements – more than one row and column – are simply that the π_i are neither of them trivial. For example, if there is only one column in S, then $\pi_2 = \top_S$.

Let us prove this properly.

7.2.5 Lemma

Neither π_1 nor π_2 is trivial.

Proof

We show π_1 is non-trivial. The argument for π_2 is similar. We argue by contradiction.

Suppose first that $\pi_1 = \perp_S$. Define $f : S \rightarrow S_1$ by $f(s) = s_{1,j}$ if and only if $\alpha(s) = (s_{1,j}, s_2)$, some s_2. For $s, s' \in S$, we have:

$$f(s) = f(s') \Leftrightarrow s, s' \in S_{1,j}, \text{ some } j \Leftrightarrow s = s'$$

since each block of π_1 has exactly one element in it. Thus $f: S \to S_1$ is an injection and hence $|S| \leq |S_1|$, a contradiction. Thus $\pi_1 \neq \perp_S$.

Likewise, $\pi_2 \neq \perp_S$.

Now suppose that $\pi_1 = \top_S$. We shall show that this implies that $\pi_2 = \perp_S$ which we already know to be false. First, $\pi_1 = \top_S$ implies that $S = S_{1,j}$, for some j and that therefore for all $s \in S$, $\alpha(s) = (s_{1,j}, s_2)$, some s_2. If $\pi_2 \neq \perp_S$, then for some $s, s' \in S$, with $s \neq s'$, we would have $s, s' \in S_{2,k}$, some k. But then, $\alpha(s) = (s_{1,j}, s_{2,k}) = \alpha(s')$ contradicting α injective. Thus $\pi_2 = \perp_S$, and we have our contradiction.

We have not yet considered outputs. In fact, as you will see, this is not necessary, mainly because the only interesting conclusions we may draw concern the output decoder θ. The conditions we have already will be enough to enable us to construct a pair of state machines (using the SP partitions) and an injective map from S into the product of their state spaces. Outputs may then be easily tacked on to give a parallel decomposition.

Putting it all together, we have the following.

7.2.6 Proposition (Necessary Conditions for Non-trivial Parallel Decomposition)

If M has a non-trivial parallel decomposition, then M has two non-trivial SP partitions, π_1 and π_2 such that:

$$\pi_1 . \pi_2 = \perp_S .$$

Proof

Use lemmas 7.2.3, 7.2.4 and 7.2.5.

7.3 SUFFICIENT CONDITIONS

Now for the converse. Given non-trivial SP partitions π_1 and π_2 with $\pi_1 . \pi_2 = \perp_S$, we shall *construct* a parallel decomposition of M. The construction is based on two facts:

(a) From the π_i we may construct Mealy machines.

(b) There is a 'natural' injection of S into the state space $\pi_1 \times \pi_2$ of the parallel composition of these two machines.

The machines of (a) are defined as follows.

7.3.1 Definition

Let M be a machine and π an SP partition on M, then the *image machine* written M_π is the machine $(\pi, I, \pi \times I, \delta_\pi, \beta_\pi)$, where:

$$\delta_\pi(X, i) = Y \Leftrightarrow \delta(X, i) \subseteq Y$$

$$\beta_\pi(X, i) = (X, i)$$

This definition may seem a little arbitrary. Why should we define our functions like that ?

The inspiration for the definition of δ_π is lemma 7.2.4. Suppose that π is actually one of the π_i of that lemma, say π_1. Let us define a mapping $\alpha_1 : \pi \rightarrow S_1$ by setting $\alpha_1(S)$ equal to the unique s such that $S = \alpha^{-1}(s)$ and $\iota_1 : I \rightarrow I_1$ by $\iota_1(i) = i_1$ if $\iota(i) = (i_1, i_2)$. Rephrasing 7.2.4 (a) gives:

$$\alpha_1(\delta_\pi(S, i)) = \delta_1(\alpha_1(S), \iota_1(i))$$

Our definition ensures that there is almost a state behaviour assignment between M_1 and M_π. We have managed to reconstruct something similar to part of one of our components.

It is not in general possible to complete the state behaviour assignment by adjoining a θ function. However, we *do* have the following proposition.

7.3.2 Proposition

Suppose π_1 and π_2 are non-trivial SP partitions of M satisfying $\pi_1 . \pi_2 = \bot_S$. Define $M_1 = M_{\pi_1}$ and $M_2 = M_{\pi_2}$. Let $o \in O$. Define functions:

$$\alpha : S \rightarrow \pi_1 \times \pi_2$$

$$\iota : I \rightarrow I \times I$$

$$\theta : (\pi_1 \times I) \times (\pi_2 \times I) \rightarrow O$$

by:

(a) $\alpha(s) = (S_1, S_2)$ if and only if $S_1 \cap S_2 = \{s\}$

(b) $\iota(i) = (i, i)$

(c) $\theta((X, i), (Y, j)) = \begin{cases} \beta(s, i) & \text{if } X \cap Y = \{s\} \text{ and } i = j \\ o & \text{if } X \cap Y = \varnothing \text{ or } 1 \neq j \end{cases}$

Let $\phi = (\alpha,\iota,\theta)$, then $\phi: M \to M_1 \,||\, M_2$ is a state behaviour assignment and in particular $M \leq M_1 \,||\, M_2$ non-trivially.

Proof

We must check that ϕ is a state behaviour assignment. For simplicity, let $M_{||} = M_1 \,||\, M_2$.

It is a simple exercise to show that functions in ϕ have the appropriate domains and ranges. To complete the proof, we need to show that α is injective and that the equations [7.1] hold.

Suppose then that $\alpha(s) = \alpha(s') = (X, Y)$. By definition of α, $\{s\} = X \cap Y = \{s'\}$ and so $s = s'$. Thus α is injective.

Next, let $s \in S$ and $i \in I$. We must show that:

$$\delta_{||}(\alpha(s),\iota(i)) = \alpha(\delta(s,i)) \qquad [7.6]$$

and

$$\theta(\beta_{||}(\alpha(s),\iota(i)) = \theta((X,i),(Y,i)) = \beta(s,i) \qquad [7.7]$$

First we show [7.6]. Since π_1 and π_2 are partitions, we may find $X, X' \in \pi_1$ and $Y, Y' \in \pi_2$ such that $s \in X \cap Y$ and $\delta(s,i) \in X' \cap Y'$.

By definition of α, we have:

$$\alpha(s) = (X, Y) \quad \alpha(\delta(s,i)) = (X', Y') \qquad [7.8]$$

We may thus calculate $\delta_{||}(\alpha(s),\iota(i))$.

$$\begin{aligned}\delta_{||}(\alpha(s),\iota(i)) &= \delta_{||}((X,Y),(i,i)) \text{ (by [7.8])}\\ &= (\delta_1(X,i),\delta_2(Y,i)) \text{ (by 6.2.1)}\end{aligned}$$

Since $\alpha(\delta(s,i)) = (X', Y')$, by [7.8], to complete the proof of [7.6] it suffices to show that:

$$\delta_1(X,i) = X' \text{ and } \delta_2(Y,i) = Y' \qquad [7.9]$$

But π_1 and π_2 are partitions and so any two elements of either of them are either disjoint or equal. Thus, to show [7.9], it suffices to show that:

$$\delta_1(X,i) \cap X' \neq \emptyset \text{ and } \delta_2(Y,i) \cap Y' \neq \emptyset \qquad [7.10]$$

By choice of X, $s \in X \cap Y \subseteq X$ and so $\delta(s,i) \in \delta(X,i)$. But by definition of δ_1 (7.3.1) $\delta(X,i) \subseteq \delta_1(X,i)$ and so $\delta(s,i) \in \delta_1(X,i)$.

But also by choice of X', $\delta(s,i) \in X' \cap Y' \subseteq X'$. Thus $\delta(s,i) \in X' \cap \delta_1(X,i)$ and so $\delta_1(X,i) \cap X' \neq \varnothing$ as required.

Similarly, $\delta(s,i) \in Y' \cap \delta_2(Y,i)$ and so $\delta_2(Y,i) \cap Y' \neq \varnothing$ as required.

We have proved [7.10]. In view of our previous remarks, this gives [7.6].

Now, we check [7.7] Calculating:

$$\begin{aligned}\theta(\beta_{||}(\alpha(s),\iota(i))) &= \theta(\beta_1(X,i),\beta_2(Y,i)) \\ &= \theta((X,i),(Y,i)) = \beta(s,i)\end{aligned}$$

(α,ι,θ) thus satisfies the conditions of 4.3.1 and is thus a state behaviour assignment. We leave the proof of non-triviality to the reader. Lemma 7.2.5 should give hints.

Note that proposition 7.3.2 not only shows that the conditions of 7.2.6 are sufficient for there to be a parallel decomposition, it also gives an algorithm for constructing parallel decompositions. The whole business may be *automated*.

To conclude the chapter, we combine propositions 7.2.6 and 7.3.2.

7.3.3 Parallel Decomposition Theorem

Let M be a machine, then M has a non-trivial parallel decomposition if and only if it has two non-trivial SP partitions π_1 and π_2 satisfying $\pi_1.\pi_2 = \bot_S$.

7.4 AN EXAMPLE OF DECOMPOSITION: A 'BOOLEAN CALCULATOR'

7.4.1 Description of the Machine

The following device calculates the logical 'and' and 'or' of two Boolean values a and b which may be set to 0 or 1. There are six commands available, to which we shall assign letters: a=0 (A), b=0 (B), a=1 (C), b=1 (D), $a.b$ (E) and $a+b$ (F). The device has three different outputs 0, 1 and #, the latter being merely an acknowledge. It has four states (corresponding to the four possible values of (a,b)).

The flow table is given in Table 7.1.

Table 7.1. The machine M

	A	B	C	D	E	F	A	B	C	D	E	F
w	w	w	y	x	w	w	#	#	#	#	0	0
x	x	w	z	x	x	x	#	#	#	#	0	1
y	w	y	y	z	y	y	#	#	#	#	0	1
z	x	y	z	z	z	z	#	#	#	#	1	1

Check, for example, that from any state the sequence a=0 b=1 a+b takes the machine to state x and produces an output ##1. It follows that x corresponds to the state $(0,1)$, i.e. in which $a = 0$ and $b = 1$. The other correspondences may be worked out like this. Try it.

7.4.2 The SP Partitions

In Chapter 9, we shall see how all the SP partitions of a machine may be computed. For the moment, we merely assert that M has two non-trivial SP partitions:

$$\pi_1 = \{\{w,x\},\{y,z\}\}$$

and

$$\pi_2 = \{\{w,y\},\{x,z\}\}$$

You should try to verify that these are indeed SP partitions. (We will check π_1 in 7.4.4).

Define $X = \{w,x\}$, $Y = \{y,z\}$, $U = \{w,y\}$ and $V = \{x,z\}$.

7.4.3 Remark

The reader should note that X corresponds to the pair of states $(0,0)$ and $(0,1)$, that is a=0 and b is anything, whereas Y corresponds to the pair $(1,0)$ and $(1,1)$, that is a=1 and b is anything. Intuitively, the partitions allow us to split the device into two, one of which is exclusively concerned with a and the other with b.

Note that:

$$\begin{aligned}\pi_1.\pi_2 &= \{X \cap U, X \cap V, Y \cap U, Y \cap V\} \\ &= \{\{w\},\{x\},\{y\},\{z\}\} = \bot\end{aligned}$$

so that we have a parallel decomposition of the device.

7.4.4 The Image Machines

Each of the SP partitions defines an image machine whose states are the elements of the partition. We shall call the Mealy machine derived from π_1, M_1 and call that derived from π_2, M_2. We use the 'recipe' of 7.3.1 to construct these machines.

For π_1, we have:

$$\delta(X,A) = X;\ \delta(X,B) \subseteq X;\ \delta(X,C) = Y$$

$$\delta(X,D) \subseteq X;\ \delta(X,E) = X;\ \delta(X,F) = X$$

$$\delta(Y,A) = X;\ \delta(Y,B) \subseteq Y;\ \delta(Y,C) = Y$$

$$\delta(Y,D) \subseteq Y;\ \delta(Y,E) = Y;\ \delta(Y,F) = Y$$

From these relations, it can be seen that π_1 is indeed SP. We may now construct δ_1. For example, since $\delta(X,B) \subseteq X$, we would define $\delta_1(X,B) = X$.

As for outputs, we have $\beta_1(s,i) = (s,i)$ for each $s \in \{X, Y\}$ and $i \in I$. To save space we will omit the parentheses and comma. The flow table for M_1 is thus that of Table 7.2.

Table 7.2. The machine M_1

	A	B	C	D	E	F	A	B	C	D	E	F
X	X	X	Y	X	X	X	XA	XB	XC	XD	XE	XF
Y	X	Y	Y	Y	Y	Y	YA	YB	YC	YD	YE	YF

Notice that it is only the inputs A (a=0) and C (a=1) that modify the state of the machine. This is quite in line with our remark 7.4.2, which identifies X with the condition that a=0 and Y with the condition that a=1.

The calculation of the transition table for M_2 is exactly the same. In this case, we get Table 7.3.

Table 7.3. The machine M_2

	A	B	C	D	E	F	A	B	C	D	E	F
U	U	U	U	V	U	U	UA	UB	UC	UD	UE	UF
V	V	U	V	V	V	V	VA	VB	VC	VD	VE	VF

7.4.5 The State Behaviour Assignment

Now let us construct the coding and decoding functions.

Recall from 7.3.2 that we define $\alpha(s)$ to be the unique pair (X,Y) such that $X \cap Y = \{s\}$. α may thus be defined as follows:

$$\alpha(w) = (X,U);\alpha(x) = (X,V);\alpha(y) = (Y,U);\alpha(z) = (Y,V)$$

ι simply maps each $i \in I$ to (i,i), while $\theta(ST,S'T')$ is defined to be $\beta(s,i)$ if $s \in S \cap S'$ and $T = i = T'$ and anything you like otherwise. Thus for the non-'don't care' values of θ we have the table:

$$\theta(XA,UA) = \#;\ \theta(XA,VA) = \#;\ \theta(YA,UA) = \#;\ \theta(YA,VA) = \#$$

$$\theta(XB,UB) = \#;\ \theta(XB,VB) = \#;\ \theta(YB,UB) = \#;\ \theta(YB,VB) = \#$$

$$\theta(XC,UC) = \#;\ \theta(XC,VC) = \#;\ \theta(YC,UC) = \#;\ \theta(YC,VC) = \#$$

$$\theta(XD,UD) = \#;\ \theta(XD,VD) = \#;\ \theta(YD,UD) = \#;\ \theta(YD,VD) = \#$$

$$\theta(XE,UE) = 0;\ \theta(XE,VE) = 0;\ \theta(YE,UE) = 0;\ \theta(YE,VE) = 1$$

$$\theta(XF,UF) = 0;\ \theta(XF,VF) = 1;\ \theta(YF,UF) = 1;\ \theta(YF,VF) = 1$$

EXERCISES

1 Prove remark 7.2.1.

2 Show that $\perp_S$ and $\top_S$ are always SP partitions. What image machines do they give rise to ?

3 Complete the proof of proposition 7.3.2.

4 Check that (α,ι,θ) defined in 7.4.5 *is* a state behaviour assignment.

5 Show that *any* machine M has a trivial parallel decomposition by constructing a machine M' such that $M \leq M \parallel M'$.

In the following exercises, we show how to reduce the size of output sets associated with a parallel decomposition.

6 Suppose $\phi = (\alpha,\iota,\theta):M \to M_1 \mid\mid M_2$. Define a relation $\approx$ on O_1 as follows. Let $o_1 \approx o_2$ if and only if for every $o \in O_2$, $\theta(o_1,o) = \theta(o_2,o)$. Prove that $\approx$ is an equivalence relation.

7 Let $\approx$ be the equivalence relation of **6**. Let $O_1/\approx$ denote the set of equivalence classes of $\approx$ and let $<o>$ denote the equivalence class of $o \in O_1$.

Define M_1' to be the machine $(S_1, I_1, O_1/\approx, \delta_1, \beta_1')$, where $\beta_1'(s,i) = <\beta_1(s,i)>$. Define $\theta'(<o_1>, o_2) = \theta(o_1, o_2)$.

Show that θ' is well defined and prove that $\phi' = (\alpha,\iota,\theta'):M \to M_1' \mid\mid M_2$ is a state behaviour assignment.

8 Consider how the arguments in **6** and **7** may be applied to M_2 and to machines produced from the parallel decomposition algorithm. Why might you feel inclined to modify the definition of θ in 7.3.2 ?

9 M is said to be a *reset machine* if there is a function $f:I \to S$ such that for all $s \in S$ and all $i \in I$:

$$\delta(s,i) = f(i)$$

Show that if M is a reset machine, then *every* partition of M is SP.

10 Show that if M is a reset machine with at least three states, then M has a parallel decomposition $M \le M' \mid\mid M_1$, where $|S_1| = 2$ and both M_1 and M' are reset machines.

11 Show using induction, **10** and appropriate results from Section 6.4 that if M is a reset machine, then M has a parallel decomposition as:

$$M \le (...(M_n \mid\mid M_{n-1}) \mid\mid ...) \mid\mid M_1$$

where each M_j is a reset machine with $|S_j| = 2$, each j and M_j is a reset machine, each j.

12 Show that if M_1 and M_2 are reset machines, then $M_1 \mid\mid M_2$ is a reset machine.

13 Show that if M is a reset machine and $M' \le M$ then M' is a reset machine.

14 Use the above to show the following proposition: M is a reset machine if and only if there exist reset machines $M_1, ..., M_n$ with $|S_j| = 2$, each j such that $M \leq (...(M_n \,||\, M_{n-1}) \,||\, ...) \,||\, M_1$.

NOTES

The material in this chapter is based on Heartmanis & Stearns (1966), section 3.5. They use 0 for the partition $\perp_S$. Our usage is consistent with the notation of computer scientists working with partial orders; $\perp_S$ will turn out to be the bottom of a partially ordered set of partitions (see Chapter 9).

Chapter 8

The Serial Decomposition Theorem

At the end of three days the clockmaker, a Mr. Towelbird, said, 'I have never met anyone like him for pulling clocks to bits. He's the best man I ever had for that branch of work. But he doesn't ever seem to put them together again. That side of the work apparently doesn't interest him.'

J. B. MORTON ('Beachcomber')
The Adventures of Charles Suet

8.1 INTRODUCTION

In the previous chapter, we showed that a machine has a parallel decomposition if and only if it has two SP partitions which are orthogonal. In this chapter we prove a theorem which explains the situation in the serial case.

The notion of serial decomposition is entirely analogous with that of parallel decomposition.

8.1.1 Definition

Suppose M is a machine. M will be said to have a serial decomposition if and only if there exist machines M_1 and M_2 and a function $\kappa: O_1 \rightarrow I_2$ such that:

$$M \leq M_1 \ominus_{\kappa} M_2$$

Again, the decomposition will be said to be *non-trivial* if $|S_1| < |S|$ and $|S_2| < |S|$.

Our strategy will be the same as in the parallel case; we begin by taking an arbitrary machine, suppose that it has a serial decomposition and deduce consequences. The reasoning is very similar to that in the parallel case.

To show the converse we will again present a construction.

The main result is theorem 8.3.3.

8.2 NECESSARY CONDITIONS

Let M be a Mealy machine and suppose that M has a non-trivial serial decomposition. This means that we have two machines M_1 and M_2 and a state behaviour assignment $\phi = (\alpha, \iota, \theta)$, $\phi: M \to M_{\ominus}$, where we are defining:

$$M_{\ominus} = M_1 \ominus_{\kappa} M_2$$

The first part of the analysis of section 7.2 goes through unchanged. In this case also, α is an injective function:

$$\alpha: S \to S_{\ominus} = S_1 \times S_2$$

and so we have the following.

8.2.1 Lemma

Define:

$$S_{1,j} = \{s \in S \mid \alpha(s) = (s_{1,j}, s') \textit{ some } s'\} \qquad [8.1]$$

$$S_{2,k} = \{s \in S \mid \alpha(s) = (s', s_{2,k}) \textit{ some } s'\}$$

and let $\pi_1 = \{S_{1,j} \mid s_{1,j} \in S_1\}$, $\pi_2 = \{S_{2,k} \mid s_{2,k} \in S_2\}$, then π_1 and π_2 are partitions satisfying $\pi_1 . \pi_2 = \perp_S$.

Again, because the argument only concerned α as a function, we may take over 7.2.5, lock, stock and barrel.

8.2.2 Lemma

Neither π_1 nor π_2 is trivial.

Turning to the state transition behaviour, we see from 8.2.1 that S inherits the egg-box structure from $S_1 \times S_2$ and that because of the usual state behaviour assignment condition:

$$\alpha(\delta(s, i)) = \delta_{\ominus}(\alpha(s), \iota(i)) \qquad [8.2]$$

we would expect the dynamics of $M_{\ominus}$ to be reflected in the subset of S corresponding to $\alpha(S)$ exactly as in the parallel case. This is indeed true – it is what [8.2] says. Unfortunately, the dynamics of $M_{\ominus}$ are not quite as straightforward as in the parallel case. The reason is that while changes in M_1 are closely related to changes in M, changes in M_2 are more complicated because they depend on outputs from M_1.

We may concoct a lemma corresponding to 7.2.4, however.

8.2.3 Lemma

With the above notation, if $S_{1,j} \neq \varnothing$ then:

$$\delta(S_{1,j}, i) \subseteq S_{1,l} \Leftrightarrow \delta(s_{1,j}, \iota(i)) = s_{1,l}$$

In particular π_1 is an SP partition.

Proof

The proof is very similar to that of 7.2.4. First, we show the '$\Leftarrow$' part.

Suppose $\delta(S_{1,j}, i) \subseteq S_{1,l}$. By 8.2.1, this means that whenever $\alpha(s) = (s_{1,j}, s')$, some s', then $\alpha(\delta(s,i)) = (s_{1,l}, s'')$, some s''. So, we suppose that $\alpha(s) = (s_{1,j}, s')$, some s'.

By [8.2], $\alpha(\delta(s,i)) = \delta_{\ominus}(\alpha(s), \iota(i))$. Since $\alpha(s) = (s_{1,j}, s')$, some s', then by definition of serial composition (6.3.1), we have:

$$\delta_{\ominus}(\alpha(s), \iota(i)) = <\delta_1(s_{1,j}, \iota(i)), \delta_2(s', \kappa[\beta_1(s_{1,j}, \iota(i))])> \qquad [8.3]$$

and since $\alpha(\delta(s,i)) = \delta_{\ominus}(\alpha(s), \iota(i))$, we have:

$$\alpha(\delta(s,i)) = <\delta_1(s_{1,j}, \iota(i)), \delta_2(s', \kappa[\beta_1(s_{1,j}, \iota(i))])> \qquad [8.4]$$

But by hypothesis, since $\alpha(s) = (s_{1,j}, s')$, some s', we have $\alpha(\delta(s,i)) = (s_{1,l}, s'')$, some s''. Substituting into [8.4] gives:

$$<\delta_1(s_{1,j}, \iota(i)), \delta_2(s', \kappa[\beta_1(s_{1,j}, \iota(i))])> = (s_{1,l}, s'')$$

Comparing coordinates, $\delta_1(s_{1,j}, \iota(i)) = s_{1,l}$.

This proves the 'only if' part of the lemma. Now we prove the 'if' part.

Suppose that $\delta_1(s_{1,j}, \iota(i)) = s_{1,l}$. We must show that $\delta_1(S_{1,j}, i) \subseteq S_{1,l}$, that is, whenever $\alpha(s) = (s_{1,j}, s')$, some s', then $\alpha(\delta(s,i)) = (s_{1,l}, s'')$, some s''.

Suppose, therefore that $\alpha(s) = (s_{1,j}, s')$, some s'. We compute $\alpha(\delta(s,i))$.

By [8.2] and our assumption:

$$\alpha(\delta(s,i)) = \delta_{\ominus}(\alpha(s), \iota(i)) = \delta_{\ominus}((s_{1,j}, s'), \iota(i)) \qquad [8.5]$$

$= \langle \delta_1(s_{1,j}, \iota(i)), \delta_2(s', \kappa[\beta_1(s_{1,j}, \iota(i))]) \rangle$ (by [8.3])

$= \langle s_1, \delta_2(s', \kappa[\beta_1(s_{1,j}, \iota(i))]) \rangle$ (by hypothesis)

$= (s_{1,l}, s'')$

setting $s'' = \delta_2(s', \kappa[\beta_1(s_{1,j}, \iota(i))])$.

This concludes the proof.

What about π_2 ? If $s \in S_{2,k}$ is there anything we can say about $\delta(s, i)$? The answer is 'no' in general. It might therefore seem that the conditions on π_2 would have to be more complicated than those on π_1. Strangely enough, this is not the case (see proposition 8.3.1). Any partition will do for π_2 providing it is non-trivial and orthogonal to π_1.

Putting together what we have so far we have the following.

8.2.4 Proposition (Necessary Conditions for Serial Decomposability)

Let M be a machine, then if M has a non-trivial serial decomposition then it has a non-trivial SP partition.

8.3 SUFFICIENT CONDITIONS

Now we must prove the converse. This proof will be constructive, that is, gives a method for constructing a serial decomposition, given an SP partition.

Let M be given and let π be a non-trivial SP partition. From 7.3.1, we know that π determines a Mealy machine, M_π. Recall that $M_\pi = (\pi, I, \pi \times I, \delta_\pi, \beta_\pi)$ where:

$$\delta_\pi(X, i) = Y \Leftrightarrow \delta(X, i) \subseteq Y$$

$$\beta_\pi(X, i) = (X, i)$$

This will be the head machine in the decomposition. How can we build the tail machine ? Part of the answer is given in the following proposition.

8.3.1 Proposition

Let π_1 be a non-trivial SP partition of S and suppose π_2 is any non-trivial partition satisfying $\pi_1.\pi_2 = \perp_S$. Suppose $Y_o \in \pi_2$ and $o \in O$.

Let $M_1 = M_{\pi_1}$ and define $M_2 = (\pi_2, \pi_1 \times I, O, \delta_2, \beta_2)$ where:

(a) $$\delta_2(X, (Y, i)) = \begin{cases} Y' & \text{if } X \cap Y \neq \emptyset \text{ and } \delta(X \cap Y, i) \subseteq Y' \\ Y_o & \textit{otherwise} \end{cases}$$

(b) $\beta_2(X,(Y,i)) = \begin{cases} \beta(s,i) & \text{if } X \cap Y = \{s\} \\ o & \textit{otherwise} \end{cases}$

Define functions:

$$\alpha : S \to \pi_1 \times \pi_2$$
$$\iota : I \to I$$
$$\theta : O \to O$$

by

$$\alpha(s) = (X,Y) \text{ if } X \cap Y = \{s\}$$
$$\iota(i) = i \quad \theta(o) = o$$

Then $\phi = (\alpha,\iota,\theta)$ is a state behaviour assignment $\phi : M \to M_1 \ominus M_2$ and in particular M has a non-trivial serial decomposition.

Proof

Let $M_\ominus = M_1 \ominus M_2$. Let $s \in S$ and $i \in I$. We must show that:

$$\delta_\ominus(\alpha(s),\iota(i)) = \alpha(\delta(s,i)) \qquad [8.6]$$

and

$$\theta[\beta_\ominus(\alpha(s),\iota(i))] = \beta(s,i) \qquad [8.7]$$

First, we show [8.6].

Since π_1 and π_2 are partitions, we may find $X,X' \in \pi_1$ and $Y,Y' \in \pi_2$ such that $s \in X \cap Y$ and $\delta(s,i) \in X' \cap Y'$. Thus, by definition of α.

$$\alpha(s) = (X,Y) \quad \alpha(\delta(s,i)) = (X',Y') \qquad [8.8]$$

We use equation [8.8] to calculate $\delta_\ominus(\alpha(s),\iota(i))$.

$$\begin{aligned} \delta_\ominus(\alpha(s),\iota(i)) &= \delta_\ominus((X,Y),i) \\ &= [\delta_1(X,i),\delta_2(Y,\beta_1(X,i))] \text{ (by 6.3.1)} \\ &= [\delta_1(X,i),\delta_2(Y,(X,i))] \end{aligned}$$

Thus:

$$\delta_{\oplus}(\alpha(s),\iota(i)) = [\delta_1(X,i),\delta_2(Y,(X,i))] \qquad [8.9]$$

But, we also have from [8.8], that $\alpha(\delta(s,i)) = (X',Y')$ and so in view of this fact and [8.9], to conclude the proof of [8.6] it suffices to show that:

$$\delta_1(X,i) = X' \text{ and } \delta_2(Y,\beta_1(X,i)) = Y' \qquad [8.10]$$

First, we show that:

$$\delta_1(X,i) = X' \qquad [8.11]$$

Since $\delta_1(X,i)$ and X' both belong to the partition π_1, it suffices to prove that $\delta_1(X,i) \cap X' \neq \emptyset$. The proof is entirely analogous to the corresponding part of 7.3.2.

By choice of X, $s \in X \cap Y \subseteq X$, so $\delta(s,i) \in \delta(X,i)$. But by definition of δ_1 (6.3.1), $\delta(X,i) \subseteq \delta_1(X,i)$. Thus $\delta(s,i) \in \delta_1(X,i)$. But by choice of X', $\delta(s,i) \in X'$ and so $\delta(s,i) \in \delta_1(X,i) \cap X'$. This proves that $\delta_1(X,i) \cap X' \neq \emptyset$ and hence [8.11].

Next, we show that:

$$\delta_2(Y,\beta_1(X,i)) = Y' \qquad [8.12]$$

By definition of δ_2 this holds if and only if $\delta(X \cap Y,i) \subseteq Y'$ But by choice of X,Y, $X \cap Y = \{s\}$, and by choice of Y', $\delta(s,i) \in Y'$. Thus $\delta(X \cap Y,i) = \delta(\{s\},i) = \{\delta(s,i)\} \subseteq Y'$, giving [8.12].

From [8.11] and [8.12], we derive [8.10], from which [8.6] follows.

Now, we show [8.7] Calculating:

$$\begin{aligned} \theta[\beta_{\oplus}(\alpha(s),\iota(i))] &= \beta_{\oplus}((X,Y),i) \\ &= \beta_2[Y,\kappa(\beta_1(X,i))] \\ &= \beta_2(Y,(X,i)) \\ &= \beta(s,i) \end{aligned}$$

since $s \in X \cap Y$.

This concludes the proof.

Proposition 8.3.1 depended on the existence of a partition orthogonal to π_1. The following lemma, which says that such a partition always exists, is purely set-theoretical.

8.3.2 Lemma

Suppose X is a non-empty set and that π is a non-trivial partition of X, then there exists a non-trivial partition τ such that $\pi.\tau = \bot_X$.

Proof

Suppose that π consists of the following sets:

$$X_1 = \{s^{1,1}, ..., s^{1,m_1}\}$$

$$. \quad . \quad .$$

$$X_i = \{s^{i,1}, ..., s^{i,m_i}\}$$

$$. \quad . \quad .$$

$$X_n = \{s^{n,1}, ..., s^{n,m_n}\}$$

Let τ consist of the sets :

$$Y_i = \{s^{1,i}, ..., s^{n,i}\}$$

for those $s^{j,i}$ which actually exist. The reader should be able to see that if $X_i \cap Y_j \neq \varnothing$ then $X_i \cap Y_j \neq \{s^{i,j}\}$.

Since $\pi \neq \bot_X$, some X_i has at least two elements, say $X_1 = \{s^{1,1}, s^{1,2}, ...\}$. It follows that τ has at least two elements Y_1 and Y_2. Thus $\tau \neq \top_X$. Similarly, since $\pi \neq \top_X$, π has at least two elements, say X_1 and X_2. Thus $Y_1 = \{s^{1,1}, s^{2,1}, ...\}$ has at least two elements and therefore $\tau \neq \bot_X$.

Therefore, τ is non-trivial.

This concludes the proof.

Putting 8.2.4, 8.3.1 and 8.3.2 together gives, finally, the following.

8.3.3 Serial Decomposition Theorem

Let M be a machine, then M has a non-trivial serial decomposition if and only if it has a non-trivial SP partition.

8.4 EXAMPLE: SERIAL DECOMPOSITION OF THE BOOLEAN CALCULATOR

As we saw in section 7.4, the so-called 'Boolean Calculator' has two SP Partitions, which we called π_1 and π_2. Both are non-trivial and we may use either to construct a serial decomposition of M.

Let us use π_1 to construct the serial decomposition. The first thing to note is that the construction of the head machine is exactly the same as that of M in the previous section – so half the work has already been done.

We also need to find a partition (not necessarily SP) τ such that $\pi_1.\tau = \perp_S$. But π_2 has this property.

Thus we already have the head machine in the decomposition, and as far as the tail machine – which we shall call M_2 – goes, we have its state set π_2, its input set O_1 (the outputs of M_1) and its output set, O (the outputs of M). Furthermore, because the principle behind the construction of the state behaviour assignment is the same for parallel and serial decomposition – a state s maps to the pair (X, Y) such that s is the unique element in $X \cap Y$ – we have that too.

It only remains, therefore, to construct the next-state and output functions for M_2. Let us take as an example the calculation of $\delta_2(U, XC)$ and $\beta_2(U, XC)$.

For M_2 to receive this input from M_1, it must be the case that M_1 was in state X, M_2 was in state U and M_1 has received input C.

Now, $U \cap X = \{w, y\} \cap \{w, x\} = \{w\}$, so the corresponding situation in M is that M was in state w and received input C. From Table 7.1, we see that M moves to state y and outputs #.

Thus, M_2 must output #, that is:

$$\beta_2(U, XC) = \#$$

and must move to a new state whose intersection with the new state of M_1 is $\{y\}$. There is only one such state, namely U, the unique block of π_2 that contains y. Thus:

$$\delta_2(U, XC) = U$$

Let us look at another example to try to bring the point home. We shall compute $\delta_2(U, YD)$ and $\beta_2(U, YD)$. $Y \cap U = \{y\}$ and $\delta(y, D) = z$ and $\beta(y, D) = \#$, so we set $\delta_2(U, YD) = V$, the block of π_2 containing z, and $\beta_2(U, YD) = \#$.

Applying this construction gives the tail machine, M_2, whose state table is given in Tables 8.1 and 8.2.

Table 8.1. The machine M_2: state transitions

	XA	XB	XC	XD	XE	XF	YA	YB	YC	YD	YE	YF
U	U	U	U	V	U	U	U	U	U	V	U	U
V	V	U	V	V	V	V	V	U	V	V	V	V

Table 8.2. The machine M_2: outputs

	XA	XB	XC	XD	XE	XF	YA	YB	YC	YD	YE	YF
U	#	#	#	#	0	0	#	#	#	#	0	1
V	#	#	#	#	0	1	#	#	#	#	1	1

EXERCISES

The first set of exercises show how the output set of M_{π_1} and the input set of M_{π_2} may be decreased in size. Suppose $\phi = (\alpha,\iota,\theta):M \to M_1 \ominus_\kappa M_2$.

1 Define a relation $\approx_1$ on O_1 by $o_1 \approx_1 o_2$ if and only if for all $s \in S_2$, $\delta_2(s,\kappa(o_1)) = \delta_2(s,\kappa(o_2))$ and $\beta_2(s,\kappa(o_1)) = \beta_2(s,\kappa(o_2))$.
Prove that $\approx_1$ is an equivalence relation.

2 Define a relation $\approx_2$ on I_2 by $i_1 \approx_2 i_2$ if and only if for all $s \in S_2$, $\delta_2(s,i_1) = \delta_2(s,i_2)$ and $\beta_2(s,i_1) = \beta_2(s,i_2)$.
Prove that $\approx_2$ is an equivalence relation.

3 Let $O_1/\approx_1$ denote the set of equivalence classes of $\approx_1$ and let $<o>_1$ denote the $\approx_1$ class of o. Let $I_2/\approx_2$ denote the set of equivalence classes of $\approx_2$ and let $<i>_2$ denote the $\approx_2$ class of i.
Show that if $o_1 \approx_1 o_2$, then $\kappa(o_1) \approx_2 \kappa(o_2)$. Conclude that we may define a function $\kappa':O_1/\approx_1 \to I_2/\approx_2$ by $\kappa'(<o>_1) = <\kappa(o)>_2$.

4 Define $M'_1 = (S_1,I_1,O_1/\approx_1,\delta_1,\beta'_1)$, where $\beta'_1(s,i) = <\beta_1(s,i)>_1$. Define $M'_2 = (S_2,I_2/\approx_2,O_2,\delta'_2,\beta'_2)$, where $\delta'_2(s,<i>_2) = \delta_2(s,i)$ and $\beta'_2(s,<i>_2) = \beta_2(s,i)$.
Show that β'_1, δ'_2 and β'_2 are well-defined and that $\phi = (\alpha,\iota,\theta):M \to M'_1 \ominus_{\kappa'} M'_2$ is a state behaviour assignment, that is $M \le M'_1 \ominus_{\kappa'} M'_2$.

By applying the construction to the machines produced in Section 8.4, show that the Boolean Calculator has a serial decomposition $M \leq M'_1 \ominus_{\kappa'} M'_2$ in which M'_1 has six outputs and M'_2 has six inputs.

5 Formalise the discussion in Section 1.4 concerning the decomposition of Great Aunt Eugenia.

6 Verify that the partition $\{\{00,01\},\{10,11\}\}$ of the machine M_{front} given in Table 6.4, is SP, and construct a serial decomposition.

NOTES

The material in this chapter is based on Heartmanis & Stearns, (1966) section 2.2. Holcombe (1982) presents the results in terms of state machines in section 3.3.

Chapter 9

The Lattice of SP Partitions

9.1 INTRODUCTION

In the preceding chapters we have seen how what one might call the external structure of a machine M – how M may be simulated by a system of simpler machines combined by serial and parallel composition – is related to what one may call its internal structure – the existence of SP partitions related in various ways.

In this chapter, we shall look more closely at the set of all SP partitions belonging to an arbitrary machine. It will turn out that they may be partially ordered in a natural kind of way and indeed form what is known as a *lattice*.

This will enable us to perform operations on SP partitions, resembling, in some respects, arithmetic operations on numbers. These will enable us to construct all the SP partitions of a given machine.

9.2 LATTICES

Recall that a partially ordered set (or 'poset') is a pair $(X,\leq)$, where $\leq$ is a reflexive, asymmetrical transitive relation, that is, it satisfies the three laws:

For all $x \in X, x \leq x$ (Reflexivity)
For all $x,y \in X, x \leq y \ \& \ y \leq x \Rightarrow x = y$ (Asymmetry)
For all $x,y,z \in X, x \leq y \ \& \ y \leq z \Rightarrow x \leq z$ (Transitivity)

We shall write $x < y$ to indicate that $x \leq y$ and $x \neq y$.

It is sometimes convenient to represent posets pictorially using so-called Hasse diagrams. A Hasse diagram is a directed graph, whose nodes are labelled by elements of X and where there is an arc from a node labelled x to a node labelled y if $x < y$ and for no z do we have $x < z$ and $z < y$.

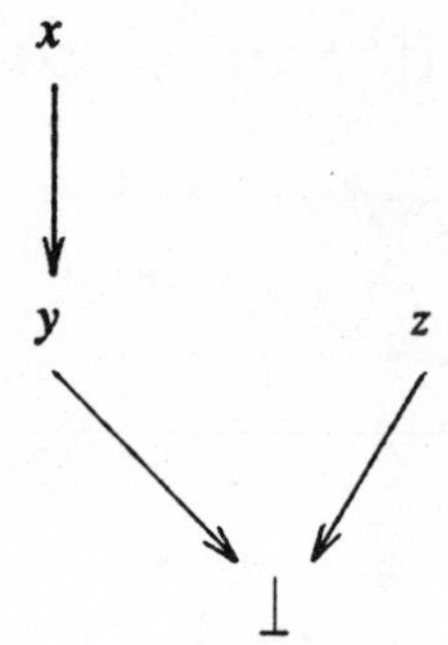

Fig. 9.1

Thus, Fig. 9.1 represents a poset $(X,\leq)$ in which $X = \{\bot, x, y, z\}$ and in which:

$$\bot \leq x \quad \bot \leq y \quad \bot \leq z \quad y \leq x$$
$$\bot \leq \bot \quad y \leq y \quad z \leq z \quad x \leq x$$

9.2.1 Examples

If X is any set, then $(\underline{P}(X),\subseteq)$ is a poset.

If $\mathbf{N}^+$ denotes the set of all positive, non-zero whole numbers, then $(\mathbf{N}^+, \mid)$ is a poset, where $x \mid y$ means that x divides y.

More relevant to us is the definition of order on partitions. We shall define a relation on sets of subsets generally. We illustrate in example 9.2.4 and prove that the relation is a partial order in lemma 9.2.3.

9.2.2 Definition

Let S be a set and suppose $\sigma_1,\sigma_2 \subseteq \underline{P}(S)$* then we define:

$$\sigma_1 \leq \sigma_2 \Leftrightarrow \text{if } X \in \sigma_1 \textit{ then } X \subseteq Y \textit{ some } Y \in \sigma_2$$

* That is to say, σ_1 and σ_2 are sets of subsets of S. In the case we are interested in, they would be partitions.

In the case where σ_1 and σ_2 are partitions, it is perhaps easier to see what this means pictorially. σ_2 divides the set S into blocks. If $\sigma_1 \leq \sigma_2$, then σ_1 further subdivides S; each block of σ_2 is a union of blocks of σ_1.

9.2.3 Lemma

Suppose $\Pi(X)$ denotes the set of partitions of a set X, then $(\Pi(X),\leq)$ is a partially ordered set.

Furthermore, for all $\pi \in \Pi(X)$, $\bot_X \leq \pi$ and $\pi \leq \top_X$.

Proof

We leave the proof of reflexivity and transitivity to the reader as an exercise. For asymmetry, suppose $\pi_1,\pi_2 \in \Pi(X)$. Suppose that $\pi_1 \leq \pi_2$ and that $\pi_2 \leq \pi_1$. We show that they are equal.

Let $X \in \pi_1$, then since $\pi_1 \leq \pi_2$, there exists $Y \in \pi_2$ such that $X \subseteq Y$. Since $\pi_2 \leq \pi_1$, there exists $Z \in \pi_1$ such that $Y \subseteq Z$. Thus, $X \subseteq Z$ and since π_1 is a partition and $X,Z \in \pi_1$ with $X \cap Z = X \neq \emptyset$, it follows that $X = Z$ and so $Y \subseteq X$. Thus, $X = Y$ and consequently $\pi_1 \subseteq \pi_2$.

Analogously, $\pi_2 \subseteq \pi_1$ and hence they are equal.

It may actually be shown directly that if $\pi_1 \subseteq \pi_2$ and they are both partitions of the same set, then $\pi_1 = \pi_2$. See exercise 3.

We leave the proof that $\bot_X \leq \pi$ and $\pi \leq \top_X$ as an exercise.

9.2.4 Example

We shall use the machine M_{exam} given in Table 9.1 and the partitions π_1,π_2,π_3 and π_4 given below to illustrate the ideas introduced in this chapter.

Table 9.1

	1	2	1	2
1	2	3	a	b
2	1	3	a	b
3	4	5	b	a
4	3	2	a	b
5	1	6	b	a
6	1	5	b	a

$$\pi_1 = \{\{1,2\},\{3\},\{4\},\{5\},\{6\}\}$$

$$\pi_2 = \{\{1\},\{2\},\{3\},\{4\},\{5,6\}\}$$

$$\pi_3 = \{\{1,2\},\{3\},\{4\},\{5,6\}\}$$

$$\pi_4 = \{\{1,4\},\{2,3,5,6\}\}$$

Define $\mathbf{P} = \{\bot_{S_{exam}}, \pi_1, \pi_2, \pi_3, \pi_4, \top_{S_{exam}}\}$.

We shall construct the Hasse diagram for $(\mathbf{P}, \leq)$. First, note that when we apply 9.2.3 to two *partitions*, π_1, π_2, we only need to consider sets X such that $|X| > 1$. If $|X| = 1$, then $X = \{s\}$, some s. Since π_2 is a partition, it follows that $s \in Y$, some $Y \in \pi_2$. But then $X = \{s\} \subseteq Y$.

Now consider π_1. Only one of its blocks has more than one element, namely $\{1,2\}$. No block of π_2 or π_4 contains this set, but $\{1,2\} \in \pi_3$, so certainly there exists $Y \in \pi_3$ such that $\{1,2\} \subseteq Y$. Hence $\pi_1 \leq \pi_3$.

Next consider π_2. Only one of its blocks has more than one element, namely $\{5,6\}$. No block of π_1 contains this set, but $\{5,6\} \in \pi_3$ and so $\pi_2 \leq \pi_3$. We also have $\{5,6\} \subseteq \{2,3,5,6\} \in \pi_4$. Hence $\pi_2 \leq \pi_4$.

We now leave it as an exercise to check that $(\mathbf{P}, \leq)$ has the Hasse diagram shown in Fig. 9.2.

9.2.5 Definition

Let $(A, \leq)$ be a poset and let $x, y, z \in A$. z is an *upper bound* for $\{x,y\}$ if $x \leq z$ and $y \leq z$. It is a *least upper bound* (lub) if it is the smallest upper bound of x and y, that is, if z' is also an upper bound of x and y, then $z \leq z'$.

From this, it follows that if z and z' are both lubs of $\{x,y\}$ then $z \leq z'$ and $z' \leq z$ whence, by the asymmetry property, we must have $z = z'$. The lub of $\{x,y\}$ if it exists is thus unique. We write it as $x + y$.

There is a dual notion of *lower bound* and *greatest lower bound* (glb). z is a lower bound for $\{x,y\}$ if $z \leq x$ and $z \leq y$. z is a glb if it is the largest such lower bound, that is if z' is also a lower bound for $\{x,y\}$ then $z' \leq z$.

The same argument shows that the glb of x and y is unique – if it exists. We write $x.y$ to denotes the glb of $\{x,y\}$.

9.2.6 Examples

Returning to our examples of 9.2.1, if X is a set and $A, B \in \underline{P}(X)$, then their lub with respect to $\subseteq$ is $A \cup B$ and their glb is $A \cap B$.

Turning to $(\mathbf{N}^+, \mid)$, the lub of two numbers is their least common multiple and their glb is their highest common factor or highest common

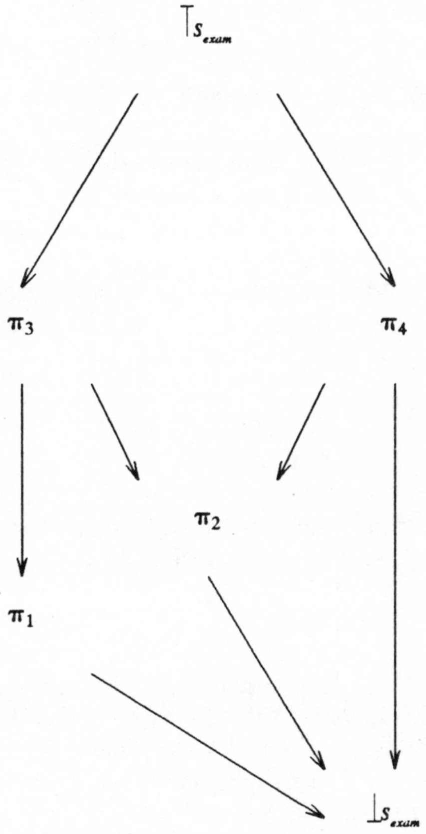

Fig. 9.2

divisor.

For example 9.2.4, we see from Fig. 9.2 that $\{\pi_1,\pi_2\}$ has $\top_{S_{exam}}$ and π_3 as upper bounds. Since $\pi_3 < \top_{S_{exam}}$, it follows that π_3 is the least upper bound and that $\pi_1 + \pi_2 = \pi_3$.

Likewise, π_2 and $\bot_{S_{exam}}$ are lower bounds for $\{\pi_3,\pi_4\}$ and $\bot_{S_{exam}} < \pi_2$. Thus $\pi_3.\pi_4 = \pi_2$.

Not every poset has the property that each pair of elements possess a lub or glb. Posets that have this property have a special name.

9.2.7 Definition

A *lattice* is a poset in which $x + y$ and $x.y$ are defined for every pair of elements x, y.

glb, . and lub, + are not the same as multiplication and addition of numbers, of course, but they do have some of the properties of these operations and we list some of them below. (They are true in any lattice.)

(a) $x + y = y + x$ $x.y = y.x$ (commutativity)

(b) $x + (y + z) = (x + y) + z$ $x.(y.z) = (x.y).z$ (associativity)

(c) $x + x = x$ $x.x = x$ (idempotency)

Since + and . have these properties, we may *unambiguously* define the sum of any finite collection of elements of a lattice.

If $X = \{x_1, ..., x_n\}$, then we define:

$$\Sigma X = x_1 + \cdots + x_n$$

$$\Pi X = x_1 . \cdots . x_n$$

Associativity and commutativity entail that the order in which the x_is are arranged makes no difference to the final answer.

9.2.8 Example

Let us now show that $(\mathbf{P}, \leq)$, of example 9.2.4 is a lattice.

It might at first be thought that we have to check for the existence of $\pi + \pi'$ and $\pi.\pi'$ for every pair $\pi, \pi' \in \mathbf{P}$ (72 tests !). However, we may reduce that number considerably using the following remarks:

(a) If $\pi \leq \pi'$ then $\pi + \pi' = \pi'$ and $\pi.\pi' = \pi$.

(b) If $\pi + \pi'$ exists then so does $\pi' + \pi$ and they are equal. Likewise, if $\pi.\pi'$ exists then so does $\pi'.\pi$ and they are equal.

Thus, we only need to check the pairs π_1, π_2, π_1, π_4 and π_3, π_4. Calculating:

$$\pi_1 + \pi_2 = \pi_3 \quad \pi_1 + \pi_4 = \top_{S_{exam}} \quad \pi_3 + \pi_4 = \top_{S_{exam}}$$

$$\pi_1.\pi_2 = \bot_{S_{exam}} \quad \pi_1.\pi_4 = \bot_{S_{exam}} \quad \pi_3.\pi_4 = \pi_2$$

Thus $(\mathbf{P}, \leq)$ is a lattice.

Now, let us concentrate our attention on SP partitions.

9.2.9 Definition

Let M be a Mealy automaton. By $SP(M)$ we will denote the set of SP partitions of M.

9.2.10 Lemma

Suppose $\pi_1, \pi_2 \in SP(M)$. Define:

$$\pi_o = \{Z \mid Z = X \cap Y,\ X \in \pi_1,\ Y \in \pi_2,\ Z \neq \emptyset\}$$

then $\pi_o \in SP(M)$ and is the glb, $\pi_1.\pi_2$ of π_1 and π_2.

Proof

First, we note that if $s \in S$, then there exist unique $X \in \pi_1$ and $Y \in \pi_2$ such that $s \in X$ and $s \in Y$. Thus, there exists a unique $Z \in \pi_o$, namely $X \cap Y$ such that $s \in Z$. Thus π_o is a partition of S.

Next, we show that it is SP. Let $Z \in \pi_o$ and let $i \in I$. By definition, $Z = X \cap Y$ for $X \in \pi_1$ and $Y \in \pi_2$. Since π_1 and π_2 are SP, there exist $X' \in \pi_1$ and $Y' \in \pi_2$ such that $\delta(X, i) \subseteq X'$ and $\delta(Y, i) \subseteq Y'$. Thus $\delta(Z, i) = \delta(X \cap Y, i) \subseteq X' \cap Y'$. But $X' \cap Y' \in \pi_o$.

It is clear that π_o is a lower bound for π_1 and π_2 since if $Z \in \pi_o$, then $Z = X \cap Y$ with $X \in \pi_1$ and $Y \in \pi_2$. Thus $Z \subseteq X \in \pi_1$ and $Z \subseteq Y \in \pi_2$.

Finally, we show that π_o is the glb for π_1 and π_2. Suppose $\pi \in SP(M)$ and suppose that $\pi \le \pi_1$ and $\pi \le \pi_2$. Let $U \in \pi$. Then there exist $X \in \pi_1$ and $Y \in \pi_2$ such that $U \subseteq X$ and $U \subseteq Y$. Thus $U \subseteq X \cap Y \in \pi_o$. Thus $\pi \le \pi_o$ as required.

Lemma 9.2.10 allows us to conclude that every pair of SP partitions has a glb. Because of certain properties of $SP(M)$, this lemma actually allows us to conclude that every pair of partitions has a lub as well.

9.2.11 Lemma

Suppose that $(L, \le)$ is a poset such that:

(a) L is finite with a $\top$ element – that is, L has an element $\top$ satisfying $x \le \top$ for all $x \in L$,

(b) $x.y$ exists for all $x, y \in L$,

then $(L, \le)$ is a lattice.

Proof

Let $x, y \in L$ and define $X = \{z \in L \mid x \leq z \text{ and } y \leq z\}$. X is non-empty since, for example, $\top \in X$. Since L is finite, X is aiso finite and so we may form $u = \Pi X$. We show $u = x + y$.

Since $x \leq z$ each $z \in X$ and u is the glb of all such z, we must have $x \leq u$. Similarly, $y \leq u$. Thus u is an upper bound for x and y. If $v \in L$ were also an upper bound for x and y, then we would have $x \leq v$ and $y \leq v$. But then $v \in X$ and so $u \leq v$. Thus $u = x + y$.

9.2.12 Proposition

$(SP(M), \leq)$ is a lattice.

Proof

From 9.2.10 and 9.2.11.

This may be nice to know, but does not help us much if we want to compute lubs directly.

Let us look at this carefully. $\pi_1 + \pi_2$ is the smallest SP partition bigger than both π_1 and π_2. It is therefore the smallest SP partition bigger than $\pi_1 \cup \pi_2$. Now $\pi_1 \cup \pi_2$ is not a partition. In fact it is only a partition if $\pi_1 = \pi_2$. But we may construct from it a unique smallest partition greater than it.

9.2.13 Definition

Let $\sigma \subseteq \underline{P}(S)$. We define a set $parti(\sigma) \subseteq \underline{P}(S)$ by the following non-deterministic algorithm.

(a) If every pair of distinct elements of σ are disjoint then set $parti(\sigma)$ equal to σ and stop.

(b) Select $X, Y \in \sigma$ such that $X \cap Y \neq \varnothing$ and set $\sigma = (\sigma - \{X, Y\}) \cup \{X \cup Y\}$. Loop back to (a).

This algorithm terminates, since at each step the cardinality of the set σ is reduced by one. In the cases in which we are interested, it also gives a unique result, as the next lemma shows.

9.2.14 Lemma

Suppose $\sigma \subseteq \underline{P}(S)$ is a *cover*, that is:

$$\bigcup_{X \in \sigma} X = S$$

then $parti(\sigma) \in \Pi(S)$ and is the smallest partition bigger than σ, that is:
(a) $\sigma \leq parti(\sigma)$.
(b) $\pi \in \Pi(S)$ and $\sigma \leq \pi \Rightarrow parti(\sigma) \leq \pi$.
In particular, $parti(\sigma)$ is well-defined.

Proof

$parti(\sigma) \in \Pi(S)$ because:

1 The algorithm terminates only if the elements of σ are pairwise disjoint.

2 If σ is a cover, then obviously for *any* $X, Y \in \sigma$, $\sigma = (\sigma - \{X, Y\}) \cup \{X \cup Y\}$ is also a cover. That σ is a cover is thus a *loop invariant** and since initially, σ was a cover, on termination σ will be a cover.

Thus on termination, σ is a cover whose elements are pairwise disjoint, that is, a partition.

We leave the proof that $\sigma \leq parti(\sigma)$ as an exercise.

For (b), suppose $\sigma \leq \pi$, where π is a partition. We shall show that this property is also a loop invariant, that is:

3 Suppose $\sigma \leq \pi$ and suppose $X, Y \in \sigma$ such that $X \cap Y \neq \emptyset$ If $\sigma' = (\sigma - \{X, Y\}) \cup \{X \cup Y\}$ then $\sigma' \leq \pi$.
Suppose $Z \in \sigma'$.
If $Z \neq X \cup Y$ then $Z \in \sigma$ and since $\sigma \leq \pi$, $Z \subseteq Z'$ some $Z' \in \pi$.
Otherwise $Z = X \cup Y$. Since $\sigma \leq \pi$, $X \subseteq X'$ and $Y \subseteq Y'$, for $X', Y' \in \pi$. But this means that $X \cap Y \subseteq X' \cap Y'$ and by hypothesis $X \cap Y \neq \emptyset$, which means that $X' \cap Y' \neq \emptyset$. Since π is a partition, it follows that $X' = Y'$. Thus, $X \cup Y \subseteq X' \cup Y' = X'$ and $Z \subseteq X'$ for $X' \in \pi$.

Thus for every $Z \in \sigma'$, $Z \subseteq Z'$ some $Z' \in \pi$, that is $\sigma' \leq \pi$ as required.

Finally, we show that $parti(\sigma)$ does not depend on the choices of X and Y in algorithm 9.2.13.

We argue by contradiction. Suppose, that $parti(\sigma)$ is not well defined. Then one sequence of choices of X, Y in 9.2.13 gives a partition π_1 and another sequence gives π_2 where $\pi_1 \neq \pi_2$.

By (a) $\sigma \leq \pi_1$ and by (b), since $\sigma \leq \pi_1$, then $\pi_1 \leq \pi_2$. The same argument, exchanging the roles of π_1 and π_2 gives $\pi_2 \leq \pi_1$. Thus, $\pi_1 = \pi_2$ by asymmetry, and we have the required contradiction.

---

* That is, it is true initially, and its truth is preserved by each execution of the loop, and hence is true upon termination.

9.2.15 Example

Let us compute $parti(\pi_1 \cup \pi_2)$ of example 9.2.4 using the methods of 9.2.13. For simplicity, we shall use the notation of Fig. 9.3 to denote that $\sigma' = (\sigma - \{X, Y\}) \cup \{X \cup Y\}$. The derivation is given in Fig. 9.4.

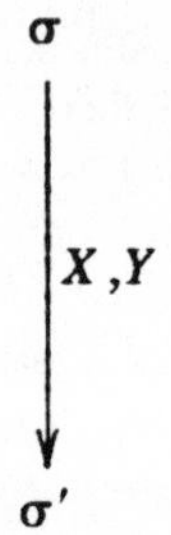

Fig. 9.3

Calculations show that $parti(\pi_1 \cup \pi_2) = \pi_3$ (which we already know to be $\pi_1 + \pi_2$ in $(\mathbf{P}, \leq)$).

Lemma 9.2.14 shows that $parti(\pi_1 \cup \pi_2)$ is a partition (since $\pi_1 \cup \pi_2$ is surely a cover). We shall show that it is SP. First, however, we shall find out more about the structure of the sets in $parti(\sigma)$ for any given σ.

Figure 9.5, may help. Here, the nodes $U_1, .., U_6$ are subsets of some set, and a line connects two nodes if and only if the corresponding sets are not disjoint. It is easy to see that the algorithm of 9.2.13 shrinks each connected piece down to a single node. All the lines will shrink too, so the resulting three sets will be disjoint.

Each of the three pieces satisfies property (b) in the following lemma.

9.2.16 Lemma

Let $\sigma \subseteq \underline{P}(S)$, and let $X \in parti(\sigma)$, then there exists $\mathbf{X} = \{X_1, ..., X_k\} \subseteq \sigma$ satisfying:

(a) $X = X_1 \cup \cdots \cup X_k$

(b) If $\mathbf{X}_1, \mathbf{X}_2 \subseteq \mathbf{X}$ are non-empty sets such that $\mathbf{X}_1 \cup \mathbf{X}_2 = \mathbf{X}$ then:

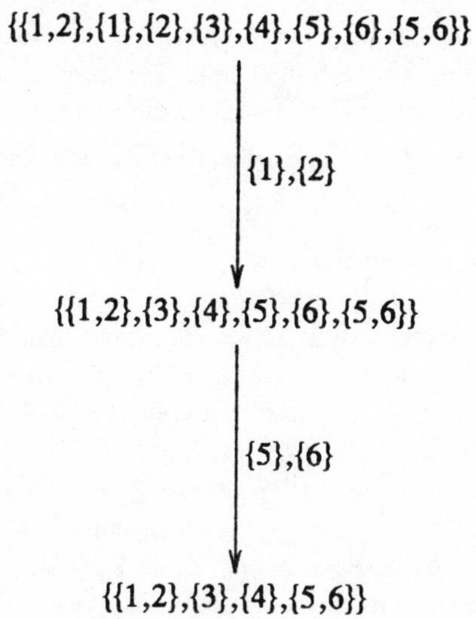

Fig. 9.4

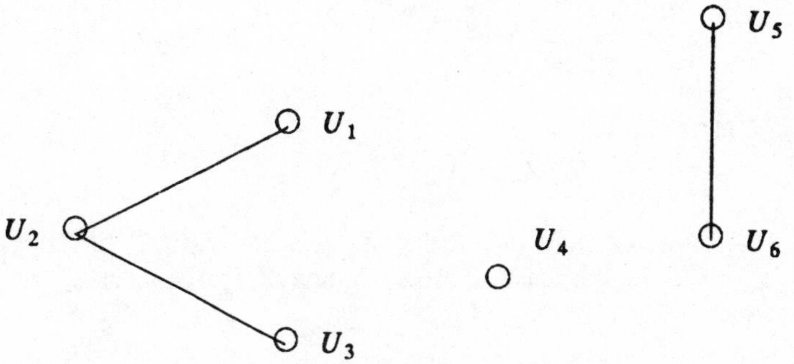

Fig. 9.5

$$(\bigcup \mathbf{X}_1) \cap (\bigcup \mathbf{X}_2) \neq \varnothing$$

We shall say that a set **X** with this property is *connected*. (Thus, in Fig. 9.5, the sets $\{U_1, U_2, U_3\}$ and $\{U_5, U_6\}$ are connected. Each is a connected component of the graph.)

Proof

This is certainly true initially since each $X \in \sigma$ satisfies $X = \bigcup\{X\}$ and it is trivial that each $\{X\}$ is connected. We may prove that the lemma's claim is a loop invariant of the algorithm of 9.2.13.

Indeed, suppose that σ has the property and suppose $X, Y \in \sigma$ such that $X \cap Y \neq \varnothing$. If $\sigma' = (\sigma - \{X, Y\}) \cup \{X \cup Y\}$, we must show that σ' also satisfies the lemma.

By hypothesis, we have $X_1, ..., X_k, Y_1, ..., Y_l \in \sigma$ such that $X = X_1 \cup \cdots \cup X_k$ and $Y = Y_1 \cup \cdots \cup Y_l$, with $\mathbf{X} = \{X_1, ..., X_k\}$ and $\mathbf{Y} = \{Y_1, ..., Y_l\}$ connected. If we can show that $\mathbf{X} \cup \mathbf{Y}$ is connected, then we may conclude that σ' does indeed satisfy the lemma.

Suppose $\mathbf{Z}_1, \mathbf{Z}_2 \subseteq \mathbf{X} \cup \mathbf{Y}$ are non empty with $\mathbf{Z}_1 \cup \mathbf{Z}_2 = \mathbf{X} \cup \mathbf{Y}$. We shall show that $(\bigcup \mathbf{Z}_1) \cap (\bigcup \mathbf{Z}_2) \neq \varnothing$.

We have that $\mathbf{Z}_1 = \mathbf{X}_1 \cup \mathbf{Y}_1$, where $\mathbf{X}_1 = \mathbf{X} \cap \mathbf{Z}_1$ and $\mathbf{Y}_1 = \mathbf{Y} \cap \mathbf{Z}_1$ and that $\mathbf{Z}_2 = \mathbf{X}_2 \cup \mathbf{Y}_2$, where $\mathbf{X}_2 = \mathbf{X} \cap \mathbf{Z}_2$ and $\mathbf{Y}_2 = \mathbf{Y} \cap \mathbf{Z}_2$.

We also haye $\mathbf{X}_1 \cup \mathbf{X}_2 = \mathbf{X}$ and $\mathbf{Y}_1 \cup \mathbf{Y}_2 = \mathbf{Y}$.

We consider two cases.

1 $\mathbf{X}_1 = \varnothing$ or $\mathbf{X}_2 = \varnothing$ and $\mathbf{Y}_1 = \varnothing$ or $\mathbf{Y}_2 = \varnothing$.

In this case, either one of $\mathbf{Z}_1$, $\mathbf{Z}_2$ is empty – contrary to hypothesis – or one of the following holds:

$$\bigcup \mathbf{Z}_1 = X \quad \bigcup \mathbf{Z}_2 = Y$$

$$\bigcup \mathbf{Z}_1 = Y \quad \bigcup \mathbf{Z}_2 = X$$

In either case:

$$(\bigcup \mathbf{Z}_1) \cap (\bigcup \mathbf{Z}_2) = X \cap Y \neq \varnothing$$

2 If 1 does not hold then either $\mathbf{X}_1 \neq \varnothing$ and $\mathbf{X}_2 \neq \varnothing$ or $\mathbf{Y}_1 \neq \varnothing$ and $\mathbf{Y}_2 \neq \varnothing$. In this case, because $\mathbf{X}$ and $\mathbf{Y}$ are connected, we would have:

$$((\bigcup \mathbf{X}_1) \cap (\bigcup \mathbf{X}_2)) \cup ((\bigcup \mathbf{Y}_1) \cap (\bigcup \mathbf{Y}_2)) \neq \varnothing \qquad [9.1]$$

Therefore:

$$\begin{aligned}
&(\bigcup \mathbf{Z}_1) \cap (\bigcup \mathbf{Z}_2) \\
&\quad = ((\bigcup \mathbf{X}_1) \cup (\bigcup \mathbf{Y}_1)) \cap ((\bigcup \mathbf{X}_2) \cup (\bigcup \mathbf{Y}_2)) \\
&\quad \supseteq ((\bigcup \mathbf{X}_1) \cap (\bigcup \mathbf{X}_2)) \cup ((\bigcup \mathbf{Y}_1) \cap (\bigcup \mathbf{Y}_2)) \neq \varnothing
\end{aligned}$$

In both cases:

$$(\bigcup \mathbf{Z}_1) \cap (\bigcup \mathbf{Z}_2) \neq \varnothing$$

so $\mathbf{X} \cup \mathbf{Y}$ is connected and we are done.

Now that we have established a connection between the elements of a cover σ and the partition *parti* (σ), we may show the following.

9.2.17 Lemma

Suppose M is a Mealy machine and σ is a cover of S having the SP property, then *parti* $(\sigma) \in SP(M)$.

Proof

Let $\mathbf{Y} = \{Y_1, ..., Y_k\} \subseteq \sigma$ be a connected set. We show that:

(a) If $i \in I$ and for $j = 1, ..., k$, $\delta(Y_j, i) \subseteq Y'_j$, then $\mathbf{Y}' = \{Y'_1, ..., Y'_k\}$ is also a connected set.

(b) If $\sigma \leq \pi$ for any partition π of S, then there exists $X \in \pi$ such that $Y_1 \cup \cdots \cup Y_k \subseteq X$.

From lemma 9.2.16, it follows that if $X \in$ *parti* (σ), then $X = Y_1 \cup \cdots \cup Y_k$, where $\mathbf{Y} = \{Y_1, ..., Y_k\}$ is a connected set. If $\delta(Y_j, i) \subseteq Y'_j$ for each j, then by (a) $\delta(X, i) \subseteq Y'_1 \cup \cdots \cup Y'_k$ where $\mathbf{Y}' = \{Y'_1, ..., Y'_k\}$ is a connected set. By (b), there exists $Y \in$ *parti* (σ) such that $Y'_1 \cup \cdots \cup Y'_k \subseteq Y$.

Thus $\delta(X, i) \subseteq Y$ and *parti* (σ) is indeed SP.

We prove (a).

Suppose $\mathbf{Y}'_1$ and $\mathbf{Y}'_2$ are non-empty and such that $\mathbf{Y}'_1 \cup \mathbf{Y}'_2 = \mathbf{Y}'$. Rearranging the Y_j, we may suppose that $\mathbf{Y}'_1 = \{Y'_1, ..., Y'_l\}$ and $\mathbf{Y}'_2 = \{Y'_{l+1}, ..., Y'_k\}$ with $1 \leq l < k$.

Let $\mathbf{Y}_1 = \{Y_1, ..., Y_l\}$ and $\mathbf{Y}_2 = \{Y_{l+1}, ..., Y_k\}$.

Since $\mathbf{Y}$ is connected, we may find $s \in S$ such that:

$$s \in (\bigcup \mathbf{Y}_1) \cap \bigcup \mathbf{Y}_2)$$

Thus $s \in Y_{j1} \cap Y_{j2}$, where $Y_{j1} \in \mathbf{Y}_1$ and $Y_{j2} \in \mathbf{Y}_2$.

But this means that $\delta(s, i) \in Y'_{j1} \cap Y'_{j2}$, where $Y'_{j1} \in \mathbf{Y}'_1$ and $Y'_{j2} \in \mathbf{Y}'_2$.

From this, it follows that:

$$(\bigcup \mathbf{Y}'_1) \cap (\bigcup \mathbf{Y}'_2) \neq \varnothing$$

and $\mathbf{Y}'$ is connected, as promised.

Now we show (b).

We argue by contradiction. Suppose (b) is false, then we may find $Y_{j1}, Y_{j2} \in \mathbf{Y}$ and $X \in \pi$ such that $Y_{j1} \subseteq X$ and $Y_{j2} \nsubseteq X$.

Let $\mathbf{Y}_1 = \{Y \in \mathbf{Y} \mid Y \subseteq X\}$ and let $\mathbf{Y}_2 = \{Y \in \mathbf{Y} \mid Y \nsubseteq X\}$. By assumption, both these sets are non-empty.

Now clearly, $(\bigcup \mathbf{Y}_1) \subseteq X$. On the other hand, if $s \in (\bigcup \mathbf{Y}_2)$, then if $Y \in \mathbf{Y}$ with $s \in Y$, then $Y \nsubseteq X$ and $Y \subseteq X'$ some other $X' \in \pi$. Since π is a partition, $X \cap X' = \emptyset$ and so $s \notin X$.

But this means that if $s \in (\bigcup \mathbf{Y}_2)$, then $s \notin X$ and hence $s \notin (\bigcup \mathbf{Y}_1)$ and this implies that:

$$(\bigcup \mathbf{Y}_1) \cap (\bigcup \mathbf{Y}_2) = \emptyset$$

which contradicts $\mathbf{Y}$ connected.

This brings us to the following proposition.

9.2.18 Proposition

Let $\pi_1, \pi_2 \in SP(M)$ and let $\pi_o = parti(\pi_1 \cup \pi_2)$, then π_o is the lub of π_1 and π_2, $\pi_1 + \pi_2$.

Proof

First of all, $\pi_1 \cup \pi_2$ is a cover with the SP property. It is a cover because:

$$\bigcup_{X \in \pi_1 \cup \pi_2} X = \bigcup_{X \in \pi_1} X \cup \bigcup_{X \in \pi_2} X = S.$$

Next, suppose $X \in \pi_1 \cup \pi_2$ and $i \in I$. Either $X \in \pi_1$ or $X \in \pi_2$. Suppose $X \in \pi_1$, then since π_1 is SP, $\delta(X, i) \subseteq Y$ some $Y \in \pi_1 \subseteq \pi_1 \cup \pi_2$. If $X \in \pi_2$, then by the same reasoning, $\delta(X, i) \subseteq Y$ some $Y \in \pi_2 \subseteq \pi_1 \cup \pi_2$. In either case, $\delta(X, i) \subseteq Y \in \pi_1 \cup \pi_2$ and $\pi_1 \cup \pi_2$ is SP.

Thus, by 9.2.17, $\pi_o \in SP(M)$. Furthermore, it is clear that π_o is an upper bound for π_1 and π_2 since any element U of either of these two sets belongs to a connected set in $\pi_1 \cup \pi_2$ whose union, an element of π_o, therefore contains U.

Finally, suppose $\pi \in SP(M)$ with $\pi_1 \leq \pi$ and $\pi_2 \leq \pi$. It easily follows that $\pi_1 \cup \pi_2 \leq \pi$. By 9.2.14, $\pi_o = parti(\pi_1 \cup \pi_2) \leq \pi$. Thus, π_o is the lub of π_1 and π_2.

9.3 PRIME PARTITIONS

Section 9.2 dealt with a kind of arithmetic that one may perform on SP partitions, allowing us to take two partitions and, from them, construct a third. So far, however, the only SP partitions we know how to construct are the trivial partitions $\perp_S$ and $\top_S$, and there's nothing much one can do with them. Indeed, since:

$$\perp_S + \top_S = \top_S \text{ and } \perp_S . \top_S = \perp_S$$

we cannot get any new partitions from them.

So, how do we derive $SP(M)$? We *could* try to generate all possible partitions and test each one. This would be ludicrously expensive for even small values of $|S|$, however. Instead we show how to generate a set of SP partitions with the property that every SP partition is the sum of elements of this set.

For this section, we shall find it convenient to make the following definition.

9.3.1 Definition

Let M be a Mealy machine and suppose $s, s' \in S$ and $\pi \in SP(M)$. We define $s \equiv s'$ (π) if and only if there exists $X \in \pi$ such that $s, s \in X$.

Note that $\equiv (\pi)$ is simply the equivalence relation induced by the partition π.

We also note the following.

9.3.2 Lemma

Let π_1, π_2 be partitions of a set S, then the following two statements are equivalent.

(a) $\pi_1 \leq \pi_2$.

(b) $s \equiv s'$ $(\pi_1) \Rightarrow s \equiv s'$ (π_2).

Proof

Suppose (b) and suppose $X \in \pi_1$ and let $s \in X$. Define $Y = \{s' \mid s \equiv s' \ (\pi_2)\}$. We prove $X \subseteq Y$. Indeed, if $s' \in X$, then $s' \equiv s$ (π_1) and hence $s' \in Y$.

Now suppose (a) and let $s, s' \in S$ with $s \equiv s'$ (π_1), then there exists $X \in \pi_1$ such that $s, s' \in X$. Since $\pi_1 \leq \pi_2$, there exists $Y \in \pi_2$ such that $X \subseteq Y$. Thus $s, s' \in Y \in \pi_2$ and so $s \equiv s'$ (π_2).

Given any pair $s, s' \in S$, there is at least one SP partition, π, such that $s = s'$ (π), namely the partition $\top_S$.

The fact that $SP(M)$ is a lattice means that there must be a unique minimal partition with this property.

To see this, suppose that $\pi_1, \pi_2 \in SP(M)$ and $s \equiv s$ (π_1) and $s \equiv s$ (π_2) then there exist $X_1 \in \pi_1$, $X_2 \in \pi_2$ such that $s, s' \in X_1$ and $s, s' \in X_2$. Thus $s, s' \in X_1 \cap X_2$. But $X_1 \cap X_2 \in \pi_1.\pi_2$. Thus:

$$s \equiv s \ (\pi_1) \ \& \ s \equiv s \ (\pi_2) \Rightarrow s \equiv s \ (\pi_1.\pi_2) \qquad [9.2]$$

Thus, if we let $X_{s,s} = \{\pi \in SP(M) \mid s \equiv s' \ (\pi)\}$, then first of all $X_{s,s'}$ is not empty, since $\top \in X_{s,s'}$. Thus $\Pi X_{s,s'}$ exists. Secondly, by [9.2] and induction, $\Pi X_{s,s'} \in X_{s,s'}$.

$\Pi X_{s,s'}$ is the smallest SP partition of M such that s and s' are in the same block.

9.3.3 Definition

Define $\pi_{s,s'} = \Pi X_{s,s'}$ and let $Prime(M) = \{\pi_{s,s'} \mid s, s' \in S\}$. We call the elements of $Prime(M)$, the *prime* partitions of M.

If $\pi \in SP(M)$ then let $Prime(\pi) = \{\pi_o \in Prime(M) \mid \pi_o \leq \pi\}$.

Prime partitions are important for two reasons. Firstly, they may be computed. Secondly, every SP partition is a sum of prime partitions. Thus *all* of $SP(M)$ may be computed. We deal with the first point first.

Take a Mealy machine M and consider $s_1, s_2 \in S$. We shall assume that $s_1 \neq s_2$ (see exercise **6**).

It is easy to see what is the smallest (not necessarily SP) partition of S in which s_1 and s_2 are in the same block. We shall call it σ_{s_1,s_2}.

$$\sigma_{s_1,s_2} = \{\{s\} \mid s \notin \{s_1, s_2\}\} \cup \{\{s_1, s_2\}\}$$

For example, if $S = \{w, x, y, z\}$, then $\sigma_{x,z} = \{\{w\}, \{y\}, \{x, z\}\}$.

We note that:

$$s_1 \equiv s_2 \ (\pi) \Leftrightarrow \sigma_{s_1,s_2} \leq \pi \qquad [9.3]$$

Now σ_{s_1,s_2} could quite well *be* an SP partition, in which case we obviously have $\sigma_{s_1,s_2} = \pi_{s_1,s_2}$.

The extent to which it fails to be SP may be seen in the set $\sigma_{s_1,s_2} \cup \Delta(\sigma_{s_1,s_2})$ where for any $\sigma \in \Pi(S)$, we define:

$$\Delta(\sigma) = \{\delta(X, i) \mid X \in \sigma \text{ and } i \in I\}$$

If σ is SP, then every set in $\Delta(\sigma)$ will be contained in some set of σ, that is $\sigma \cup \Delta(\sigma) \leq \sigma$.

9.3.4 Lemma

Suppose $\sigma \in \Pi(S)$, then:

$$\sigma \in SP(M) \Leftrightarrow parti(\sigma \cup \Delta(\sigma)) = \sigma.$$

Proof

It is clear that $\sigma \leq \sigma \cup \Delta(\sigma)$ and $\sigma \cup \Delta(\sigma) \leq parti(\sigma \cup \Delta(\sigma))$ by 9.2.14(a). Thus $\sigma \leq parti(\sigma \cup \Delta(\sigma))$. It therefore suffices to show that $\sigma \in SP(M) \Leftrightarrow parti(\sigma \cup \Delta(\sigma)) \leq \sigma$.

First, suppose σ is SP, then $\sigma \cup \Delta(\sigma) \leq \sigma$. By 9.2.14 (b), $parti(\sigma \cup \Delta(\sigma)) \leq \sigma$.

Now suppose $parti(\sigma \cup \Delta(\sigma)) \leq \sigma$ and let $X \in \sigma$ and $i \in I$. Since σ is a partition, there exists $Y \in \sigma$ such that $\delta(X, i) \cap Y \neq \varnothing$. We shall show that $\delta(X, i) \subseteq Y$ and that accordingly σ is SP.

Since $\delta(X, i) \cap Y \neq \varnothing$, there exists a connected set $\mathbf{X}$ such that $\delta(X, i), Y \in \mathbf{X}$ and $\bigcup(\mathbf{X}) = Z \in parti(\sigma \cup \Delta(\sigma))$. Thus $\delta(X, i), Y \subseteq Z$. We need only show that $Y = Z$ to complete the proof.

Since $parti(\sigma \cup \Delta(\sigma)) \leq \sigma$, there exists $Y' \in \sigma$ such that $Z \subseteq Y'$. But $Y \subseteq Z$ and so $Y \subseteq Y'$. But $Y, Y' \in \sigma$ and so $Y = Y'$. Thus, $Y \subseteq Z \subseteq Y' = Y$ and hence $Y = Z$. This completes the proof.

We observed in the proof of 9.3.4 that we always have $\sigma \leq parti(\sigma \cup \Delta(\sigma))$ Thus, if σ is not SP, then $\sigma < parti(\sigma \cup \Delta(\sigma))$. Let us simplify the notation by defining for $\sigma \in \Pi(S)$:

$$form(\sigma) = parti(\sigma \cup \Delta(\sigma)).$$

We may apply lemma 9.2.14 to this construction and obtain the following.

9.3.5 Lemma

(a) $form(\sigma)$ is a partition.

(b) For all $\pi \in \Pi(S)$, $\sigma \leq \pi \Rightarrow form(\sigma) \leq \pi$.

(c) $s_1 \equiv s_2\ (\sigma) \Rightarrow s_1 \equiv s_2\ (form(\sigma))$.

Proof

(a) and (b) follow directly from 9.2.14, given the obvious fact that $\sigma \cup \Delta(\sigma)$ is a cover.

(c) follows from the fact that by [9.3]:

$$\begin{aligned} s_1 \equiv s_2\ (\sigma) &\Rightarrow \sigma_{s_1,s_2} \le \sigma \\ &\Rightarrow \sigma_{s_1,s_2} \le form(\sigma)\ \text{(by (b))} \\ &\Rightarrow s_1 \equiv s_2\ (form(\sigma)) \end{aligned}$$

Now this is rather a useful result. Suppose we start with σ_{s_1,s_2} and repeatedly apply $form$ to it. We get a sequence of partitions:

$$\sigma_{s_1,s_2} < form(\sigma_{s_1,s_2}) < form(form(\sigma_{s_1,s_2})) < \cdots \qquad [9.4]$$

For simplicity, let us define, for a partition π, $form^0(\pi) = \pi$ and $form^{n+1}(\pi) = form(form^n(p))$. The sequence [9.4] then becomes:

$$form^0(\sigma_{s_1,s_2}) < form^1(\sigma_{s_1,s_2}) < \cdots < form^k(\sigma_{s_1,s_2}) < \cdots \qquad [9.5]$$

Now this sequence cannot go on for ever because $\Pi(S)$ is finite. So, for some n, we must have:

$$form^n(\sigma_{s_1,s_2}) = form^{n+1}(\sigma_{s_1,s_2}) \qquad [9.6]$$

But, by lemma 9.3.4, $form^n(\rho_{s_1,s_2})$ must be an SP partition.

Furthermore, a repeated application of lemma 9.3.5 (b) shows that since $\rho_{s_1,s_2} \le \pi_{s_1,s_2}$ we must have:

$$form^n(\sigma_{s_1,s_2}) \le \pi_{s_1,s_2}. \qquad [9.7]$$

Not only that, but a repeated application of 9.3.5 (c) gives that since $s_1 \equiv s_2\ (\sigma_{s_1,s_2})$ then $s_1 \equiv s_2\ (form^n(\sigma_{s_1,s_2}))$.

Thus $form^n(\sigma_{s_1,s_2}) \in X_{s_1,s_2}$

But if $form^n(\sigma_{s_1,s_2}) \in X_{s_1,s_2}$ then we must have $\Pi X_{s_1,s_2} \le form^n(\sigma_{s_1,s_2})$ and by definition $\Pi X_{s_1,s_2} = \pi_{s_1,s_2}$. Thus:

$$\pi_{s_1,s_2} \le form^n(\sigma_{s_1,s_2}). \qquad [9.8]$$

From [9.7] and [9.8], we get, finally:

$$form^n(\sigma_{s_1,s_2}) = \pi_{s_1,s_2}. \qquad [9.9]$$

We may summarize the foregoing in the following.

9.3.6 Proposition

Suppose M is a Mealy machine and $s, s' \in S$, then the following algorithm correctly calculates $\pi_{s,s'}$.

$\tau := \sigma_{s,s'}$;

REPEAT

$\tau := form(\tau)$

UNTIL $\tau = form(\tau)$;

$\pi_{s,s'} := \tau$.

We have seen how to compute basic partitions. Now let us get on to the property that we mentioned earlier, that every SP partition is a sum of basic ones. This is shown by the next result. Recall from definition 9.3.3 that $Prime(\pi) = \{\pi_o \in Prime(M) \mid \pi_o \leq \pi\}$ for $\pi \in SP(M)$.

9.3.7 Proposition

Let M be a machine and suppose $\pi \in SP(M)$, then:

$$\pi = \Sigma\, Prime(\pi).$$

Proof

Let $\pi' = \Sigma\, Prime(\pi)$. Since for each $\pi_{s,s'} \in Prime(\pi)$ we have $\pi_{s,s'} \leq \pi$ by definition, it follows that their lub must be less than π. Thus $\pi' = \Sigma\, Prime(\pi) \leq \pi$.

On the other hand, if $s = s'$ (π), then $s = s'$ (π'), since $\pi_{s,s'} \leq \pi'$. Thus $\pi \leq \pi'$.

We thus have $\pi' \leq \pi$ and $\pi \leq \pi'$ from which $\pi = \pi'$ follows by asymmetry.

This proposition guarantees that if we take all possible 'sums' of the $\pi_{s,s'}$ then we obtain all SP partitions of M. Note that we may not need to compute *all* possible sums. For example, if we know that $\pi_{s,s'} = \mathsf{T}_S$, then any sum involving $\pi_{s,s'}$ will also add up to T_S.

9.4 REDUCED MACHINES REVISITED

Recall from Chapter 5 that for any machine M, there exists an event consistent SP partition ρ_M such that M/ρ_M is the smallest machine (in terms of $|S|$) such that $M \equiv M/\rho_M$. Now that we know more about SP partitions, we may re-examine the problem of computing ρ_M.

9.4.1 Lemma

Let $\pi_1, \pi_2 \in SP(M)$, then if $\pi_1 \leq \pi_2$, then if π_2 is output consistent, then so is π_1.

Proof

Let $X \in \pi_1$ and $i \in I$. Since $\pi_1 \leq \pi_2$, there exists $Y \in \pi_2$ such that $X \subseteq Y$. Since π_2 is output consistent, there exists $o \in O$ such that $\beta(Y, i) = \{o\}$. Thus, $\beta(X, i) \subseteq \beta(Y, i) = \{o\}$, whence $\beta(X, i) \subseteq \{o\}$, and since $\beta(X, i) \neq \varnothing$, it follows that $\beta(X, i) = \{o\}$.

9.4.2 Lemma

Let $\pi_1, \pi_2 \in SP(M)$, then if π_1 and π_2 are output consistent, then so is $\pi_1 . \pi_2$.

Proof

From 9.4.1, since $\pi_1 . \pi_2 \leq \pi_2$.

9.4.3 Lemma

Let $\pi_1, \pi_2 \in SP(M)$, then if π_1 and π_2 are output consistent, then so is $\pi_1 + \pi_2$.

Proof

Let $i \in I$ and $X \in \pi_1 + \pi_2$. By 9.2.16, we know that there exists a connected set $\mathbf{X} \subseteq \pi_1 \cup \pi_2$ such that $X = (\bigcup \mathbf{X})$.

Select $U \in \mathbf{X}$. Since U must belong to either π_1 or π_2 and since both are output consistent, there must exist $o \in O$ such that

$\beta(U, i) = \{o\}$.

Let $\mathbf{X}_1 = \{U' \in \mathbf{X} \mid \beta(U', i) = \{o\}\}$ and let $\mathbf{X}_2 = \mathbf{X} - \mathbf{X}_1$. Clearly, $\mathbf{X} = \mathbf{X}_1 \cup \mathbf{X}_2$. Also note that $U \in \mathbf{X}_1$.

Let $s \in (\bigcup \mathbf{X}_1) \cap (\bigcup \mathbf{X}_2)$, then there must exist $U_1 \in \mathbf{X}_1$ and $U_2 \in \mathbf{X}_2$ such that $s \in U_1 \cap U_2$.

But since $U_1 \in \mathbf{X}_1$, then $\beta(s, i) \in \beta(U_1, i) = \{o\}$. Thus $\beta(s, i) = o$. But $U_2 \notin \mathbf{X}_1$, and so $\beta(s, i) \in \beta(U_2, i) \neq \{o\}$, whence $\beta(s, i) \neq o$. This contradiction shows that no such s may exist and so $(\bigcup \mathbf{X}_1) \cap (\bigcup \mathbf{X}_2) = \emptyset$.

But $\mathbf{X}$ is connected, and so either $\mathbf{X}_1 = \emptyset$ or $\mathbf{X}_2 = \emptyset$. We cannot have the first, for $U \in \mathbf{X}_1$

Thus $\mathbf{X}_2 = \emptyset$ and so $\mathbf{X} = \mathbf{X}_1$. It follows that $\beta(U', i) = \{o\}$ for every $U' \in \mathbf{X}$, and so $\beta(X, i) = \{o\}$.

Repeated application of 9.4.3 gives the following.

9.4.4 Corollary

Let $OR(M)$ denote the set of output consistent SP partitions of M. If $\pi_M = \Sigma\, OR(M)$, then $\pi_M \in OR(M)$.

π_M is the creature we are after.

9.4.5 Proposition

$\pi_M = \rho_M$.

Proof

Since ρ_M is output consistent, it must belong to $OR(M)$ and hence $\rho_M \leq \Sigma\, OR(M) = \pi_m$.

To prove the converse, note that if $s \equiv s'$ (π_M) then for all x, $\beta^*(s, x) = \beta^*(s', x)$, since π_M is output consistent. But this implies $s \equiv s'$ by 5.3.4 and so $s \equiv s'$ (ρ_M).

Thus $s \equiv s'$ (π_M) implies $s \equiv s'$ (ρ_m) and hence $\pi_M \leq \rho_M$.

9.4.6 Example

Returning to example 9.2.4, we see that π_1, π_2 and π_3 are output consistent and that $\pi_1 + \pi_2 + \pi_3 = \pi_3$. Thus $\rho_{M_{exam}} = \pi_3$.

EXERCISES

1 Consider the set B_3 of all Boolean functions of three variables. Define $f \leq g$ if whenever $f(x,y,z)$ evaluates to TRUE then so does $g(x,y,z)$. Show that $(B_3,\leq)$ is a lattice.

2 If $S \subseteq \underline{P}(\underline{P}(X))$, is $(S,\leq)$ a poset ? What properties would S need to possess in order that $(S,\leq)$ be a poset ?

3 Show that if $\pi_1,\pi_2 \in \Pi(X)$ and $\pi_1 \subseteq \pi_2$, then $\pi_1 = \pi_2$.

4 Give an example of a poset which is not a lattice (there is one with two elements).

5 A poset $(X,\leq)$ is called a *total order* if for every pair of elements $x,y \in X$ either $x \leq y$ or $y \leq x$. Show that every finite total order is a lattice.

6 Suppose $s = s'$. Describe $\pi_{s,s'}$.

7 Prove [9.3].

8 Prove that if $\pi_{1,2} = \top$ and $\delta(\{3,4\},i) = \{1,2\}$, then $\pi_{3,4} = \top$.

9 Let $\pi_{1,2,3}$ denote the smallest SP partition in which 1,2 and 3 are in the same block. Prove $\pi_{1,2} + \pi_{1,3} = \pi_{1,2,3}$.

The next few exercises explain our use of the word *Prime* to describe the elements $\pi_{s,s'}$.

10 Let $(L,\leq)$ be a poset. An element x of L is said to be *prime* if and only if for every non empty $X \subseteq L$, if ΣX exists and $x \leq \Sigma X$, then $x \leq y$, some $y \in X$.
Show that the elements of *Prime* (M) are prime in *SP* (M)

11 Suppose $\pi \notin$ *Prime* (M). Show that there exists $X \subseteq SP(M)$ such that $\pi \leq \Sigma X$ but for no $\pi' \in X$ do we have $\pi \leq \pi'$. (Hint, look at proposition 9.3.7).

12 A poset $(L,\leq)$ is said to be *prime algebraic* if it has a bottom element and for every element $x \in L$, the set $\{y \leq x \mid y\ '\}$ has a least upper bound and that least upper bound equals x.

13 Use **10, 11** and **12** to prove the proposition:

$(SP(M), \leq)$ is prime algebraic with *Primes* (M) as the set of primes.

NOTES

Hartmanis & Stearns (1966) does not give an explicit construction for $\pi_{s,s'}$. We have derived the algorithm of this chapter from their examples.

Partial orders are used in two areas of computer science. The first is in the theory of concurrent systems, where they are used to model non-sequential behaviour. We shall say more on this in Chapter 11.

The other area is that of programming language semantics.

The problem was to construct *denotational semantics* for programming languages, that is, to provide a means of associating with each program in the language a function which describes its input/output behaviour.

A similar problem had been encountered with the type free λ calculus. The trouble was that if λ expressions were to be interpreted as functions on a set X, then X would have to contain its own function space – which is impossible, by Cantor's theorem.

The problem was solved in 1969 by Dana Scott. Instead of a set, he constructed a special kind of partially ordered set $(D, \leq)$ and required that the functions in question be *continuous* in the sense that whenever $X \subseteq D$ and $\sum X$ existed, then so did $\sum f(X)$, and then $f(\sum X) = \sum f(X)$.

For more on this, see Stoy (1979).

Chapter 10

Analysis of Machines

That the Machine may progress, that the Machine may progress, that the Machine may progress eternally.

E. M. FORSTER
The Machine Stops

10.1 INTRODUCTION

The parallel and serial decomposition theorems tell us when we can break a machine M into two smaller machines. Sometimes, the component machines can themselves be broken down into smaller machines and, again, we can find out whether or not this is possible by constructing their lattices of SP partitions.

At this, I seem to hear a gasp of horror. 'We build this whole lattice $SP(M)$, right ? We use at most *two* partitions to break down the machine – two partitions, when the thing might have hundreds – and now you blandly talk about computing more lattices !'

Things are not as bad as that. In fact, it turns out that you only ever need to compute one lattice using the method of Chapter 9. The lattice of SP partitions of an image machine of machine M may be obtained directly and simply from that of M.

If you give me a finite lattice and say, 'That is the lattice of SP partitions of a machine', then I do not need to examine the actual sets involved to decide whether the machine has a serial or parallel decomposition. If it has a non-trivial partition, then I know it can be serially decomposed, say $M \leq M_1 \ominus M_2$. Because of the relationship between the lattice $SP(M)$ and $SP(M_1)$, I will be able to make the same kind of decision about M_1. The *shape* of the lattice $SP(M)$ tells me about the *shape* of possible decompositions.

In the next section, we investigate the relationships between partitions of a machine and the partition of its image machines.

10.2 THE THREE-STAGE-SERIAL-DECOMPOSITION-THEOREM

We shall base our investigations on a particular problem; that of extending the serial decomposition theorem to a decomposition into three machines connected in series.

Suppose that M is a Mealy machine and that there are machines M_1, M_2 and M_3 such that $M \leq (M_1 \ominus M_2) \ominus M_3$. Writing $M' = M_1 \ominus M_2$, we see that $M \leq M' \ominus M_3$ and so, by the serial decomposition theorem, Section 8.3.3, there exists $\pi_1 \in SP(M)$ such that M' is the image machine of M with respect to π_1.

But also $M' = M_1 \ominus M_2$ and so, again by the serial decomposition theorem, there exists $\pi_2 \in SP(M')$ with M_1 as the image machine of M' with respect to π_2.

Going in the other direction, let M be a Mealy machine and suppose π_1 is an SP partition of M. If π_1 is non-trivial – and we shall assume all partitions to be so unless otherwise stated – then we may form an image machine, after the recipe of Section 8.3.1, and use it to construct a serial decomposition: $M' \ominus M_3$.

If M' itself has an SP partition, π_2, then we could form an image machine, M_1, and a decomposition, $M_1 \ominus M_2$.

An application of proposition 6.4.3 allows us to conclude that M may be decomposed as $(M_1 \ominus M_2) \ominus M_3$. This gives us our first approximation to a result.

10.2.1 Three-Stage-Serial-Decomposition-Theorem (Mark I)

Suppose M is a Mealy machine, then M has a non-trivial serial decomposition:

$$M \leq (M_1 \ominus M_2) \ominus M_3$$

if and only if there exists a non-trivial $\pi_1 \in SP(M)$ and a non-trivial $\pi_2 \in SP(M_{\pi_1})$.

This result is true, but unsatisfactory. To apply it, we need to build the image machine and examine that. We would prefer the conditions for three-stage decomposability to be expressed purely in terms of M_1.

If there are decomposition theorems for decomposition into more than two components, then past form suggests that they may be expressed in terms of sets of subsets of S.

What have we actually got ? We have $\pi_1 \in SP(M)$, which is all right, and $\pi_2 \in SP(M_1)$, which is not. π_2 partitions the state space of M_1 and if you look at the definition of M_1, the state space of M_1 is π_1.

So if our 'three-stage-serial-decomposition-theorem' is to use only subsets of S, then we had better find something in S corresponding to π_2.

We shall first show how, given a partition π_2 of π_1, we may construct a partition of S. (Note that the construction has nothing to do with the fact that S is part of a machine; the construction works for arbitrary sets.)

The construction actually constructs subsets of S from subsets of π_1. Thus from a collection of subsets of π_1, we obtain a collection of subsets of S. It turns out that if the former is a partition, then so is the latter.

Suppose $X \in \pi_2$, then $X = \{U_1, ..., U_k\} \subseteq \pi_1$. Define:

$$X^*\pi_1 = U_1 \cup \cdots \cup U_k \qquad [10.1]$$

and now we have $X^*\pi_1 \subseteq S$. This associates subsets of π_1 with subsets of S. We may extend this to sets of subsets if we define:

$$\pi_2{}^*\pi_1 = \{U^*\pi_1 \mid U \in \pi_2\} \qquad [10.2]$$

then we have a subset of $\underline{P}(S)$. Let us look more closely at it.

Suppose $s \in S$, then $s \in U$, some $U \in \pi_1$, since π_1 partitions S. Hence $U \in X$, some $X \in \pi_2$, because π_2 partitions π_1. If $X = \{U_1, ..., U_k\}$, then U is one of the U_i and hence $U \subseteq (\bigcup U_i) = X^*\pi_1$. Since $s \in U$, we have $s \in X^*\pi_1$.

Thus every s belongs to at least one element of $\pi_2{}^*\pi_1$. If we can show that such an element is unique, then we may conclude that $\pi_2{}^*\pi_1$ partitions S.

We may, in fact, show that:

$$X_1{}^*\pi_1 \cap X_2{}^*\pi_1 \neq \varnothing \Rightarrow X_1 = X_2. \qquad [10.3]$$

For, suppose $X_1{}^*\pi_1 \cap X_2{}^*\pi_1 \neq \varnothing$, then we may find, $s \in X_1{}^*\pi_1 \cap X_2{}^*\pi_1$. Since $s \in X_1{}^*\pi_1$, we may find $U_1 \in X_1$ such that $s \in U_1$. Likewise, we may find $U_2 \in X_2$ such that $s \in U_2$. But this entails that $U_1 \cap U_2 \neq \varnothing$, and since both belong to a partition, π_1, it follows that $U_1 = U_2$. But this means that $U_1 \in X_1 \cap X_2$, and since both of these are members of a partition, π_2, we must have $X_1 = X_2$.

It follows from [10.3] that:

$$X_1{}^*\pi_1 \cap X_2{}^*\pi_1 \neq \varnothing \Rightarrow X_1{}^*\pi_1 = X_2{}^*\pi_1. \qquad [10.4]$$

and hence the following.

10.2.2 Lemma

$\pi_2 * \pi_1 \in \Pi(S)$.

We also note that if $U \in \pi_1$, then there exists $V \in \pi_2 * \pi_1$ such that $U \subseteq V$. Simply take $X \in \pi_2$ such that $U \in X$ and set $V = X * \pi_1$. This leads to the following.

10.2.3 Lemma

$\pi_1 \leq \pi_2 * \pi_1$.

What if $\pi_1 = \pi_2 * \pi_1$? Suppose this is the case and let $X \in \pi_2$. Let $X = \{U_1, ..., U_k\}$, then $X * \pi_1 = U_1 \cup \cdots \cup U_k$. But $\pi_1 = \pi_2 * \pi_1$ and hence $X * \pi_1 = U$, some $U \in \pi_1$. We thus have $U = U_1 \cup ... \cup U_k$. It follows that $U \cap U_j \neq \emptyset$, for each j. But U and each U_j belongs to the partition π_1 and so we must have $U = U_j$, each j and, hence, $X = \{U\}$. Since X can be any element of π_2, we deduce that if $\pi_1 = \pi_2 * \pi_1$ then $\pi_2 = \perp_{\pi_1}$.

But π_2 is non trivial in $SP(M_{\pi_1})$, by Section 10.2.1. Thus:

$$\pi_1 < \pi_2 * \pi_1 \qquad [10.5]$$

Next, what if $\pi_2 * \pi_1 = \top_S$? If that is the case, if $X_1, X_2 \in \pi_2$, then $X_1 * \pi_1, X_2 * \pi_1 \in \pi_2 * \pi_1 = \top_{\pi_1}$ and thus $X_1 * \pi_1 = X_2 * \pi_1 = S$. But, by [10.3], this entails $X_1 = X_2$. It follows that any two elements of π_2 are equal, or equivalently that π_2 contains a single element. This is only possible for a partition of π_1 if π_2 equals $\top_{\pi_1}$, which is impossible, since π_2 is non-trivial, by 10.2.1.

Thus:

$$\pi_2 * \pi_1 < \top_S \qquad [10.6]$$

[10.5] and [10.6] together give the following.

10.2.4 Lemma

$\pi_1 < \pi_2 * \pi_1 < \top_S$.

Let us finally see whether or not $\pi_2 * \pi_1$ has the SP property.

Let $X \in \pi_2$. Since π_2 is SP in M_{π_1}, we find $Y \in \pi_2$ such that. $\delta_{\pi_1}(X, i) \subseteq Y$. We shall show that $\delta(X * \pi_1, i) \subseteq Y * \pi_1$.

Let $s \in X * \pi_1$, then there exists $U \in X$ such that $s \in U$. Since $U \in X \subseteq \pi_1$, and π_1 is SP, there exists $V \in \pi_1$ such that $\delta(U, i) \subseteq V$.

Now, by definition of image machine, $\delta_1(U, i) = V$ and since $\delta_{\pi_1}(X, i) \subseteq Y$ by hypothesis, we have $V \in Y$ and so $V \subseteq Y^* \pi_1$.

Thus $\delta(s, i) \in \delta(U, i) \subseteq V \subseteq Y^* \pi_1$. Since s is an arbitrary member of $X^* \pi_1$, it follows that $\delta(X^* \pi_1, i) \subseteq Y^* \pi_1$ as required.

This leads to the following.

10.2.5 Lemma

$\pi_2^* \pi_1 \in SP(M)$.

We may summarize our discoveries so far as follows.

10.2.6 Proposition (Necessary Conditions for Three-Stage-Serial-Decomposition)

If M has a non-trivial serial decomposition:

$$M \le (M_1 \ominus M_2) \ominus M_3$$

then there exists $\pi_1, \pi_3 \in SP(M)$ such that $\bot_S < \pi_1 < \pi_3 < \top_S$.

Proof

Let $\pi_3 = \pi_2^* \pi_1$, then $\pi_3 \in SP(M)$ by 10.2.5 and $\bot_S < \pi_1 < \pi_3 < \top_S$ by 10.2.4 and the non-triviality of π_1.

Let us now try to find sufficient conditions. Evidently, in view of 10.2.1, we must find something in M which gives rise to a non-trivial SP partition of M_{π_1}. The first clue is provided by the fact that given $\pi_2^* \pi_2$ and π_1, we may reconstruct π_2. The key fact here is that if $X \in \pi_2$ and $U \in \pi_1$, then:

$$U \subseteq X^* \pi_1 \Leftrightarrow U \in X. \qquad [10.7]$$

For it is certainly the case that if $U \in X$ then $U \subseteq X^* \pi_1$. It is a consequence of [10.1]. If on the other hand, we have $U \subseteq X^* \pi_1$, then $U \cap U' \neq \varnothing$, some $U' \in X$. But $U, U' \in \pi_1$, a partition, and so $U = U' \in X$. From [10.7], we deduce:

$$\{U \in \pi_1 \mid U \subseteq X^* \pi_1\} = X \qquad [10.8]$$

[10.8] suggests a construction for making elements of π_2 from elements of $\pi_2^* \pi_1$. Suppose $V \subseteq S$. Define:

$$V/\pi_1 = \{U \in \pi_1 \mid U \subseteq V\} \qquad [10.9]$$

then in this notation, [10.8] becomes:

$$(X^* \pi_1)/\pi_1 = X$$

and so if we define:

$$\pi_2/\pi_1 = \{U/\pi_1 \mid U \in \pi_2\}$$

then we have the following.

10.2.7 Lemma

$(\pi_2{}^* \pi_1)/\pi_1 = \pi_2$

We may obviously use this '/' operator on arbitrary partitions. In the case in which $\pi_1 \leq \pi_3$, we have the following.

10.2.8 Lemma

Suppose $\pi_1, \pi_3 \in \Pi(S)$ with $\pi_1 \leq \pi_3$, then $\pi_3/\pi_1 \in \Pi(\pi_1)$.

Proof

Suppose $U \in \pi_1$. We must show that there exists a unique $V \in \pi_3$ such that $U \in V/\pi_1$. Since $\pi_1 \leq \pi_3$, we have $U \subseteq V$ some $V \in \pi_3$. Now, by definition, $U \in V/\pi_1$ if and only if $U \subseteq V$. Thus $U \in V/\pi_1$. To show that this V is unique, we note simply that if $U \subseteq V'$, $V' \in \pi_3$, then $V \cap V' \neq \varnothing$, since U is in the intersection, and hence $V = V'$.

Just as lemma 10.2.7 allowed us to reconstruct π_2 from π_1 and $\pi_2{}^* \pi_1$, so we may also reconstruct π_3 from π_1 and π_3/π_1.

10.2.9 Lemma

Suppose π_1, $\pi_3 \in \Pi(S)$ with $\pi_1 \leq \pi_3$, then $(\pi_3/\pi_1)^* \pi_1 = \pi_3$.

Proof

It suffices to show that for all $V \in \pi_3$:

$$(V/\pi_1)^* \pi_1 = V. \qquad [10.10]$$

So let $s \in V$. Since π_1 partitions S, we must have $s \in U$, some $U \in \pi_1$. Since $\pi_1 \leq \pi_3$, there must exist V' such that $U \subseteq V'$. Now, $s \in U \subseteq V'$ and $s \in V$ and so $s \in V \cap V'$ and hence $V = V'$, since π_3 is a partition.

Thus, for any $s \in V$, we may find $U \in \pi_1$ such that $s \in U \subseteq V$. By definition [10.9], $U \in V/\pi_1$ and hence by definition [10.2], $U \subseteq (V/\pi_1)^* \pi_1$ and hence $s \in (V/\pi_1)^* \pi_1$.

Thus $V \subseteq (V/\pi_1)^* \pi_1$.

On the other hand, if $s \in (V/\pi_1)^* \pi_1$, then $s \in U$, some $U \in V/\pi_1$, by [10.2]. But, if $U \in V/\pi_1$, then $U \subseteq V$, by [10.9].

Thus $(V/\pi_1)^* \pi_1 \subseteq V$.

This completes the proof.

Next, we examine the question of non-triviality of π_3. First, we need the following lemma, whose proof will be left as an exercise.

10.2.10 Lemma

(a) $\top_{\pi_1} * \pi_1 = \top_S$.

(b) $\bot_{\pi_1} * \pi_1 = \pi_1$.

10.2.11 Lemma

Suppose $\pi_1 < \pi_3 < \top_S$, then π_3/π_1 is non-trivial.

Proof

If $\pi_3/\pi_1 = \top_{\pi_1}$, then:

$$\begin{aligned} \pi_3 &= (\pi_3/\pi_1)^* \pi_1 \text{ (by lemma 10.2.8)} \\ &= \top_{\pi_1} * \pi_1 \text{ (hypothesis)} \\ &= \top_S \text{ (by lemma 10.2.10(a))} \end{aligned}$$

contradicting $\pi_3 < \top_S$.

If $\pi_3/\pi_1 = \bot_{\pi_1}$, then:

$$\begin{aligned} \pi_3 &= (\pi_3/\pi_1)^* \pi_1 \text{ (by lemma 10.2.8)} \\ &= \bot_{\pi_1} * \pi_1 \text{ (hypothesis)} \\ &= \pi_1 \text{ (by lemma 10.2.10(b))} \end{aligned}$$

contradicting $\pi_1 < \pi_3$.

Finally, we show that π_3/π_1 is SP.

10.2.12 Lemma

Let $\pi_1, \pi_3 \in SP(M)$ with $\pi_1 \leq \pi_3$, then $\pi_3/\pi_1 \in SP(M_{\pi_1})$.

Proof

Let $X \in \pi_3/\pi_1$ and $i \in I$. We must show that $\delta_{\pi_1}(X, i) \subseteq Y$, some $Y \in \pi_3/\pi_1$. Now, $X = X'/\pi_1$ for some $X' \in \pi_3$. Since π_3 is SP, there exists $Y' \in \pi_3$ such that $\delta(X', i) \subseteq Y'$. Let $Y = Y'/\pi_1$. We shall show that $\delta_{\pi_1}(X, i) \subseteq Y$.

We need to show that if $U \in X$, then $\delta_{\pi_1}(U, i) \in Y$. Now, $U \in \pi_1$ and $\delta_{\pi_1}(U, i) = U'$, where U' is the unique block of π_1 such that $\delta(U, i) \subseteq U'$. But $U \subseteq X'$ and so $\delta(U, i) \subseteq Y'$. Thus $U' \cap Y' \neq \varnothing$ since $\pi_1 \leq \pi_3$, each block of π_1 is either contained in a block of π_3 or disjoint from it. Thus $U \subseteq Y'$ and hence $U \in Y'/\pi_1 = Y$. We have shown:

$$U \in X \Rightarrow \delta_{\pi_1}(U, i) \in Y$$

as required.

Putting lemmas, 10.2.11 and 10.2.12 together, we get the following.

10.2.13 Proposition (Sufficient Conditions for Three-Stage-Serial-Decomposition)

If there exists $\pi_1, \pi_3 \in SP(M)$ such that $\perp_S < \pi_1 < \pi_3 < \top_S$ then M has a non-trivial serial decomposition:

$$M \leq (M_1 \ominus M_2) \ominus M_3.$$

Propositions 10.2.6 and 10.2.13 now give us the final version of the following.

10.2.14 Three-Stage-Serial-Decomposition-Theorem

Suppose M is a Mealy machine, then M has a non-trivial serial decomposition:

$$M \le (M_1 \ominus M_2) \ominus M_3$$

if and only if there exists non-trivial $\pi_1, \pi_3 \in SP(M)$, such that $\bot_S < \pi_1 < \pi_3 < \top_S$.

10.3 THE SP PARTITIONS OF IMAGE MACHINES

We have constructed our three-stage-serial-decomposition-theorem at last and the cunning reader may have spotted that it generalizes the two-stage-decomposition theorem (8.3.3) in a very simple way. This reader may also have conjectured the full generalization, as follows.

10.3.1 The n-Stage-Serial-Decomposition-Theorem

Let M be a Mealy machine, then M has an non-trivial n-stage serial decomposition, that is:

$$M \le ((...(M_1 \ominus M_2) \ominus ...) \ominus M_{n-1}) \ominus M_n$$

with $|S_j| < |S|$, each j, if and only if there exist $\pi_1, ..., \pi_{n-1} \in SP(M)$ such that $\bot_S < \pi_1 < \cdots < \pi_{n-1} < \top_S$.

Proof

See exercise **1**.

There is no reason why we cannot go on adding theorems to our belt. Here, for example is the parallel version. It is possibly less obvious than the serial.

10.3.2 The n-Stage-Parallel-Decomposition-Theorem

Let M be a Mealy machine, then M has an non-trivial n-stage parallel decomposition, that is:

$$M \le ((...(M_1 \,||\, M_2) \,||\, ...) \,||\, M_{n-1}) \,||\, M_n$$

with $|S_j| < |S|$, each j, if and only if there exist non-trivial $\pi_1, \pi'_1, ..., \pi_{n-1}, \pi'_{n-1} \in SP(M)$ such that:

$$\pi_i . \pi'_i = \pi_{i-1},\ i = 2, ..., n-1$$

$$\pi_1 . \pi'_1 = \bot_S$$

Proof

See exercise 2.

The reader may be beginning to realize, however, that it is not so much the theorems that we can hack out that is important, but rather the method that we use to systematically dismantle a given Mealy machine. This method has something to do with the relationship between the lattice $SP(M)$ and the lattice $SP(M_\pi)$.

Lemmas 10.2.7 and 10.2.9, taken together, show that there is a bijection between SP partitions of M greater than a partition π and the SP partitions of M_π. This correspondence actually 'preserves' the order structure, as we see from the next lemma.

10.3.3 Lemma

Let X be a set and suppose $\pi_1, \pi_2, \pi_3 \in \Pi(X)$ and suppose that $\pi_1 \leq \pi_2$ and $\pi_1 \leq \pi_3$, then:

$$\pi_2 \leq \pi_3 \Leftrightarrow \pi_2/\pi_1 \leq \pi_3/\pi_1$$

Proof

It suffices to show that if $U \in \pi_2$ and $V \in \pi_3$ then:

$$U \subseteq V \Leftrightarrow U/\pi_1 \subseteq V/\pi_1. \qquad [10.11]$$

for suppose we have shown [10.11], then:

$$\begin{aligned}\pi_2 \leq \pi_3 &\Leftrightarrow \text{if } U \in \pi_2 \text{ then } U \subseteq V, \text{ some } V \in \pi_3\\ &\Leftrightarrow \text{if } U/\pi_1 \in \pi_2/\pi_1 \text{ then } U/\pi_1 \subseteq V/\pi_1, \text{ some } V \in \pi_3/\pi_1\\ &\Leftrightarrow \pi_2/\pi_1 \leq \pi_3/\pi_1\end{aligned}$$

We prove [10.11].

First, suppose $U \subseteq V$ and let $X \in U/\pi_1$, then by definition, $X \subseteq U$ and so, since $U \subseteq V$, we have $X \subseteq V$ and hence $X \in V/\pi_1$. Thus $U/\pi_1 \subseteq V/\pi_1$.

Next, suppose $U/\pi_1 \subseteq V/\pi_1$ and let $s \in U$. There exists $X \in \pi_1$ such that $s \in X \in U/\pi_1$. Since $U/\pi_1 \subseteq V/\pi_1$, we have $s \in X \in V/\pi_1$ and thus $s \in X \subseteq V$. Thus $U \subseteq V$.

We may summarize our findings in the following.

10.3.4 Theorem

Let M be a Mealy machine and let $\pi \in SP(M)$. Let $SP_\pi(M)$ denote the set of all SP partitions τ such that $\pi \leq \tau$, then there exists a bijection:

$$f_\pi : SP_\pi(M) \to SP(M_\pi)$$

given by $f(\tau) = \tau/\pi$ such that for all τ :

$$\tau' \in SP_\pi(M) : \tau \leq \tau' \Leftrightarrow f_\pi(\tau) \leq f_\pi(\tau') \qquad [10.12]$$

Proof

First, f is onto, for if $\pi' \in SP(M_\pi)$, then, by lemma 10.2.7, $f(\pi' * \pi) = \pi'$.

Secondly, f is injective, for if $f(\pi_1) = f(\pi_2)$, then using lemma 10.2.9, $\pi_1 = f(\pi_1) * \pi = f(\pi_2) * \pi = \pi_2$.

Finally [10.12] is lemma 10.3.3.

10.3.5 Remark

Pictorially, theorem 10.3.4 has the following significance. Take the Hasse diagram of $SP(M)$. Remove every node below π. Then replace each label τ by τ/π. The resulting Hasse diagram is that of the image machine M_π.

10.4 AN EXAMPLE

In the introduction to this chapter, we said that one may obtain an idea of the shape of possible decompositions of a machine M from the shape of lattices. Hopefully, the reader now has a better idea of what we meant.

1 From the lattice, we may determine whether or not M is decomposable at all.

2 Selecting a non-trivial SP partition from the lattice for use in whatever kind of decomposition, the lattice of the corresponding image machine is derivable from that of M via theorem 10.3.4 (pictorially, via remark 10.3.5).

We illustrate with the lattice whose Hasse diagram is pictured in Fig. 10.1 and which we suppose to be that of $SP(M)$ for some machine M. Note that the whole of the following exercise is carried out without knowing anything about M other than the structure of $SP(M)$.

From this, we see that M has a non-trivial SP-partition π_5 and that it therefore has a serial decomposition $M_1 \ominus M_2$ where $M_1 = M_{\pi_5}$. It fol-

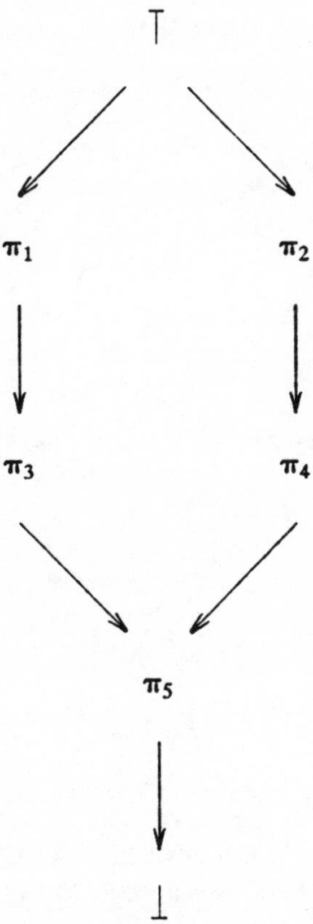

Fig. 10.1

lows from theorem 10.3.4 that it has $SP(M_{\pi_5})$ as its set of SP partitions and that this lattice must be as shown in Fig. 10.2.

From this, we see that M_1 has two non-trivial SP partitions namely π_3/π_5 and π_4/π_5 such that $(\pi_3/\pi_5).(\pi_4/\pi_5) = \bot_{\pi_5}$. By the parallel decomposition theorem, M_1 has a parallel decomposition $M_3 \mid\mid M_4$, where $M_3 = M_{1\pi_3/\pi_5}$ and $M_4 = M_{1\pi_4/\pi_5}$.

We have proved that:

$$M \leq M_1 \ominus M_2 \qquad [10.13]$$

and

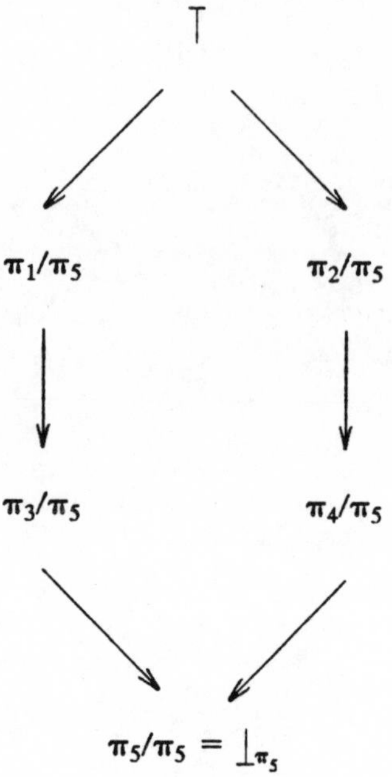

Fig. 10.2

$$M_1 \le M_3 \mid\mid M_3 \qquad [10.14]$$

and we know that $M_2 \le M_2$ from exercise **2** of Chapter 4. We may therefore apply proposition 6.4.3(a) to substitute [10.14] into [10.13] and obtain:

$$M_1 \ominus M_2 \le (M_3 \mid\mid M_4) \ominus M_2 \qquad [10.15]$$

We may now use the transitivity of ≤ (exercise **2**, Chapter 4) to combine [10.13] and [10.15] to get:

$$M \le (M_3 \mid\mid M_4) \ominus M_2 \qquad [10.16]$$

There is no reason why we should stop here. We may use theorem 10.3.4 again on M_3 and M_4. Their lattices are given in Fig. 10.3.

M_3 and M_4 both have non trivial SP partitions and so M_3 and M_4 both have non trivial serial decompositions:

$$M_3 \le M_5 \ominus M_6 \text{ and } M_4 \le M_7 \ominus M_8 \qquad [10.17]$$

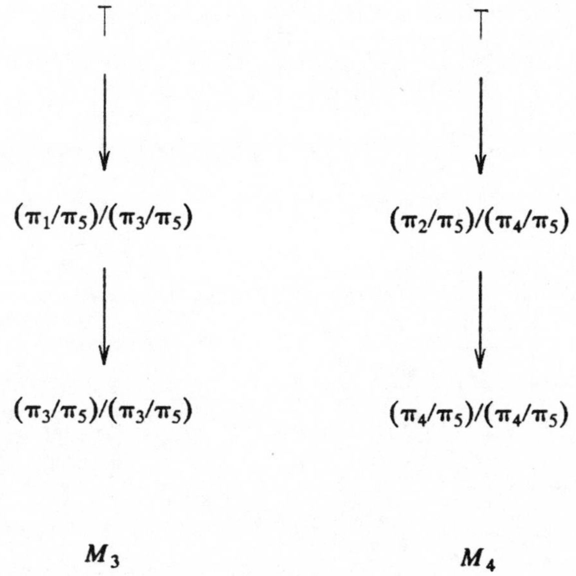

Fig. 10.3

Now we may use proposition 6.4.3(b) to conclude from [10.17] that:

$$M_3 \,||\, M_4 \leq (M_5 \ominus M_6) \,||\, (M_7 \ominus M_8) \qquad [10.18]$$

and use the proposition again to combine [10.18] and the fact that $M_2 \leq M_2$ to obtain:

$$(M_3 \,||\, M_4) \ominus M_2 \leq ((M_5 \ominus M_6) \,||\, (M_7 \ominus M_8)) \ominus M_2 \qquad [10.19]$$

and hence, from [10.16] and [10.19] and the transitivity of $\leq$, we get:

$$M \leq ((M_5 \ominus M_6) \,||\, (M_7 \ominus M_8)) \ominus M_2$$

From the lattice of [10.1], therefore, we may deduce – without even knowing the flow table of M – that it may be decomposed as in Fig. 10.4.

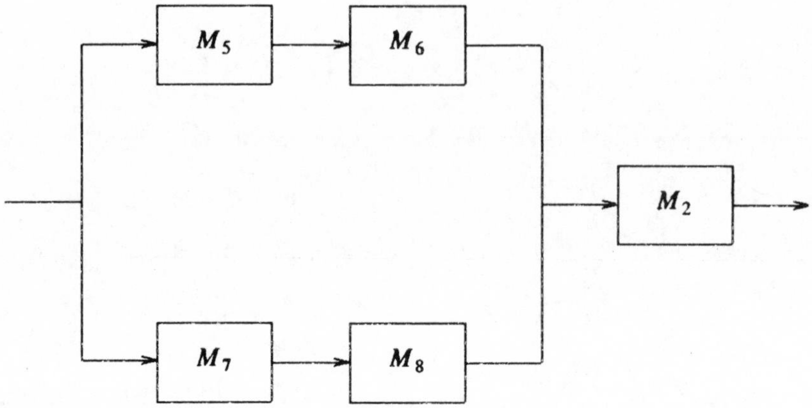

Fig. 10.4

EXERCISES

1 Suppose $\pi_1, \ldots, \pi_{n-1} \in SP(M)$ such that $\perp_S < \pi_1 < \cdots < \pi_{n-1} < \top_S$. Let M' be the image machine M_{π_1}.

Show that $\pi_2/\pi_1, \ldots, \pi_{n-1}/\pi_1 \in SP(M')$ and
$\perp_{\pi_1} = < \pi_1/\pi_1 < \cdots < \pi_{n-1}/\pi_1 < \top_S/\pi_1 = \perp_{\pi_1}$.

Use this fact and induction on n to prove theorem 10.3.1.

2 Suppose $\pi_1, \pi'_1, \ldots, \pi_{n-1}, \pi'_{n-1} \in SP(M)$ such that
$\pi_i . \pi'_i = \pi_{i-1}$, $i = 2, \ldots, n-1$ and $\pi_1 . \pi'_1 = \perp_S$.
Prove that $\pi_1 \leq \pi_j$, $j = 1, \ldots, n$ and $\pi_1 \leq \pi'_j$, $j = 2, \ldots, n-1$.

Let M' be the image machine M_{π_1}.

Show that $\pi'_1/\pi_1, \ldots, \pi_{n-1}/\pi_1, \pi'_{n-1}/\pi_1 \in SP(M')$ such that
$\pi_i/\pi_1 . \pi'_i/\pi_1 = \pi_{i-1}/\pi_1$, $i = 3, \ldots, n-1$ and $\pi_2/\pi_1 . \pi'_2/\pi_1 = \perp_{\pi_1}$.

Use this fact and induction on n to prove theorem 10.3.2.

3 We will call a machine *indecomposable* if it has no non-trivial serial or parallel decomposition. What does $SP(M)$ look like for undecomposable M ? Prove the proposition: Let M be a machine, then M may be realized by serial and parallel composition of indecomposable machines.

4 $\pi \in SP(M)$ is *minimally non-trivial* if π is non-trivial and is such that, if $\tau \in SP(M)$ and $\tau < \pi$, then $\tau = \perp_S$. Which machine lacks minimally non-trivial SP partitions ?

The next few exercises are to do with tail machines in a serial decomposition.

5 Suppose $M \le M' \ominus M_3$ and $M' \le M_1 \ominus M_2$. Prove that $M \le M_1 \ominus (M_2 \ominus M_3)$.

6 In **5**, let π_1 be the SP partition of M induced by M_1 and π' be the partition of M induced by M'. Prove that if none of the decompositions are trivial, then $\pi_1 < \pi'$. Conclude the following proposition: Let $\pi \in SP(M)$ and let $M \le M_1 \ominus M_2$ using π to construct M_1, then, if π is minimally non-trivial, M_2 is indecomposable.

7 Using the proposition of **6**, prove that the machines constructed in the decomposition discussed in Section 10.4 must be indecomposable.

8 Using 10.3.4 show that if $\pi_1, \pi_2, \pi_3 \in \Pi(X)$, some set X, and $\pi_1 \le \pi_2$ and $\pi_1 \le \pi_3$, then:

$$(\pi_2/\pi_1).(\pi_3/\pi_1) = (\pi_2.\pi_3)/\pi_1$$

$$(\pi_2/\pi_1) + (\pi_3/\pi_1) = (\pi_2 + \pi_3)/\pi_1$$

9 Using 10.3.4 show that, if $\pi_1 \in \Pi(X)$ and $\pi_2, \pi_3 \in \Pi(\pi_1)$, some set X, then:

$$(\pi_2 * \pi_1).(\pi_3 * \pi_1) = (\pi_2.\pi_3) * \pi_1$$

$$(\pi_2 * \pi_1) + (\pi_3 * \pi_1) = (\pi_2 + \pi_3) * \pi_1$$

NOTES

This chapter has discussed the use of $SP(M)$ in decomposing a given machine M. The more advanced theory of machine decompositions considers the decomposition of arbitrary machines. (In fact they consider state machines rather than Mealy machines). Just as any positive integer may be decomposed as a product of primes, so, it has been shown that any state machine may be decomposed into serial and parallel composites of machines of one of two types:

(a) two state reset machines;

(b) simple grouplike machines whose groups are covered by the semi-group of the original machine.

A reset machine is a state machine such that for each $i \in I$, there exists s_i such that $\delta(s, i) = s_i$ for each $s \in S$. (See exercises, Chapter 7.)

(b) is more difficult to explain. Very briefly, in the more advanced theory, each state machine may be associated with an object called a *semi-group* acting on it state set. Simple grouplike machines are machines whose semi-group has also the property of being what is know as a *simple group*. For more details see Holcombe (1982).

Chapter 11

Concurrent Systems: Net Theory

Slepe he neuer so fast, his nette catches for hym.

ERASMUS

11.1 INTRODUCTION

All the machines we have considered so far have been sequential. They did one thing at a time. Many useful systems may safely be considered to be sequential.

However, in some cases it is not sensible or practical to think of a system sequentially. In such cases, we need something more sophisticated than the sequential model.

This chapter describes the first of two, rather different, approaches to the description and analysis of concurrent systems, namely *net theory*, which dates from 1962 when it was introduced in the doctoral thesis of the theory's inventor, Dr C.A. Petri. The second, CCS, was introduced in 1980 by Professor R. Milner of Edinburgh University and will be described in the next chapter.

11.2 NETS

Net Theory is a theory of *concurrent* systems,* systems in which several things may be going on at the same time. This is in contrast to systems which may be described by finite state automata, in which only one thing at a time (an input received/ an output generated) is possible.

This theory was one of the first to attack systems which are not merely sequential. The central objects in the theory are called *nets*. First, we give the formal definition of a net and then we explain some of the symbols and the intuition behind the model.

* Such systems are also sometimes described as 'distributed' or as exhibiting 'parallelism'.

11.2.1 Definition

A net is a triple $\mathbf{N} = (P, T, F)$, where:
(a) P is a non-empty set of *places*;
(b) T is a non-empty set of *transitions*;
(c) $F \subseteq (P \times T) \cup (T \times P)$ is the *flow relation*; we write $x\ F\ y$ to denote that $(x, y) \in F$;
(d) $domain(F) \cup range(F) = P \cup T \neq \emptyset$ and $P \cap T = \emptyset$.
Here $domain(F) = \{x \mid (x, y) \in F \text{ some } y\}$ and $range(F) = \{x \mid (y, x) \in F \text{ some } y\}$.

11.2.2 Explanation

Nets are often represented pictorially, and so as well as explaining the significance of places, transitions and the flow relation, we will tell you how they are pictured.

1 Transitions, usually drawn as boxes, represent the actions of a system. Whether or not an action may occur (or, in the usual jargon, 'fire') depends on the availability of certain resources. The firing of a transition may cause a change to the type and number of resources available.

2 Places, usually drawn as circles, represent types of resource. At any time, a place may contain a number of markers of *tokens*, indicating that there are that many of that type of resource currently available.

3 The interdependencies of actions and resources are given in the flow relation F. Pictorially, if $x\ F\ y$, then an arrow is draw from x to y.

Suppose $p \in P$ and $t \in T$.

If $p\ F\ t$ then p is said to be an *input place* of t and t is said to be an *output transition* of p. $p\ F\ t$ indicates that a resource of type p must be available for t to fire. Pictorially, p must contain at least one token. When t fires, it takes one token from p.

If $t\ F\ p$ then t is said to be an *input transition* of p and p is said to be an *output place* of t. $t\ F\ p$ indicates that a resource of type p will be created after t has fired. Pictorially, after t has fired, p will contain an extra token.

Note that if $p\ F\ t$ and $t\ F\ p$, then there will be no change to the number of tokens on p if t fires, but there must be at least one token on p for t to fire.

4 The first clause of 11.2.1 (d) says that every place and transition occurs in at least one of the two coordinates in some pair, that is, every circle or box has an arrow attached to it. The second says that nothing can be both a circle and a box.

11.2.3 Convention

As with automata and homomorphisms, we make the convention that coordinates inherit subscripts. For example $\mathbf{N}'_3 = (P'_3, T'_3, F'_3)$.

11.2.4 Example

As an illustration, consider an industrial process in which components are being bolted together to form a finished product. A particular action in this process may involve bolting together a component of type A and a component of type B using an instrument C to produce an object D. We may picture this by the net in Fig. 11.1. Note that $P = \{A, B, C, D\}$, $T = \{t\}$ and:

$$F = \{(A,t), (B,t), (C,t), (t,C), (t,D)\}$$

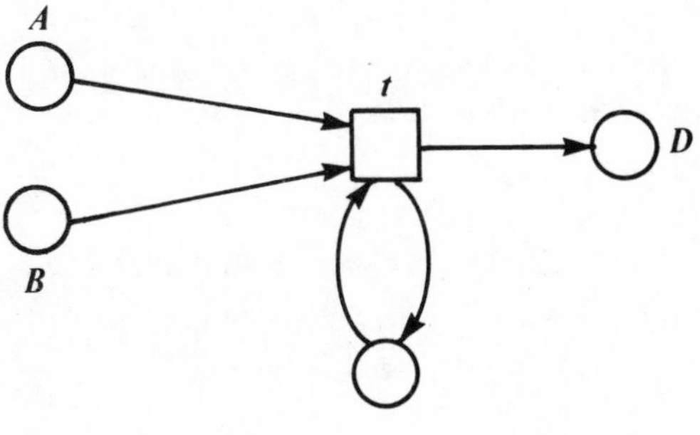

Fig. 11.1

Note the way in which it is necessary for there to be a token in C, even though it is always 'put back' after use. Note also that one token from A and B is lost for every item of type D that is created.

One of the most important differences between nets and the machines we have looked at so far is in the notion of state. In the machines described in Chapter 2, a state is something atomic. The corresponding notion in net theory is that of the distribution of tokens, because it is this which determines which transitions are eligible to fire. This distribution may be changing locally in different parts of the net at the same time. It is this that allows the possibility of concurrent execution.

A distribution of tokens on a net is called a marking.

11.2.5 Definition

Let **N** be a net. A *marking* of **N** is a mapping:

$$M : P \rightarrow \{0, 1, 2, ...\}$$

A marking M associates every place $p \in P$ with a number $M(p)$, the number of tokens in that place at that time. As transitions 'fire', the number of tokens on places change according to the rule about consuming and producing tokens, known as the firing rule.

11.2.6 Definition

Let **N** be a net, M a marking of **N**, $t \in T$; t has *concession* in M if and only if:

$$\text{For all } p \in P, \text{ if } p \; F \; t \text{ then } M(p) > 0$$

We write $M\ [t>$ to denote that t has concession in M.

If $M\ [t>$, then t may *fire*, transforming the marking M into a new marking M', where:

$$M'(p) = \begin{cases} M(p) - 1 & \text{if } p \; F \; t \text{ and } \textit{not } t \; F \; p \\ M(p) + 1 & \text{if } t \; F \; p \text{ and } \textit{not } p \; F \; t \\ M(p) & \textit{otherwise} \end{cases}$$

Thus, for example, $M'(p)$ has one less token than $M(p)$ if $p \; F \; t$ (t consumes a token from p) and we do not have $t \; F \; p$ (which would put a token back onto p again).

Write $M\ [t> M'$ to denote that t may fire at marking M transforming it to marking M'.

The behaviour of a net consists of the firing of transitions as resources are consumed and created.

We illustrate the firing of a transition, pictorially, in Fig. 11.2.

Does t have concession after it has fired ? If not, why not ?

We may extend 11.2.6 to deal with sequences of transitions.

11.2.7 Definition

Let **N** be a net and let M be a marking of **N**. A sequence $\sigma = t_1 \cdots t_n$ of transitions is a *firing sequence* from M to a marking M', and we write

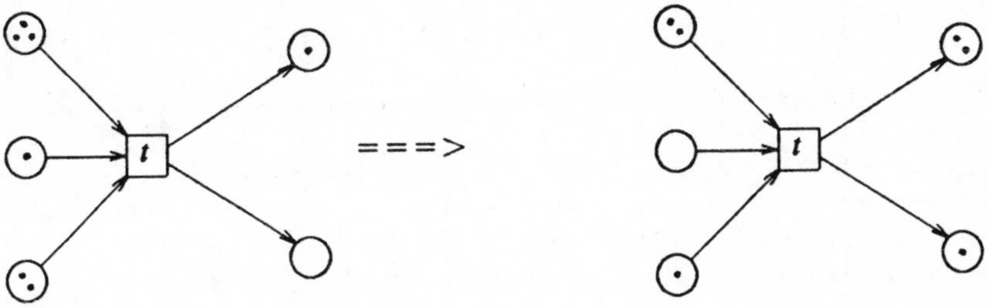

Fig. 11.2. The firing rule

M $[\sigma > M'$, if either of the following is the case:

(a) if $\sigma = \varepsilon$ (the empty string, that is, if σ is the empty sequence) – and in that case $M' = M$.

(b) if there exists a marking M'' such that M $[t_1 > M''$ and M'' $[t_2 \cdots t_n > M'$.

11.2.8 Definition

Let **N** be a net and let M be a marking of **N**. We define $[M]_{\mathbf{N}}$ (or just $[M]$ if **N** is understood from context) to be the set of all markings *reachable* from M, that is:

$$[M] = \{M' \mid M \ [\sigma > M' \ \textit{some} \ \sigma\}.$$

11.2.9 Example

In the net of Fig. 11.3, with the marking shown, the following are firing sequences: a, *bcda*, *cbda*, *bcdbcdbcdbcd*.... Note that *bcda* and *cbda* really define the *same* behaviour – b and c concurrently followed by d and a in sequence.

We shall now look at some dynamic properties of nets. Consider the net pictured in Fig. 11.3.

1 First, notice that a, b and c all have concession in the marking shown. However, if a fires, then the token on place 1 is consumed and b no longer has concession. Similarly, if b fires, then the token on place 1 is consumed and a no longer has concession. Only one of the two

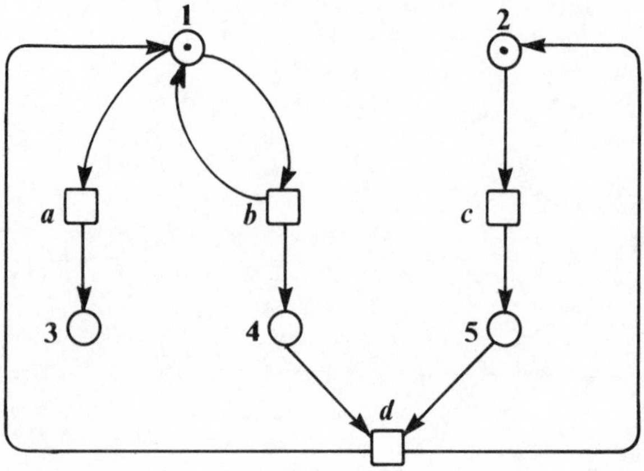

Fig. 11.3. A net

transitions, a or b, may fire in this marking, and the firing of one *disables* the firing of the other. a and b are said to be in *conflict*. Note also, that nothing determines which of the two fire. The net is *non-deterministic*.

2 c, however, is not in conflict with either a or b. In fact, the firing of c happens independently of either, 'at the same time as' whichever fires, or *concurrently* with it. The ability to represent concurrency is one of the chief features distinguishing the net theory from other systems theories.

3 If a and c fire concurrently, then the result is to place tokens on places 3 and 5. There are no tokens on 1 or 2, and so a, b and c do not have concession in this marking. Furthermore, there is no token on 4. Since d may only fire if *all* its input places are marked (namely 4 and 5), it follows that d does not have concession either. The net is stuck – nothing else can happen. This is an example of *deadlock*. Detecting deadlock is a non-trivial problem in systems design, which we shall be looking at later.

4 Finally, suppose we fire b and c concurrently. Both input places of d receive tokens; it therefore has concession and may fire. Note also that the firing of b replaces a token on 1. After the firing of d, we have *two* tokens on 1 and one token on 2. Repeating this, we would end up with *three* tokens on 1 and one token on 2. Repeating this again would give *four* tokens on 1 and one on 2. Evidently, we may repeat this process as often as we like and the number of tokens on 1 would grow without bound. This is an example of *unsafe-ness* or *unbounded-ness*. Since in most respects the real world is finite, such a system could never be implemented – sooner or later it would grind to a halt as we ran out of tokens.

We shall formalize some of these properties in Section 11.4.

Finally, we shall find the following notation useful.

11.2.10 Definition

Let $x \in P \cup T$ and define:
(a) $^\bullet x = \{y \in P \cup T \mid y \; F \; x\}$
(b) $x^\bullet = \{y \in P \cup T \mid x \; F \; y\}$.
Let $X \subseteq P \cup T$. Define:
(c) $^\bullet X = \{y \in P \cup T \mid y \; F \; x \; \textit{some} \; x \in X\}$
(d) $X^\bullet = \{y \in P \cup T \mid x \; F \; y \; \textit{some} \; x \in X\}$.

11.3 CONCURRENT BEHAVIOUR

The more prominent work involving net theory has (for historical reasons) involved the analysis of systems properties such as deadlock. For these purposes, it suffices to understand the dynamics of nets in terms of firing sequences.

Indeed, from this point of view, net theory appears an extension of automata theory, because such properties may be deduced from a (partial) state machine which may be derived from a net and its initial marking. This state machine, sometimes called the *marking graph* of the net and marking, is $SM(\mathbf{N},M) = ([M],T,\delta)$, where $\delta(M',t)$ is defined and equals M'' if and only if $M' \; [t> M''$.

So-called liveness and safeness properties may be defined in terms of $SM(\mathbf{N},M)$.We therefore have a general problem; to infer properties of $SM(\mathbf{N},M)$ from properties of $\mathbf{N}$ and M. This is the general domain of what has been called *token mathematics* because it centres on the firing rule, which allows one to transfer concern between aspects of net dynamics and state-machine dynamics.

We shall spend most of the rest of this chapter on token mathematics. To avoid an imbalance, in this section we shall say something about the other aspects of net theory, principally the notion of concurrency.

First, we must explain that the general theory, developed by Petri and his colleagues, uses nets for systems description on different levels of abstraction.

For example, on the lowest level, places represent *atomic propositions* which are either true (have one token in them) or false (have no token). Transitions represent atomic events, which may take place only if certain propositions are true. We remark that for these *condition/event* nets, the firing rule is modified to prevent more than one token ever residing in a place. Also, side conditions (places p such that $p^\bullet \cap {}^\bullet p \neq \emptyset$) are not allowed.

Higher level nets may then be interpreted in terms of lower level nets. For example, the type of net we look at in this chapter is called a *place/transition* net. Each place may be considered as standing for a set of propositions, for example asserting that some particular instance of a type of resource is available. n tokens on this place is equivalent to n of these propositions being true.

In higher level nets, tokens may be given individual names or 'colours' and transitions are associated with predicates which entail that only tokens of a certain colour or type may be used to fire the transition and to dictate what kind of tokens are produced on firing the transition. This leads to very compact representations of systems which would otherwise require very large condition/event nets.

Each level (except the bottom one, of course) is interpreted in the level below. This means that each net and marking on a higher level may be associated with a net of the lower level, which 'defines the same system'.

We remark that the formal machinery by which these levels of interpretation are established uses category theory.

The lowest level is given meaning by a behavioural semantic model. That is to say, for a given condition/event net and initial marking, we may define a set of objects, each of which describes a possible period of behaviour of the system.

These objects themselves involve nets, having two properties.

Firstly, there is no conflict; neither the forwards conflict seen in 11.2.9, where there exists $p \in P$ and $t_1, t_2 \in T$ such that $p\ F\ t_1$ and $p\ F\ t_2$ for $t_1 \neq t_2$, nor *backwards* conflict, where there exists $p \in P$ and $t_1, t_2 \in T$ such that $t_1\ F\ p$ and $t_2\ F\ p$.

Secondly, it is not possible to find a sequence of arrows starting from and ending at some place or transition. (In the jargon of 11.4.5, the net contains no circuits).

Such nets are called *occurrence nets*.

Let us explain the use of occurrence nets. First, let F^* denote the reflexive, transitive closure of F, that is, we define $x\ F^*\ x$ for each x and let $x\ F^*\ y$ if and only if we have $x = x_1\ F\ x_2\ \cdots\ x_{n-1}\ F\ x_n = y$, some $n \geq 1$. $(P \cup T, F^*)$ now becomes a partially ordered set ! The order relation may now be interpreted as meaning 'occurred before' for transitions and 'was the case before' for places. An occurrence net may therefore be used to display the condition holdings and event occurrences in the order in which they were held or occurred.

Now we may note that if a set is partially ordered and not totally ordered then there exist elements x and y for which neither $x \leq y$ nor $y \leq x$. Such elements are said to be incomparable in the order $\leq$. If x, y are elements of an occurrence net, incomparable with respect to F^*, then they are said to be *concurrent*.

The ability to represent concurrency formally distinguishes net theory from other approaches to the study of parallelism, which tend to adopt a 'firing- sequence' way of describing the behaviour of systems.*

Given a net **N** and a marking M, we may construct a collection of occurrence nets describing possible behaviour of **N** from M. The places and transitions of these nets will be labelled with the names of places and transitions of **N**. The interpretation of this is as follows. Suppose **N′** is one of these labelled occurrence nets. Suppose $p' \in P'$ is labelled by $p \in P$ and t' T' is labelled by $t \in T$, then in the behaviour of **N** represented by **N′**, p is a *holding* of condition p and t' is an *occurrence* of event t.

An occurrence net with such a labelling is called a *process* of **N** – providing it accurately represents the order in which conditions may hold and transitions fire as determined by the firing rule.

Without going into too much detail, let us describe how to generate finite processes from a net. We illustrate the method with the net shown in Fig. 11.4.

Initially, we have nothing (and therefore no net). For each transition t having concession from M, we construct a net as follows:

1 It has a transition labelled t.

2 For each input place p of t, construct a place labelled p and an arrow from it to the transition.

3 For each output place p of t, construct a place labelled p and an arrow to it from the transition.

The only transition of the net in Fig. 11.4 that can fire is b. The process which describes the behaviour involving the firing of b is pictured in Fig. 11.4.

Next, observe that every finite process has a set of places with no output transitions. Call these *terminal* places. It is true after the firing of the first transition, and by induction remains true, that every such place will contain a token at the conclusion of the behaviour represented by the process. If other places are also marked, then these will be places marked by M initially and have not yet given up a token. Call these *undisturbed* places.

We may now describe how to construct new processes from old. Let **N′** be such a process.

Say that $t \in T$ has concession from **N′** if for every $p \in {}^{\bullet}t$, p labels either a terminal place or an undisturbed place. This corresponds to t having concession in the marking determined by the process **N′** and so is quite

* The two may be reconciled, since processes may be regarded as generalized strings in which certain symbols commute. See Shields (1985).

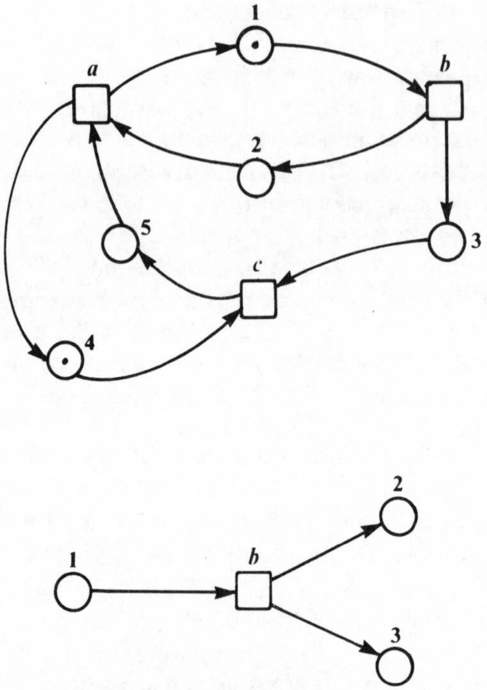

Fig. 11.4

consistent with our earlier use of the term.

A new process, representing the behaviour **N′** together with a subsequent firing of t is obtained as follows.

1 If $p \in {}^{\bullet}t$ labels an undisturbed place, adjoin a new place to **N′** labelled p.

2 Adjoin to **N′** a new transition t' labelled t.

3 For each $p' \in P'$ which is either a terminal place or a place added in 1 labelled by some element of ${}^{\bullet}t$, construct an arrow from p' to t'.

4 For each output place p of t, construct a place labelled p and an arrow to it from t'.

This construction is illustrated by Fig. 11.5. Note that in the b process, places labelled 2 and 3 are terminal and place 4 is undisturbed.

Processes give the 'correct' semantics for nets, rather than firing sequences, which do not in general exhibit properties, such as concurrency, for the formal description of which nets were originally invented ! It is true that for many purposes, firing sequences are adequate. From the net theoretic point of view, however, this remark is a general theorem about

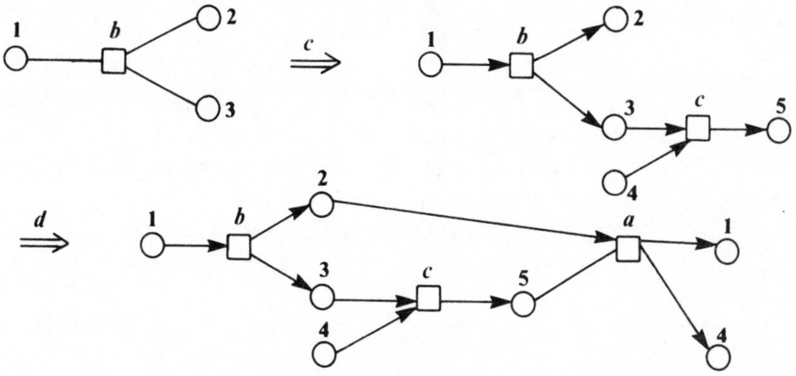

Fig. 11.5

nets, not a postulate about formal representation of concurrency in general.

11.4 DYNAMIC PROPERTIES OF NETS

One of the first envisaged *uses* of net theory was in the analysis of concurrent systems to detect unwanted properties, such as deadlock. In this section we present some general results about such properties.

11.4.1 Definition

(a) **N** is *n-safe* with respect to M if and only if for every $M' \in [M]$, and for every $p \in P$, $M'(p) \leq n$ (p never accumulates more than n tokens whatever happens).

(b) **N** is *safe* with respect to M if and only if it is 1-*safe* with respect to M.

(c) **N** is *bounded* with respect to M if and only if there exists a number n such that **N** is n-*safe* with respect to M.

As we have explained, a system which is not bounded may not be implemented. It is therefore reasonably important to ascertain whether or not a system, described by a net, is bounded or not.

11.4.2 Theorem (Karp & Miller)

Let **N** be a net and let M be a marking of **N**. If **N** is finite (i.e., P and T are finite sets), then it is decidable whether **N** is bounded with respect to

M.

Proof

We sketch the proof, which is based on the construction of a directed tree whose nodes are labelled by vectors $\mathbf{v} = (v_1, ..., v_n)$, where each coordinate i corresponds to a place p_i and where each v_i belongs to the set $\{0, 1, 2, ...\} \cup \{\infty\}$. ∞ may be read 'infinity'. It is a symbol equipped with the property that $n < \infty$ for all natural numbers n.

$\mathbf{v}$ may be regarded as a marking, $M_\mathbf{v}$, where $M_\mathbf{v}(p_i) = v_i$, and the usual firing rule applies, with the understanding that $\infty + 1 = \infty$ and $\infty - 1 = \infty$.

Let $\mathbf{v} = (v_1, ..., v_n)$ and $\mathbf{v}' = (v'_1, ..., v'_n)$. Define $\mathbf{v} \leq \mathbf{v}'$ if and only if $v_i \leq v'_i$, each i.

The point behind the construction is as follows. Suppose $\mathbf{v} \leq \mathbf{v}'$ and $\mathbf{v}\ [\sigma\!>\ \mathbf{v}'$ with, say, $v'_1 = v_1 + m$, some $m > 0$. One may show that for any k, there exists $\mathbf{v}''$ such that $\mathbf{v}\ [\sigma^k\!>\ \mathbf{v}''$ and that $v''_1 = v_1 + k.m$, where $\mathbf{v}'' = (v''_1, ..., v''_n)$.

Thus, in this situation, **N** is not bounded with respect to M. (We have seen an example of this phenomenon in 4 of 11.2.9.)

Now for the construction.

Label the root node with the vector $(M(p_1), ..., M(p_n))$ corresponding to the initial marking.

Now suppose we have constructed part of the tree. Some leaves may have become 'ticked' during the construction. If *all* leaves have been ticked, then stop. Otherwise, select an unticked leaf, labelled by $\mathbf{v}$, say, and adjoin directed edges from it to nodes labelled $\mathbf{v}_1, ..., \mathbf{v}_k$, where this is the set of all markings $\mathbf{v}'$ such that $\mathbf{v}\ [t\!>\ \mathbf{v}'$, some t.

Now for each new leaf, perform the following:

1 If the vector $\mathbf{v}$ labelling this leaf already labels some node which is not a leaf, then tick that node (we have already started to deal with this vector and do not need to do it twice).

2 If there exists a node between this leaf and the root, such that the node is labelled $\mathbf{v}'$, and $\mathbf{v}' \leq \mathbf{v}$ and $\mathbf{v}' \neq \mathbf{v}$, then replace each v_i such that $v'_i < v_i$, by ∞. As we have seen, the corresponding places p_i are unbounded and this is what ∞ indicates.

It may be shown that this tree is finite. The argument goes as follows. Since **N** is finite, the out valency of each node is bounded above (by $|T|$). If the tree were infinite, then by *Koenig's lemma*, there would have to be an infinite path through it. But this would mean that there would be an infinity of vectors such that for no two of them $\mathbf{v} \leq \mathbf{v}'$ and this is known to be impossible.

Indeed, one may prove that any infinite set of n-vectors has an infinite subset which is totally ordered with respect to $\leq$. The proof is by induction on n. It is certainly true for $n = 1$, since such a set of vectors would essentially be the natural numbers with their usual ordering.

Suppose we have an infinite set V of n vectors. Each vector may be regarded as a pair $(\mathbf{v},x)$, where $\mathbf{v}$ is an $n-1$ vector. By induction, there exists an infinite subset W of the set of $\mathbf{v}$ totally ordered with respect to $\leq$. Let V' be the set of vectors $(\mathbf{v},x) \in V$ such that $\mathbf{v} \in W$.

Now we will be able to construct an infinite total order $V'' \subseteq V'$ if we have the property that for every $\mathbf{w} \in V'$, we may find $\mathbf{w}' \in V'$ such that $\mathbf{w} \leq \mathbf{w}'$ and $\mathbf{w} \neq \mathbf{w}'$.

If this is true for *no* $\mathbf{w}$, then take an arbitrary $\mathbf{w} = (\mathbf{v},x)$. There are an infinite number of $\mathbf{v}'$ such that $\mathbf{v} \leq \mathbf{v}'$ and $(\mathbf{v}',x') \in V'$, by definition of V'. Since we do not have $(\mathbf{v},x) \leq (\mathbf{v}',x')$, it follows that $x > x'$.

Since there are a finite number of such x's but an infinite number of such $\mathbf{v}'$, it follows that for some $x_o < x$, $(\mathbf{v}',x_o) \in V'$ for an infinite number of $\mathbf{v}'$. The set of all such $(\mathbf{v}',x_o) \in V'$ is now an infinite total order.

If the tree has no ∞ coordinates, then it may be shown that all reachable markings occur as labels to the tree – and therefore the net is bounded with respect to M. Otherwise, the net is not bounded, by a previous remark.

Thus, boundedness may be decided from this tree.

Now, we turn to liveness properties of nets.

11.4.3 Definition

Let **N** be a net and let M be a marking of **N**.

(a) A transition t is *live* with respect to M if and only if, for all $M' \in [M]$, there exists $M'' \in [M']$ such that $M''\ [t>$. In other words, whatever happens, it is always possible to fire t in the future.

(b) **N** is *live* with respect to M if and only if, every transition t is live with respect to M.

(c) A transition t is *dead* with respect to M if and only if for all $M' \in [M]$, t does not have concession with respect to M'.

(d) **N** is *deadlock-free* with respect to M if and only if, at least one transition t is live with respect to M. In other words, **N** may never reach *deadlock*, a marking in which all transitions are dead.

We have seen that there is an algorithm which determines whether or not a given net is safe at a given marking. We now go on to look at some elementary results on liveness.

First, if a net is finite and bounded, then it has only a finite number of possible markings from a given marking. This leads to the following proposition.

11.4.4 Proposition

Suppose **N** is finite. If **N** is bounded with respect to a marking M, then it is decidable whether or not **N** is live or is deadlock-free with respect to M.

Proof

N is finite, thus $|P| = k$, some k.

Since **N** is bounded with respect to M, **N** is n-safe with respect to M for some n. It follows that $[M] \subseteq [S \rightarrow \{0,...,n\}]$, that is, each $M' \in [M]$ is a function from S to the set $\{0,...,n\}$. There are k^{n+1} such functions. Thus, $|[M]| \leq k^{n+1}$ and so $[M]$ is finite.

It follows that for each $M' \in [M]$, we may construct the sets $[M']$ and $tr(M')$, where $tr(M') = \{t \in T \mid M''[t> some\ M'' \in [M']\}$.

It may therefore be checked, for any given $M' \in [M]$ whether or not $tr(M') = T$ or $tr(M') = \varnothing$.

But now the proposition follows, because, as may easily be shown:

(a) **N** live is with respect to $M \Leftrightarrow tr(M') = T$ for each $M' \in [M]$;

(b) **N** is deadlock free with respect to $M \Leftrightarrow tr(M') \neq \varnothing$ for each $M' \in [M]$;

This completes the proof.

Since in practice, we are only working with finite systems, it would appear that checking for liveness is always possible. Use 11.4.2 to determine whether or not the net is bounded (if it is not, we can not implement it) and then use 11.4.4 to check liveness.

Unfortunately, this is not always possible in practice. Brams (p.78), gives an example of a bounded net with 21 places, 23 transitions with more reachable markings than the estimated number of atoms in the Universe. We could not use 11.4.4 to analyse it.

We can sometimes get *some* information about liveness by looking at the graphical structure of the net. For example, we may look at the extent to which it is interconnected. We shall see that the Brams net is not live.

11.4.5 Definition

(a) A *path* through a net **N** from x_1 to x_n is a sequence $\pi = x_1 \cdots x_n$ such that $x_i \ F \ x_{i+1}$ for $i = 1,2,...,n-1$. Write $x_1 \ \pi \ x_n$ to indicate that there is a path from x_1 to x_n.

(b) A *circuit* in **N** is a path π with $x \ \pi \ x$ and $\pi \neq x$, some x, i.e., it goes back to where it started.

(c) **N** is *connected* if for every $x, y \in P \cup T$, there exists a path π such that either $x \ \pi \ y$ or $y \ \pi \ x$.

(d) **N** is *strongly connected* if for every $x, y \in P \cup T$, there exists paths π and π' such that $x \ \pi \ y$ and $y \ \pi' \ x$.

(e) If π_1 is the path $x_1 \cdots x_n$ and π_2 is the path $x_n \cdots x_m$ then $\pi_1 \pi_2$ is defined to be the path $x_1 \cdots x_n \cdots x_m$.

11.4.6 Definition

Let **N′**, **N** be nets, **N′** is a *subnet* of **N** if and only if $P' \subseteq P$ and $x, y \in P' \cup T', x \ F' \ y \Leftrightarrow x \ F \ y$. Write $\mathbf{N}' \subseteq \mathbf{N}$.

11.4.7 Proposition

Suppose **N** is finite and connected. If **N** is live and bounded for some marking M then **N** is strongly connected.

Proof

Suppose that **N** is not strongly connected. We show that **N** is either unbounded or not live with respect to M.

There are three cases to consider.

1 $^\bullet t = \varnothing$, some $t \in T$. Note that t always has concession, since the statement 'all input places of t are marked' is always trivially true, and that therefore for all m, then exists M' such that $M \ [t^m > M'$. Since $^\bullet t = \varnothing$, by 11.2.1(d), $t^\bullet \neq \varnothing$. Let $p \in t^\bullet$, then if $M \ [t^m > M'$, then $M'(p) = M(p) + m$ and so **N** is not m-safe with respect to M for any m, i.e. not bounded with respect to M.

2 $^\bullet p = \varnothing$, some $p \in P$. Again, by 11.2.1(d), $p^\bullet \neq \varnothing$ and so $t \in p^\bullet$, some $t \in T$. It is clear that t cannot fire more than $M(p)$ times, since there is no way of returning tokens to p. Thus, t is not live with respect to M and hence **N** is not live with respect to M (11.4.3(b)).

3 In the third case, neither 1 nor 2 is the case. Our strategy here is as follows:

(a) We show that N must contain a connected subnet N_{min} not strictly contained in any other connected subnet of N (a maximal strongly connected subnet).

(b) We show that N_{min} may be chosen so that it has no inputs from the rest of the net but has outputs to it (via 'fringe' elements).

(c) We show that if N is live then so is N_{min} and that therefore it may export an unlimited number of tokens out through its fringe places. These tokens may actually be left on these fringe places. Hence N is unbounded.

Since neither 1 nor 2 is the case, then we may pick any place p_1 and construct a sequence $t_1, p_1, t_2, ...$ such that $t_i \in {}^\bullet p_i$ and $p_{i+1} \in {}^\bullet t_i$, Since N is finite, we must have $p_m = p_n$, some $m < n$. The sequence $p_n t_{n-1} p_{n-1} \cdots p_{m+1} t_m p_m$ is thus a circuit in N. Therefore, the subnet of N, N′, such that $P' = \{p_{m+1}, ..., p_n\}$ and $T' = \{t_m, ..., t_{n-1}\}$, is strongly connected.

Therefore N contains a strongly connected subnet.

We say that N′ ⊆ N is a maximal strongly connected subnet (msc subnet) if and only if, whenever N′ ⊆ N″ ⊆ N and N″ is strongly connected, then either N″= N or N″ = N′.

If N_1 and N_2 are nets, define
$N_1 \cup N_2 = (P_1 \cup P_2, T_1 \cup T_2, F_1 \cup F_2)$.

We may verify that $N_1 \cup N_2$ is a net and that if N_1 and N_2 are strongly connected and $(P_1 \cup T_1) \cap (P_2 \cup T_2) \neq \emptyset$, then $N_1 \cup N_2$ is strongly connected.

If N contains a strongly connected subnet N″, then it contains an msc subnet N′ such that N″ ⊆ N′. Take N′ as the union of all strongly connected subnets containing N″. (If N is itself strongly connected, then N is its own msc subnet).

Thus, if N contains a strongly connected subnet, then it contains an msc subnet. In fact the argument above shows more than this, namely that for any $y \in P \cup T$, there exists an msc subnet N′ and element x of N′ and a path $x \, \pi \, y$.

We shall refer to the above construction as the *backtracking construction*.

Define a relation on the msc subnets of N. $N_1 \rightarrow N_2$ if and only if there is a path $x \, \pi \, y$, where x is in N_1 and y is in N_2.

We show that → is a partial order. Reflexivity is obvious. If $N_1 \rightarrow N_2$ via a path π_1 and $N_2 \rightarrow N_1$ via a path π_2, then the subnet N′ composed of the elements of N_1, N_2 and π_1 and π_2 is strongly connected. Since $N_1 \subseteq N'$ and $N_2 \subseteq N'$ and both N_1 and N_2 are msc and N is not strongly connected, it follows that $N_1 = N' = N_2$.

Finally, suppose $N_1 \to N_2$ via a path $w\ \pi_1\ x$ and $N_2 \to N_3$ via a path $y\ \pi_2\ z$, then since N_2 is strongly connected, there exists a path $x\ \pi\ y$ in N_2. Thus $N_1 \to N_3$ via the path $w\ \pi_1 \pi' \pi_2\ z$. Thus, $\to$ is transitive.

Since **N** is finite, the number of msc subnets of **N** is finite and we may choose an msc subnet N_{min} such that $N'' \to N_{min}$ for no msc subnet $N'' \neq N_{min}$. We shall express this property by saying that N_{min} is minimal.

Let $X_{min} = P_{min} \cup T_{min}$.

Next we show that if $x, y \in X_{min}$ and $x\ \pi\ y$, then all of π is in N_{min}. This will entail that N_{min} has no inputs from outside.

Suppose $\pi = xx_1...x_r y$. Let N_π be the net obtained by adjoining the x_i to N_{min}. If z is any element of N_{min} then there are paths ρ_1 and ρ_2 within N_{min} such that $z\ \rho_1\ x$ and $y\ \rho_2\ z$, because N_{min} is strongly connected. Therefore, for all i, j:

$$x_i\ \pi_i\ z \text{ where } \pi_i = x_i ... x_r . \rho_2$$

$$z\ \pi'_j\ x_j \text{ where } \pi'_i = \rho_1 . x_1 ... x_j$$

$$x_i\ \pi'_{ij}\ x_j \text{ where } \pi'_{ij} = x_i ... x_r . \rho_2 . \rho_1 . x_1 ... x_j$$

Thus, N_π is strongly connected. Since $N_{min} \subseteq N_\pi$ and N_{min} is an msc subnet, we must have either $N_{min} = N_\pi$ or $N = N_\pi$. The latter impossible, since **N** is assumed not strongly connected. Thus $N_{min} = N_\pi$ and so $x_i \in X_{min}$ for all i.

Now suppose $x \in X_{min}$ and suppose $y\ F\ x$. Applying the backtracking construction gives an msc subnet N' and a path π such that $N' \to N_{min}$ via π and $\pi = x_1 ... x_i yx$, some x_i. Since N_{min} is minimal, it follows that $N' = N_{min}$. By our previous argument, $y \in X_{min}$.

Thus, N_{min} has no inputs from outside. On the other hand, it must have outputs to the outside, otherwise either $N = N_{min}$ – which is impossible, because **N** is not strongly connected – or **N** is not connected. Thus there exists $x \in X_{min}$ and $y \notin X_{min}$ such that $x\ F\ y$.

We now make two observations about the relationships between the behaviour of N_{min} and **N**. Let M_{min} denote the restriction of M to P_{min}.

Suppose $\sigma \in T_{min}{}^*$ and $t \in T_{min}$. Let $p \in T_{min}^{\bullet} - P_{min}$ (p is a 'fringe' place) and define:

$$\#_1(\varepsilon, p) = 0$$

$$\#_1(\sigma . t, p) = \begin{cases} \#_1(\sigma, p) & \text{if } t \notin {}^{\bullet}p \\ \#_1(\sigma, p) + 1 & \text{if } t \in {}^{\bullet}p \end{cases}$$

The point of this is that if σ were a firing sequence, then it would put $\#_1(\sigma,p)$ tokens on p – and take none off, since p has no outputs to T_{min}. We use this to show that if **N** is live then p is unbounded. The proof uses the following observation.

Lemma A

Suppose M_{min} $[\sigma>$ M_{min}' in $\mathbf{N}_{min}$, then M $[\sigma>$ M' in **N** where:

$$M'(p) = \begin{cases} M_{min}'(p) & \text{if } p \in P' \\ M(p) & \text{if } p \in (P - P') - T'^{\bullet} \\ M(p) + \#_1(\sigma,p) & \text{if } p \in (P - P') \cap T'^{\bullet} \end{cases}$$

Lemma A says that every firing sequence of $\mathbf{N}_{min}$ is also a firing sequence of **N**. We may also go in the opposite direction and construct firing sequences of $\mathbf{N}_{min}$ from those of **N**.

Let $\sigma \in T^*$, $t \in T$. We define $\sigma \mid T_{min}$ to be the string obtained from σ by striking out all elements not of T_{min}. Formally:

$$\varepsilon \mid T_{min} = \varepsilon$$

$$\sigma.t \mid T_{min} = \begin{cases} \sigma \mid T_{min} & \text{if } t \in T - T_{min} \\ (\sigma \mid T_{min}).t & \text{if } t \in T_{min} \end{cases}$$

If $p \in P'$, then $\#_2(\sigma,p)$ counts the number of ts deleted from σ such that $p \in {}^{\bullet}t$. Formally:

$$\#_2(\varepsilon,p) = 0$$

$$\#_2(\sigma.t,p) = \begin{cases} \#_2(\sigma) & \text{if } p \notin {}^{\bullet}t \text{ or } t \in T_{min} \\ \#_2(\sigma) + 1 & \text{if } p \in {}^{\bullet}t \;\&\; t \notin T_{min} \end{cases}$$

The point is, that if we take a firing sequence of **N**, σ and remove all non T_{min} transitions, then the $\#_2(\sigma,p)$ tokens that would have been removed remain in p. We may use this to show unboundedness of p – providing, of course, that $\sigma \mid T_{min}$ is a firing sequence. This leads to the following.

Lemma B

Suppose $M\ [\sigma> M'$ in $\mathbf{N}$, then $M_{\min}\ [\sigma \mid T_{\min}> M_{\min}'$ in $\mathbf{N}_{\min}$, where:

$$M_{\min}'(p) = \begin{cases} M'(p) & \text{if } p \in P' - {}^\bullet(T - T_{\min}) \\ M'(p) + \#_2(\sigma, p) & \text{if } p \in P' \cap {}^\bullet(T - T_{\min}) \end{cases}$$

We are now nearing the end of the proof. Suppose that $\mathbf{N}$ is live with respect to M. We will show that $\mathbf{N}$ is unbounded.

We have argued that there exist $x \in X_{\min}$ and $y \notin X_{\min}$ such that $x\ F\ y$. We consider two cases.

Case I: $x \in P$ and $y \in T$

Since $\mathbf{N}$ is live with respect to M, for any m we may construct $\sigma \in T^*$ such that $M\ [\sigma> M'$ and y occurs m times in σ. It follows that $\#_2(\sigma, x) \geq m$. Let $\sigma' = \sigma \mid T_{\min}$,. By lemma B, $M_{\min}\ [\sigma'> M_{\min}'$ in $\mathbf{N}_{\min}$, with $M_{\min}'(x) = M'(y) + \#_2(\sigma, x) \geq m$. By lemma A, $M\ [\sigma'> M''$ in $\mathbf{N}$, with $M''(p) = M_{\min}'(p) \geq m$.

Thus, $\mathbf{N}$ is not m-safe with respect to M for any m, and hence $\mathbf{N}$ is not bounded with respect to M.

Case II: $x \in T$ and $y \in P$

Since $\mathbf{N}$ is live with respect to M, for any m we may construct $\sigma \in T^*$ such that $M\ [\sigma> M'$ and x occurs m times in σ. It follows that $\#_1(\sigma, y) \geq m$. Let $\sigma' = \sigma \mid T_{\min}$,. By lemma B, $M_{\min}\ [\sigma'> M_{\min}'$ in $\mathbf{N}_{\min}$. By lemma A, $M\ [\sigma'> M''$ in $\mathbf{N}$, with $M''(y) = M_{\min}'(y) + \#_1(\sigma, y) \geq m$.

Thus, $\mathbf{N}$ is not m-safe with respect to M for any m, and hence $\mathbf{N}$ is not bounded with respect to M.

This completes the proof.

We remark that the net presented by Brams, whose set of markings is of such an astronomical size, is known to be bounded but is also not strongly connected. We may use 11.4.7 to conclude that this net is not live.

Now let us consider a net $\mathbf{N}$ and a marking M such that $\mathbf{N}$ is not deadlock-free with respect to M. This means that we may find M' in the set $[M]$ of markings reachable from M such that all transitions are dead with respect to M'.

We shall show that it is possible to construct a sequence of sets $D_1 \subseteq D_2 \subseteq \cdots \subseteq P$ and $T_1 \subseteq T_2 \subseteq \cdots \subseteq T$ such that for every j:

(a) For all $p \in D_j$, $M'(p) = 0$;

(b) $T_j = {}^\bullet D_j$;

(c) $T_j \subseteq D_{j+1}{}^\bullet$;

The construction is iterative. Suppose that we have constructed $D_1, ..., D_k$ and $T_1, ..., T_{k-1}$ (initially, we have no T_1, only D_1) and that they satisfy (a), (b) and (c).

Define $T_k = {}^\bullet D_k$ (this ensures (b)). Also note that $T_{k-1} = {}^\bullet D_{k-1} \subseteq {}^\bullet D_k = T_k$, so $T_{k-1} \subseteq T_k$.

Now let $D_{k+1} = D_k \cup D'_k$, where D'_k consists of the set of all $p \in P$ such that $M'(p) = 0$ and $p \in {}^\bullet t$ for some $t \in T_k - T_{k-1}$. This will ensure (a) and the property that $D_k \subseteq D_{k+1}$.

Finally, we prove that $T_k \subseteq D_{k+1}{}^\bullet$.

Since $T_{k-1} \subseteq D_k{}^\bullet$, it suffices to show that $T_k - T_{k-1} \subseteq D'_k{}^\bullet$. Let $t \in T_k - T_{k-1}$. Since **N** is deadlocked at marking M', it follows that t is not live in M' and so we must have $M'(p) = 0$, some $p \in {}^\bullet t$. But then $p \in D'_k{}^\bullet$, by definition and $t \in p^\bullet$. Thus, $t \in D'_k{}^\bullet$, as required.

To start this construction, we select $p \in P$ such that $M'(p) = 0$ - such a p exists because **N** is deadlocked at marking M - and set $D_1 = \{p\}$.

The point of the construction is that, because **N** is finite, at some stage we must have $D_j = D_{j+1}$. But then:

$$ {}^\bullet D_j = T_j \subseteq D_{j+1}^\bullet = D_j^\bullet $$

and so ${}^\bullet D_j \subseteq D_j^\bullet$

Such a set is called a *deadlock* or *siphon* (we shall use the latter term to avoid confusion with the dynamic property of deadlock).

11.4.8 Definition

Let **N** be a net. A siphon in **N** is a set of places D such that:

$$ {}^\bullet D \subseteq D^\bullet $$

We shall say that a siphon D is *emptyable* from M if there is a marking $M' \in [M]$ such that $M'(p) = 0$ for each $p \in D$.

Our previous argument gives the first part of the following proposition.

11.4.9 Proposition

(a) If **N** is not deadlock-free with respect to M then **N** contains a siphon emptyable from M.

(b) If D is a siphon of **N** and M is a marking of **N** such that D is empty in M, then D remains empty.

(c) If **N** contains an siphon emptyable from M, then **N** is not live with respect to M.

Proof

2 A token may only enter D if a transition in ${}^{\bullet}D$ fires. But since each such transition has an input place inside D and D is empty, no such transition may fire.
3 By 2, once D is empty, every transition in $D^{\bullet}$ has an input place which remains perpetually unmarked.

We note that the problem of determining whether, in general, a siphon is emptyable, has not been solved. Note also that the presence of an emptyable siphon does not guarantee deadlock.

A backtracking argument allowed us to deduce the presence of emptyable siphons for nets that were not deadlock-free. We could try the same argument for nets which are not live but are perhaps deadlock-free.

We can begin the construction, because we know that there must be a marking in which there is at least one dead transition. Where the construction goes wrong is that we cannot assume that all elements of $T_k - T_{k-1}$ are dead.

The culprit in this case is the kind of transition which is dead, not because some subset of its input set has become permanently unmarked, but because not all of them are marked at the same time. Such transitions are called *locked transitions*.

11.4.10 Definition

$t \in T$ is said to be locked from M if and only if:
(a) t is not live with respect to M;
(b) for all $M' \in [M]$, if $p \in {}^{\bullet}t$ and $M'(p) = 0$, then for some $M'' \in [M']$, $M''(p) > 0$.

We now may state the following proposition.

11.4.11 Proposition

Let **N** be a finite net and M a marking of **N**, then **N** is live with respect to M if and only if:
(a) **N** contains no siphon emptyable from M;
(b) **N** contains no transition locked with respect to M.

Proof

First we show the 'only if' part. Indeed, if **N** contains a siphon emptyable from M, then **N** is not live with respect to M, by 11.4.9(c). If **N** contains a transition t locked from M, then *a fortiori*, t is not live with respect to

M and hence **N** is not live with respect to M.

Now we show the 'if' part. We shall in fact show that if **N** is not live with respect to M and has no transitions locked from M, then it contains a siphon emptyable from M.

The construction is similar to the one leading to 11.4.9(a). We construct sets $D_1 \subseteq D_2 \subseteq \cdots \subseteq P$ and $T_1 \subseteq T_2 \subseteq \cdots \subseteq T$ and markings $M_1, M_2, M_3, \ldots$ such that for each j:

(a) $T_j = {}^\bullet D_j$;

(b) $T_j \subseteq D_{j+1}{}^\bullet$;

(c) $M_{j+1} \in [M_j]$;

(d) for all $M' \in [M_j]$, D_j is unmarked by M'.

Since **N** is finite, $D_i = D_{i+1}$ for some i and then ${}^\bullet D_i = T_i \subseteq D_{i+1}{}^\bullet = D_i{}^\bullet$ and D_i is therefore a siphon unmarked by M_i.

Suppose we have constructed $D_1, \ldots, D_k$, $T_1, \ldots, T_{k-1}$ and $M_1, \ldots, M_k$ satisfying (a), (b), (c), (d) above. (Initially, we will have a set $\{p\}$ and marking $M_1 = M$ and no T_1).

Define $T_k = {}^\bullet D_k$. This will guarantee (a). Note also that $T_{k-1} = {}^\bullet D_{k-1} \subseteq {}^\bullet D_k = T_k$, so $T_{k-1} \subseteq T_k$.

If $T_{k-1} = T_k$, then ${}^\bullet D_k = T_k = T_{k-1} \subseteq D_k{}^\bullet$ and we are done, since D_k is unmarked by M_k.

If not, then $T_k - T_{k-1} = \{t_1, \ldots, t_n\}$. We note that all the t_i are dead with respect to M_k. If not, then there exists $M', M'' \in [M_k]$ and t_i such that $M' [t_i > M''$. But $t_1 \in {}^\bullet p$, some $p \in D_k$ and hence $M''(p) \geq 1$, contradicting (d).

Since t_1 is dead but not locked from M, we must be able to find $p_1 \in {}^\bullet t_1$ and $M_{k,1} \in [M_k]$ such that $M_{k,1}(p_1) = 0$ and for all $M' \in [M_{k,1}]$, $M''(p_1) = 0$. Similarly, since t_2 is dead but not locked from M, we must be able to find $p_2 \in {}^\bullet t_2$ and $M_{k,2} \in [M_{k,1}]$ such that $M_{k,2}(p_2) = 0$ and for all $M' \in [M_{k,2}]$, $M'(p_2) = 0$.

Inductively, we may construct $D'_k = \{p_1, \ldots, p_n\}$ and $M_{k+1} = M_{k,n}$ such that for each i, $p_i \in {}^\bullet t_i$ and for all $M' \in [M_{k+1}]$, $M'(p_i) = 0$. Note that such an M_{k+1} satisfies (c).

Note that $T_k - T_{k-1} \subseteq {}^\bullet D'_k$ so that if we define $D_{k+1} = D_k \cup D'_k$, then $T_k = (T_k - T_{k-1}) \cup T_{k-1} \subseteq D'_k{}^\bullet \cup D_k{}^\bullet = D_{k+1}{}^\bullet$, satisfying (b). It is now clear that M_{k+1} satisfies (d).

Since **N** is not live from M and contains no locked transitions, we may find $M' \in [M]$ and $t \in T$ such that t is dead with respect to M' and since t is not locked from M, there must exist $p \in {}^\bullet t$ and $M_1 \in [M']$ such that for all $M'' \in [M_1]$, $M''(p) = 0$.

Let $D_1 = \{p\}$. We may now iteratively apply the above construction until we find $D_i = D_{i+1}$, which we have shown to be an emptyable siphon.

This result is not all that useful in general, because it is not easy to discover whether a given siphon is emptyable or whether a given transition is locked. However, for certain subclasses of net, things are much simpler.

11.5 SPECIAL CLASSES OF NETS

The first studies of the liveness property were made for special kinds of nets, for which necessary and/or sufficient conditions could be obtained which allowed static analysis of the net to determine this property. We define the three principal classes below.

11.5.1 Definition

(a) **N** is a *marked graph* if for every place p, $|{}^{\bullet}p| \leq 1$ and $|p^{\bullet}| \leq 1$.
The definition says that each place has at most one input and one output transition.

(b) **N** is a *free choice* if for every place p, if $|p^{\bullet}| > 1$ then for each $t \in p^{\bullet}$, ${}^{\bullet}t = \{p\}$.

(c) **N** is an *asymmetric choice* net* if for every pair of places p, q, if $p^{\bullet} \cap q^{\bullet} \neq \emptyset$ then either $p^{\bullet} \subseteq q^{\bullet}$ or $q^{\bullet} \subseteq p^{\bullet}$. We abbreviate 'asymmetric choice' to 'AC'.
The relationship between the classes is as follows.

11.5.2 Remark

(a) **N** is a marked graph $\Rightarrow$ **N** is free choice.

(b) **N** is free choice $\Rightarrow$ **N** is AC.

AC nets are in some sense on a boundary. As opposed to the general case, the absence of an emptyable siphon is both necessary and sufficient for liveness. This is because of the following proposition.

11.5.3 Proposition

Suppose **N** is a finite AC net, then for no marking M does **N** contain a transition locked from M.

* These nets have also been called 'simple'. The above terminology (which is due to Eike Best), is preferable, firstly because the nets are not simple, in the sense that they are well understood, and secondly because the word 'simple' has an alternative meaning in net theory.

Proof

Suppose t is locked from M and suppose that **N** is AC. We derive a contradiction.

First of all, define S' to be the set of all $p \in {}^\bullet t$ such that if $M' \in [M]$ and $M'(p) > 0$, then for all $M'' \in [M']$ $M''(p) > 0$. S' is the set of inputs to t such that once marked, they remain marked.

It follows from (b) of 11.4.10 that there exists $M' \in [M]$ such that $M'(p) > 0$ for all $p \in S'$.

Now, consider $S'' = {}^\bullet t - S'$. Since for any pair $p', p'' \in S''$, $t \in p'^\bullet \cap p''^\bullet$, it follows, by 11.5.1(c), that the sets $p^\bullet$, with $p \in S''$ are totally ordered by inclusion. Thus $S'' = \{p_1, ..., p_r\}$ with $p_1^\bullet \subseteq p_2^\bullet \subseteq \cdots \subseteq p_r^\bullet$.

Now consider p_1. By 11.4.10(b), there exists $M'' \in [M']$ such that $M''(p_1) > 0$. Since $p_1 \notin S''$, there must exist $M''' \in [M'']$ such that $M'''(p_1) = 0$. So there is a firing sequence from M'' to M''' which removes all the tokens from p_1. Thus, there must be some transition whose firing removes the last token. That is, there exists $M_1, M_2 \in [M'']$ and $t' \in T$ such that $M_1(p_1) = 1$, $M_2(p_1) = 0$ and $M_1\ [t'> M_2$.

It follows that $t' \in p_1^\bullet$. But $p_1^\bullet \subseteq p_i^\bullet$ for all i and thus $S'' \subseteq {}^\bullet t'$. Since $M_1\ [t'> M_2$, we must have $M_1(p_i) > 0$ for all $p_i \in S'$. But $M_1(p) > 0$ for all $p \in S'$. Since ${}^\bullet t = S' \cup S''$, it follows that t also has concession in M_1.

This contradicts the assumption that t is locked with respect to M and we are done.

From 11.4.11 and 11.5.3, we obtain the following proposition.

11.5.4 Proposition

Suppose **N** is a finite AC net, then **N** is live with respect to M if and only if **N** does not contain a siphon emptyable from M.

As we have said, detecting that a siphon is emptyable is a difficult problem. On occasions, however, we may be able to ascertain that a siphon is not emptyable. Recall that a siphon once empty remains empty. There is a dual notion – a set of places that, once marked, remains marked.

11.5.5 Definition

A set S of places of **N** is called a *trap* if:

$$S^\bullet \subseteq {}^\bullet S$$

A marked trap may never be emptied of tokens (see exercise **4**). Therefore, if a siphon contained a marked trap, then that siphon could never be emptied. We thus have the following from proposition 11.5.4.

11.5.6 Proposition

Suppose **N** is a finite AC net, then **N** is live with respect to M if every siphon of **N** contains a trap marked by M.

Note that the condition is only sufficient – it is possible that **N** contains a siphon which does not contain a marked trap and yet **N** is still live. Note also that by remark 11.5.2, proposition 11.5.6 also holds for free choice nets and marked graphs. For free-choice nets, however, the condition is both necessary and sufficient.

11.5.7 Theorem (Commoner)

Suppose **N** is a finite free choice net, then **N** is live with respect to M if and only if every siphon of **N** contains a trap marked by M.

Proof

Since **N** is free choice, it is also AC, by 11.5.2(b). Thus, if every siphon of **N** contains a trap marked by M then **N** is live from M by 11.5.6.

For the converse, we will suppose that $D \subseteq P$ is a siphon which does not contain a trap marked by M. We show that **N** is not live from M.

Let $D_o = D$. We define, iteratively:

(a) $T_{i+1} = D_i^\bullet - {}^\bullet D_i$;

(b) $D_{i+1} = D_i - {}^\bullet T_{i+1}$.

Since **N** is finite and $D_o \supseteq D_1 \supseteq D_2 \cdots$, we must have $D_i = D_{i+1}$ for some i. Thus, we have:

$$D_o \supset D_1 \supset D_2 \supset \cdots \supset D_{k+1} = D_{k+2}$$

for some k. Thus, ${}^\bullet T_{k+2} = \emptyset$ and hence, by (a) either $D_{k+1} = \emptyset$ or $D_{k+1}^\bullet \subseteq {}^\bullet D_{k+1}$. In the latter case, D_{k+1} is a trap, and hence unmarked, by hypothesis.

Next, consider $t \in T_{i+1}$, $i \leq k$. By definition, $t \notin {}^\bullet D_j$, for any $j \geq i$, otherwise, since $D_j \subseteq D_i$, we would have $t \in {}^\bullet D_i$, contradicting (a). Thus, if $M'\ [t> M''$, then:

(c) $$M''(p) = \begin{cases} M'(p) & \text{if } p \in D_i - {}^\bullet t \\ M'(p) - 1 & \text{if } p \in {}^\bullet t \end{cases}$$

The second part follows from 11.2.6 and the fact that if $p \in D_i$ and $p \in {}^\bullet t$, then $p \notin t^\bullet \cap {}^\bullet t$ by (a).

Thus, the firing of t strictly reduces the number of tokens on D_i. It follows that we may construct sequences $\sigma_{k+1}, \sigma_k, ..., \sigma_1$, with $\sigma_i \in T_i{}^*$, each i, and markings $M_{k+1}, ..., M_o$, such that for each i:

(d) M_{i+1} $[\sigma_{i+1}> M_i$;

(e) for no $t \in T_j$, $j \geq i$ is it the case that $M_i [t>$;

(f) if $p \in D_j$ and $j > i$, then $M_{i+1}(p) = M_i(p)$.

Now, we show that $M_o [t>$ for no $t \in {}^\bullet D$. We argue by contradiction.

Suppose that $M_o [t>$ with $t \in {}^\bullet D$. By (e), $t \notin T_i$ for any i. Also, since D is a siphon, we must have $t \in D^\bullet$. Let $p \in D$ with $p \in {}^\bullet t$. We must have $M_o(p) > 0$, since $M_o [t>$, and so $p \notin D_{k+1}$, which is either empty or an unmarked trap.

Thus, for some j, $p \in D_j - D_{j+1}$ and so $p \in {}^\bullet T_{j+1}$. Thus $p \in {}^\bullet t'$, some $t' \in T_{j+1}$.

We may at last wheel out the free choice hypothesis, because we now have $t, t' \in p^\bullet$ and $t \neq t'$, since $t' \in T_{j+1}$ and $t \notin T_i$ for all i. It follows that ${}^\bullet t' = \{p\} = {}^\bullet t$. But, we have already remarked that $M^o(p) > 0$. Thus, $M_o [t'>$, contradicting (e).

Finally, we use this to show that all transitions in ${}^\bullet D$ are dead in M_o. This will complete the proof.

Suppose the contrary, that is that for some $t \in {}^\bullet D$ and $\sigma \in T^*$, M_o $[\sigma.t>$.

We may assume that $\sigma \in (T - {}^\bullet D)^*$. But now, we note that if $t' \in T - {}^\bullet D$ and M' $[t'> M''$ for any M', M'', then $M'(p) \geq M''(p)$ for all $p \in D$, since $t' \notin {}^\bullet D$. By induction, if $M_o [\sigma> M'$, where $\sigma \in (T - {}^\bullet D)^*$, then for all $p \in D$, $M_o(p) \geq M'(p)$. But this means that if M' $[t>$, then M_o $[t>$. But we know this to be impossible.

Thus, all elements of ${}^\bullet D$ are dead with respect to M and, in particular, **N** is not live with respect to M.

This completes the proof.

From remark 11.5.2, this theorem will also hold for marked graphs, but because of their relatively simple structure, it may be expressed much more directly. (Historically, theorem 11.5.8 was discovered before theorem 11.5.7.)

Recall that a *circuit* in **N** is a path π with $x \; \pi \; x$, some x. We shall say that it is *simple* if the only element appearing in it more than once is x.

11.5.8 Theorem

Suppose **N** is a finite, connected marked graph, then **N** is live and bounded with respect to M if and only if **N** is strongly connected and every simple circuit of **N** contains at least one token.

Proof

By proposition 11.4.7, if **N** is live and bounded, then it is strongly connected. Furthermore, if **N** contains an unmarked circuit, then **N** cannot be live, by proposition 11.4.9 (c), since such a circuit would be a siphon. Thus, if **N** is live and bounded with respect to M, then **N** is strongly connected and every circuit of **N** contains at least one token.

Conversely, if **N** is not live with respect to M, then the backtracking argument sketched prior to 11.4.8 allows us to find a circuit which is not marked by some successor marking of M. But the places of a circuit form a trap, so this circuit must have been unmarked initially. Thus, if **N** is not live with respect to M then **N** contains an unmarked circuit. Thus, if **N** does not contain an unmarked circuit, then it is live.

Finally, if **N** is strongly connected, then every place lies on a circuit. Note (exercise 6) that firing a transition in a marked graph does not change the number of tokens on any circuit. Accordingly, if there were n tokens initially on a given circuit, then for each place p on that circuit and for each $M' \in [M]$, $M'(p) \leq n$. There can only be a finite number of simple circuits in **N**, because a simple circuit cannot have more than $|P| + |T| + 1$ elements and there are a finite number of such sequences. Thus, we may find a number m such that there are not more than m tokens initially on any circuit. It follows that **N** is m-safe and hence bounded.

EXERCISES

1 Prove (a) and (b) of Section 11.4.4.

2 Prove lemma A of 11.4.7. Use induction on $lnth(\sigma)$. A key fact is that if $p \in T_{\min}{}^{\bullet} - P_{\min}$, then $p \notin {}^{\bullet}t$ for all $t \in T_{\min}$, since $\mathbf{N}_{\min}$ is msc and has no inputs from the rest of the net.

3 Prove lemma B of 11.4.7. Use induction on $lnth(\sigma)$.

4 Suppose S is a trap and $M(p) > 0$, some $p \in S$. Prove that for all $M' \in [M]$, there exists $p' \in S$, such that $M'(p') > 0$.

5 Prove that every simple circuit in a marked graph is both a siphon and a trap.

6 Show that in a marked graph, the number of tokens on any given simple circuit remains constant.

NOTES

There is a growing literature about nets, mostly concerning token mathematics. The first book in English to be published on this was Peterson (1981), which is good on token mathematics. There is also a good account in Brams (1983) (in French), which describes other methods for analysing nets such as reduction – transformations which make the net smaller but preserve some interesting property – and the use of linear algebra to construct formulae involving variables representing place markings which are invariant under transition firing.

For other aspects of net theory, the reader is directed to Brauer (1979), particularly Genrich, Lautenbach & Thiagarajan and the essays by Petri himself.

Chapter 12

Concurrent Systems: The Calculus of Communicating Systems

Evil communications corrupt good manners.

I Corinthians, 15:33

12.1 INTRODUCTION

In CCS, a system is considered to be composed of a set of interacting *agents*. The agents interact by exchanging messages. Agents may also absorb messages from the environment of the system (input) and send messages to the environment (output).

Many real systems are like this. Consider, for example, the telephone network. This is built up from many individual machines, such as telephone exchanges and receivers of various kinds, which cooperate by sending and receiving signals. There is no 'central control' in a telephone network – it would make things rather awkward if there were – and many actions may go on at the same time.

CCS involves a language of *expressions*, which may be used to define the behaviours of agents. The behaviour of an agent consists of communications with its environment or with other agents. Communications take place through labelled *port*s. We shall use lower case greek letters for labels. One label, τ, has a special interpretation, which we shall describe shortly.

There is a special agent, called *NIL*, which does nothing at all. It may seem odd to have such an agent in one's system, but remember that at one time, the number zero was regarded in certain quarters as a diabolical invention; *NIL* plays a role in CCS similar to that of zero.

Expressions are built up from port names and behaviour identifiers (names for agents) with certain operators. We shall give a syntax for the language in definition 12.2.1, but first let us see some examples.

12.2 THE LANGUAGE OF BEHAVIOUR EXPRESSIONS

$$b <= \alpha(x).NIL \qquad [12.1]$$

[12.1] gives an example of the forming of one agent from another by *guarding*. It is to be read 'b is an agent which accepts an input x through a port α and then behaves like *NIL*'. b is a *behaviour identifier*.

Definitions can be recursive. Consider [12.2], for example:

$$b <= \alpha(x).b \qquad [12.2]$$

This can be read 'b is an agent which accepts an input x through a port labelled α and then behaves like b'. And how does b behave ? Well, it inputs x through α and then inputs x through α and then. . . In other words, b loops infinitely.

To each label λ is associated a unique *complementary label*, denoted $\overline{\lambda}$. Barred labels represent output ports. Thus in [12.3], b takes in a pair of numbers x,y through its α port and delivers their product through its $\overline{\beta}$ port.

$$b <= \alpha(x,y).\overline{\beta}(x * y).b \qquad [12.3]$$

The complementation operation provides us with a means of determining inter-agent communication. If an agent p may make an output through a port $\overline{\lambda}$ and another agent q may receive an input through a port λ then the two agents combined have the option of communicating through the ports. If they do, the intercommunication is considered to be hidden from the rest of the world. A *silent action* takes place, for which we use the letter τ. The agent which results from the combination of p and q is denoted $p \mid q$.

Suppose we define p by [12.4]:

$$p <= \gamma(u,v,w,x).\overline{\alpha}(u+v,w+x).p \qquad [12.4]$$

then $p \mid b$ may behave as follows: p receives the numbers u,v,w,x and outputs the sums of u,v and w,x through an $\overline{\alpha}$ port. b *may* receive this output through its α port and then output the value of $(u+v)*(w+x)$.

We wrote *may*, because it is also possible that the two agents completely ignore each other. b, for example, retains the option of taking its input from the environment. What actually happens in such a case, whether p takes its input from b or elsewhere is resolved non-deterministically; either could happen.

We can force the agents to communicate by removing all possibility for an α or $\overline{\alpha}$ communication (the intercommunication could take place because it involves a τ action not an α action). This is the process of *hiding*. The resulting system is described by the expression $(p \mid b)\backslash\alpha$. If A is a set of labels $\{\lambda_1,...,\lambda_n\}$, then we write $b \backslash A$ to denote $b \backslash\lambda_1\backslash\lambda_2...\backslash\lambda_n$.

Thus, $(p \mid b)\backslash\alpha$ *must* perform a τ action corresponding to exchange of data across α ports. It no longer has the option of performing visible α or $\overline{\alpha}$ communications.

It is important to note that $\mid$ is very different from parallel composition of Mealy machines. Apart from the fact that there is no intercommunication of information in Mealy machines, parallel composition is *synchronous*; the system 'clocks' simultaneously. In CCS, two agents with no possibility of intercommunicating do not have to 'keep in step'. Synchronization does not come for free in CCS.*

Non-determinism can arise from $\mid$ composition, but it may also be programmed explicitly. Consider the following equations:

$$rand <= b(1) \qquad [12.5]$$

$$b(n) <= \tau.b(n+1) + \overline{\beta}(n).NIL$$

'+' stands for non-deterministic choice; $b(n)$ may either perform a τ action to become an agent $b(n+1)$ or it may choose to output n and die; *rand* is a random number generator.

Sometimes, however, we would like to make choice dependent on some Boolean condition. CCS contains an <u>if</u>–<u>*then*</u>–<u>*else*</u> construct to allow this. For example, in [12.6], the agent *parity* uses the construct to test the parity of a stream of input numbers.

$$parity <= \alpha(n).\underline{\text{if}}\ (n\ DIV\ 2)*2 = 2 \qquad [12.6]$$

$$\underline{then}\ \overline{\beta}(even).parity\ \underline{else}\ \overline{\beta}(odd).parity$$

There is one final operation, which is useful in cases where a system contains multiple copies of a single agent. This is the renaming operation. Again, we illustrate with an example. A simple binary cell could be described by:

$$cell <= \alpha(n).\overline{\beta}(n).cell \qquad [12.7]$$

* There is a version of CCS, *synchronous CCS*, in which this is not the case.

Suppose you want to define a number of cells $cell_i$. Defining:

$$cell_i <= cell\,[\alpha_i/\alpha,\beta_i/\beta] \qquad [12.8]$$

produces a copy of *cell* in which α is replaced by α_i and β is replaced by β_i.

We now give the rules for forming CCS expressions.

Agents pass values around. We assume a set of variable names, $x, y, \ldots$ and constants and function symbols standing for known total functions over values. With these, we may construct expressions involving both variables and constants.

We assume a set Λ of port names and $\overline{\Lambda}$ of their complementary names.

12.2.1 Definition

(a) *NIL* is a behaviour expression; it is an agent that does nothing.

(b) If B is a behaviour expression then $\tau.B$ is a behaviour expression. If $\mu \in \Lambda$ and $x_1, \ldots, x_n$ are variables, then $\mu(x_1, \ldots, x_n).B$ is a behaviour expression. If $\mu \in \Lambda$ and $E_1, \ldots, E_n$ are value expressions, then $\overline{\mu}(E_1, \ldots, E_n).B$ is a behaviour expression.

(c) If B and B' are expressions, then $B + B'$ is a behaviour expression.

(d) If B and B' are expressions, then $B \mid B'$ is a behaviour expression.

(e) If B is a behaviour expression and $A \subseteq \Lambda \cup \overline{\Lambda} - \{\tau\}$, then $B \backslash A$ is a behaviour expression.

(f) If B is a Boolean predicate and B_1, B_2 are expressions, then <u>if</u> B <u>then</u> B_1 <u>else</u> B_2 is a behaviour expression.

(g) If B is a behaviour expression and α and α' are distinct port names, then $B\,[\alpha/\alpha']$ is a behaviour expression. We will write $B\,[\alpha_1, \ldots, \alpha_n/\alpha'_1, \ldots, \alpha'_n]$ for $B\,[\alpha_1/\alpha'_1] \ldots [\alpha_n/\alpha'_n]$.

(h) Behaviour identifiers are expressions.

Finally, if b is a behaviour identifier and B is a behaviour expression then we write $b <= B$ as an equation signifying that b is to have the behaviour determined by B.

Let us now look at another example, which not only uses most of the operations we have defined but also illustrates how much more powerful CCS is than the language of finite state automata.

12.2.2 Example: Eratosthenes

The sieve of Eratosthenes is a well-known way of generating the list of prime numbers. The method goes like this.

(a) Initially, we have $p_1 = 2$; 2 is the first prime number.

(b) At step n, you have discovered p_n to be the nth prime number. Strike out all higher multiples of p_n, i.e. $2.p_n$, $3.p_n$ etc. Let p_{n+1} be the smallest remaining number bigger that p_n.

Any number between p_n and p_{n+1} has been struck out and is therefore composite (is the product of two smaller numbers each bigger than 1). Since, by induction, $2,...,p_n$ are the first n prime numbers, either p_{n+1} is prime or divisible by one of the p_i, for $i \le n$. But if the latter were true, p_{n+1} would have been struck out. Thus, p_{n+1} is prime and since the numbers between p_n and p_{n+1} are composite, it is the n+1th prime.

We shall describe a distributed form of this algorithm based on a version due to Professor C.A.R. Hoare.

The system is composed of various kinds of agent. The first, which we call *source* simply generates the sequence of integer:

$$source(n) <= \overline{\alpha}_0(n).source(n+1) \qquad [12.9]$$

The rest of the system is dynamically generated from an agent called *rest*; *rest* has the task of generating a sequence of linked cells each of whose task is to sieve out multiples of a particular prime number.

$$rest(n) <= (cell_n \mid rest(n+1))\backslash\alpha_n \qquad [12.10]$$

The life cycle of a typical cell is as follows. It receives a stream of numbers through an α port. The first number it receives, it assumes to be prime, and broadcasts it through a $\overline{\beta}$ port. This number becomes 'its' prime number. From then on, it will copy incoming numbers through to an $\overline{\alpha}$ port providing they are not multiples of its prime number.

A generic cell thus has the form:

$$cell <= \alpha(x).\overline{\beta}(x).cell(x) \qquad [12.11]$$

$$cell(x) <= \alpha(y).\underline{if}\ (x\ DIV\ y)*y = x \qquad [12.12]$$

$$\underline{then}\ cell(x)\ \underline{else}\ \overline{\gamma}(y).cell(x)$$

A typical cell is now obtained by:

$$cell_n <= cell[\alpha_{n-1}/\alpha, \beta_n/\beta, \alpha_n/\gamma] \qquad [12.13]$$

The whole system may now be defined:

$$Eratosthenes <= (source\,(2) \mid rest\,(1))\backslash\alpha_0 \qquad [12.14]$$

Eratosthenes can be thought of as defining an infinite sequence of cells connected together as in Fig. 12.1.

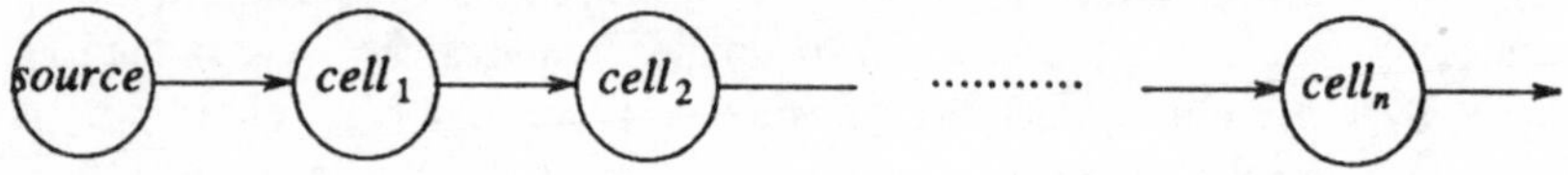

Fig. 12.1

We have yet to explain the formal machinery by which the behaviour of CCS systems are described, but we might see intuitively how the sieve works by considering the 'life cycle' of an individual cell, say $cell_1$.

Initially, it will receive an input 2 from *source*. It will output this through $\overline{\beta_1}$ and turn into $cell_1(2)$. From then on, it will transfer only odd numbers from α_0 to $\overline{\alpha}_1$. Thus, for example, the first input to $cell_2$ will be 3; $cell_2$ will therefore sieve out all numbers which are multiples of 3, and so on.

We see one very obvious difference between CCS and automata theory. As *Eratosthenes* progresses, it generates more and more states. CCS allows us to model 'dynamic process creation', which certainly may not be done with Mealy machines.

We note also that each cell has an infinite input set and an infinite output set. Specifically, cell n will receive as inputs, all numbers not divisible by the first n primes and will produce as ouputs, the n+1th prime and all numbers not divisible by the first n+1 primes. Both these sets are infinite. We could not describe cells using Mealy machines.

We will resume our discussion of the relationship between the two theories after a discussion of the semantics of CCS.

12.3 THE BEHAVIOUR OF CCS SYSTEMS

A behaviour expression determines sequences of communications, representing the visible behaviour of some agent. In CCS, a system is characterized by the patterns of communications they offer to an environment or 'observer'.

We may describe this behaviour by derivations of the form:

$$B_1 \rightarrow^{\mu\underline{v}} B_2$$

to indicate that an agent described by B_1 has the capability of making a $\mu\underline{v}$ communication, after which the agent behaves like B_2. $\underline{v}$ is a vector of values $(v_1, ..., v_n)$ being passed in or out of μ.

For example:

$$cell_5 \rightarrow^{\alpha_4(11)} \overline{\beta_5(11)}.cell(11)$$

To each construction of definition 12.2.1, there corresponds a rule showing how such a system behaves in one 'step'.

12.3.1 Definition

Let B, B' B'', B_i, B'_i be expressions, μ a label and b a behaviour identifier.

1 *NIL* has no actions: $NIL \rightarrow^{\mu} B$ is false for all μ, B.

2 There are three cases:

$$\mu(x_1, ..., x_n).B \rightarrow^{\mu(v_1, ..., v_n)} B\{v_1/x_1, ..., v_n/x_n\}$$

$$\overline{\mu}(v_1, ..., v_n).B \rightarrow^{\overline{\mu}(v_1, ..., v_n)} B$$

$$\tau.B \rightarrow^{\tau} B$$

3 Summation: the composite agent has the capabilities of both:

$$\frac{B \rightarrow^{\mu\underline{v}} B''}{B + B' \rightarrow^{\mu\underline{v}} B''} \qquad \frac{B' \rightarrow^{\mu\underline{v}} B''}{B + B' \rightarrow^{\mu\underline{v}} B''}$$

4 Communication: the composite may allow its composites to behave independently or handshake, producing a silent (τ) action:

$$\frac{B \rightarrow^{\mu\underline{v}} B''}{B \mid B' \rightarrow^{\mu\underline{v}} B'' \mid B'} \qquad \frac{B' \rightarrow^{\mu\underline{v}} B''}{B \mid B' \rightarrow^{\mu\underline{v}} B \mid B''}$$

$$\frac{B_1 \rightarrow^{\mu\underline{v}} B'_1 \text{ and } B_2 \rightarrow^{\overline{\mu}\underline{v}} B'_2}{B_1 \mid B_2 \rightarrow^{\tau} B'_1 \mid B'_2}$$

5 Restriction: the agent may perform any action which is not indicated by the restriction set:

$$\frac{B \rightarrow^{\mu\underline{v}} B' \text{ and } \{\mu,\overline{\mu}\} \cap A = \varnothing}{B \setminus A \rightarrow^{\mu\underline{v}} B' \setminus A}$$

6 Conditional choice:

$$\frac{B \rightarrow^{\mu\underline{v}} B''}{\underline{\text{if}}\ \textbf{true}\ \underline{then}\ B\ \underline{else}\ B' \rightarrow^{\mu\underline{v}} B''}$$

$$\frac{B' \rightarrow^{\mu\underline{v}} B''}{\underline{\text{if}}\ \textbf{false}\ \underline{then}\ B\ \underline{else}\ B' \rightarrow^{\mu\underline{v}} B''}$$

7 Relabelling:

$$\frac{B \rightarrow^{\mu\underline{v}} B'}{B\,[\nu\backslash\mu] \rightarrow^{\nu\underline{v}} B'\,[\nu\backslash\mu]}$$

8 Assignment: the behaviour identifier is associated with the behaviour of the defining expression:

$$\frac{b \mathrel{<=} B\,\{v_1/x_1, \ldots, v_{n(b)}/x_{n(b)}\} \text{ and } B \rightarrow^{\mu\underline{v}} B'}{b\,(v_1, \ldots, v_{n(b)}) \rightarrow^{\mu\underline{v}} B'}$$

We give an example: for simplicity, we will not bother with value passing.

$$b \mathrel{<=} \alpha.b_1 + (\beta.\overline{\gamma}.b_2 \mid \gamma.b_2)\backslash\gamma \qquad [12.15]$$

(a) $\alpha.b_1 \rightarrow^{\alpha} b_1$, by 12.3.1(2).

(b) Thus, $\alpha.b_1 + (\beta.\overline{\gamma}.b_2 \mid \gamma.b_2)\backslash\gamma \rightarrow^{\alpha} b_1$, by (a) and 12.3.1(3).

(c) Thus, $b \rightarrow^{\alpha} b_1$, by (b) and 12.3.1(8).

(d) Also, $\beta.\overline{\gamma}.b_2 \rightarrow^{\beta} \overline{\gamma}.b_2$, by 12.3.1(2).

(e) Thus, $(\beta.\overline{\gamma}.b_2 \mid \gamma.b_3) \rightarrow^{\beta} (\overline{\gamma}.b_2 \mid \gamma.b_3)$, by (d) and 12.3.1(4).

(f) Thus, $(\beta.\overline{\gamma}.b_2 \mid \gamma.b_3)\backslash\gamma \rightarrow^{\beta} (\overline{\gamma}.b_2 \mid \gamma.b_3)\backslash\gamma$, by (e) and 12.3.1(5).

(g) Thus, $\alpha.b_1 + (\beta.\overline{\gamma}.b_2 \mid \gamma.b_3)\backslash\gamma \rightarrow^{\beta} (\overline{\gamma}.b_2 \mid \gamma.b_3)\backslash\gamma$, by (f) and 12.3.1(3).

(h) Thus, $b \rightarrow^{\beta} (\overline{\gamma}.b_2 \mid \gamma.b_3)\backslash\gamma$, by (g) and 12.3.1(8).

(i) We also have $\overline{\gamma}.b_2 \rightarrow^{\overline{\gamma}} b_2$ and $\gamma.b_2 \rightarrow^{\gamma} b_2$ by 12.3.1(2) and hence $(\overline{\gamma}.b_2 \mid \gamma.b_3) \rightarrow^{\tau} (b_2 \mid b_3)$, by 12.3.1(4).

(j) Thus, $(\overline{\gamma}.b_2 \mid \gamma.b_3)\backslash\gamma \rightarrow^{\tau} (b_2 \mid b_3)\backslash\gamma$, by (i) and 12.3.1(5).

We may now define sequences of communications possible to a behaviour expression.

12.3.2 Definition

Let $s \in (\Lambda \cup \overline{\Lambda})^*$. If B and B' are expressions and μ is a label, then we define:

(a) $B \mid\Rightarrow^{\varepsilon} B$ where ε denotes the null string.

(b) $B \mid\Rightarrow^{\mu.s} B'$ if and only if there exists B'' such that $B \rightarrow^{\mu} B''$ and $B'' \mid\Rightarrow^{s} B'$.

Now, the string s in an expression $B \mid\Rightarrow^{s} B'$ may very well contain τ actions. Indeed, the only systems which do not produce τ actions are systems in which no communication takes place. But τ actions are supposed to be invisible. We shall say that s is a visible sequence of actions from B to B' and write $B \Rightarrow^{s} B'$ if $s \in (\Lambda \cup \overline{\Lambda})^* - \{\tau\}$ and there exists $s' \in (\Lambda \cup \overline{\Lambda})^*$ such that $B \mid\Rightarrow^{s'} B'$ and $s' \mid_{\tau} = s$. Here, $s' \mid_{\tau}$ denotes the string obtained from s' by erasing all τs.

For example $\sigma\tau\alpha\tau\tau\overline{\beta}\mid_{\tau} = \sigma\alpha\overline{\beta}$.

Let us now define $\Lambda(B) = \{\lambda \mid B \mid\Rightarrow^{s.\lambda},\ \textit{some } s\}$.

12.4 CCS COMPARED TO AUTOMATA THEORY

CCS is obviously more powerful than the theory of Mealy machines. For example, it has value passing and a form of dynamic process creation which allows it to handle systems, like *Eratosthenes*, which have an unbounded number of 'states'. Indeed, even without value passing, it is possible to simulate any given Turing machine in CCS. Most importantly, CCS may be interpreted as describing *distributed systems*.

CCS is not a generalization of automata theory to the same extent as net theory; its origins lie closer to λ-calculus. However, it may be instructive to examine some correspondences.

Given a Mealy machine M it is easy enough to simulate M in CCS. Define:

$$b_M(s) <= \iota(i).\overline{\theta}(\beta(s,i)).b_M(\delta(s,i))$$

Can we transfer ideas of homomorphism, behavioural equivalence, composition and decomposition from automata theory to CCS ?

As for composition, it is plainly unnecessary to erect such a theory on top of CCS, because CCS is built round composition. We may use the operations that are already there to simulate serial and parallel composition. For example, serial composition may be defined:

$$b_M(s) \ominus b_{M'}(s') <= (b_M(s)[\gamma/\theta] \mid b_{M'}(s')[\gamma/\iota])\backslash\gamma$$

Such constructs add nothing to the power of synthesis of the calculus. The question of behavioural equivalence is much more interesting.

In Chapter 5, we said that two machines are behaviourally equivalent if they have exactly the same potential input/output behaviour. Two such machines would be interchangeable.

If we were to attempt to generalize this to CCS agents, then the first thing we would notice is that CCS agents can be non-deterministic, so that the relationship between input and output is not necessarily functional. We also notice that whereas a Mealy machine has only one input and one output port, a CCS agent may have several (or none !) of each. Lastly, inputs and outputs do not strictly alternate.

Instead of comparing input/output, we compare the sequences of inputs and outputs intermixed. For this we may use either the $\mid\Rightarrow$ or $\Rightarrow$ relations described above. We then might be tempted to define:

$$B \equiv B' \text{ if and } \textit{only} \text{ if for } \textit{all } s,\ B \mid\Rightarrow^s \Leftrightarrow B' \mid\Rightarrow^s \qquad [12.16]$$

or

$$B \equiv B' \text{ if and } \textit{only} \text{ if for } \textit{all } s,\ B \Rightarrow^s \Leftrightarrow B' \Rightarrow^s \qquad [12.17]$$

[12.16] is rather too strong. For example, we would like to regard *Eratosthenes* as being equivalent to an agent that simply spits out the sequence of primes. [12.16] would distinguish between the two, because *Eratosthenes*, as well as spitting out primes, also performs numerous τ actions. We therefore turn to [12.17].

Unfortunately, there are problems here as well. The trouble is that unlike Mealy machines, in which each input/output sequence determines a unique final state, a CCS agent may be capable of performing a sequence which could lead to two different states. Consider the following example, which is adapted from Milner (1980) p.9.

$$S <= \alpha.(\beta.NIL + \gamma.\delta.S)$$

$$T <= \alpha.\beta.NIL + \alpha.\gamma.\delta.T$$

Both agents have the same 'language' of strings, but we may argue that they have different behaviour. In S, we have perfect control over the termination of the machine. After α, we can decide whether to stop it, by performing a β action or allowing it to continue, by performing a γ action. In T we have no such control. On input α, the machine itself decides which branch to go along. Termination is out of our control.

We therefore need a more subtle way of comparing agents. This is the observational equivalence, defined in the next section.

12.5 OBSERVATIONAL EQUIVALENCE AND OTHER BEHAVIOURAL EQUIVALENCES

In our explanation of the *Eratosthenes* system, we explained that we believed that the behaviour of the system, ignoring τ *actions* was a sequence $\overline{\omega}_2\overline{\omega}_3\overline{\omega}_5 \cdots$. Another way of saying this is that *Eratosthenes* is a device which spits out the prime numbers in sequence. Yet another way of saying this is that if we *had* such a device and compared it with *Eratosthenes*, then they would be indistinguishable from each other. Formally, we would say that they were *observationally equivalent*.

12.5.1 Definition

Let B_1, B_2 be expressions. We shall say that they are observationally equivalent (and write $B_1 \approx B_2$) if $B_1 \approx_n B_2$, for all natural numbers n, where:

(a) We always have $B_1 \approx_0 B_2$.

(b) $B_1 \approx_{n+1} B_2$ if and only if,

  (i) if $B_1 \Rightarrow^s B'_1$ then there exists B'_2 such that $B_2 \Rightarrow^s B'_2$ and $B'_1 \approx_n B'_2$

  (ii) if $B_2 \Rightarrow^s B'_2$ then there exists B'_1 such that $B_1 \Rightarrow^s B'_1$ and $B'_1 \approx_n B'_2$.

We may now explain precisely what we intend *Eratosthenes* to do. Suppose we define:

$$primes <= primes(1)$$

$$primes(n) <= \overline{\beta}_n(p_n).primes(n+1)$$

where p_n denotes the nth prime number.

Our requirement that *Eratosthenes* generates the sequence of prime numbers may now be stated formally as:

$$Eratosthenes \approx primes$$

Incidentally, if there are objections to our definition of *primes*, that it requires a knowledge of the sequence of primes, then we may use a result from number theory called *Wilson's Theorem*, which states that a number n is prime if and only if n divides $(n - 1)! + 1$, to produce a more 'computational' definition.

$$primes \Leftarrow primes_1(2)$$

$$primes_k(n) \Leftarrow \underline{if}\ [((n-1)!+1)\ DIV\ n]*n = (n-1)!+1$$
$$\underline{then}\ \overline{\beta_k}(n).primes_{k+1}(n+1)$$
$$\underline{else}\ primes_k(n+1)$$

Returning to the example, we see here an illustration of a very important use of observational equivalence and behavioural equivalence generally. It allows us to assert that an agent representing a specification of some system is indistinguishable from an agent representing an implementation of that system. In other words, it gives us a precise way to assert that an implementation meets a specification. (Compare the discussion in Chapter 4.)

It is not always easy to show directly that two agents are observationally equivalent. Some of the work may be eased by the use of the identities presented in the next proposition.

12.5.2 Proposition

1 $\approx$ is an equivalence relation.

2 Let B_1, B_2, B_3 be agents, then:
(a) $B_1 + B_2 \approx B_2 + B_1$
(b) $B_1 + (B_2 + B_3) \approx (B_1 + B_2) + B_3$
(c) $B + NIL \approx B$
(d) $B + B \approx B$.

3 Let B_1, B_2, B_3 be agents, then:
(a) $B_1 \mid B_2 \approx B_2 \mid B_1$
(b) $B_1 \mid (B_2 \mid B_3) \approx (B_1 \mid B_2) \mid B_3$

(c) $B \mid NIL \approx B$.

4 Let B, B_1, B_2 be agents, then:
(a) If $\alpha, \bar{\alpha} \notin \Lambda(B)$, then $B \approx B \backslash \alpha$
(b) $NIL \backslash \alpha \approx NIL$
(c) $(B_1 + B_2) \backslash \alpha \approx B_1 \backslash \alpha + B_2 \backslash \alpha$
(d) If $\alpha, \bar{\alpha} \notin \Lambda(B_1) \cap \overline{\Lambda(B_2)}$, then $(B_1 \mid B_2) \backslash \alpha \approx B_1 \backslash \alpha \mid B_2 \backslash \alpha$.

5 Let B, B_1, B_2 be agents, then if $B_1 \approx B_2$ then:
(a) $\alpha.B_1 \approx \alpha.B_2$
(b) $B_1 \mid B \approx B_2 \mid B$
(c) $B_1 \backslash A \approx B_2 \backslash A$
(d) $B_1[S] \approx B_2[S]$, where S is a relabelling.

6 $\tau.B \approx B$.

Since + is commutative and associative, we may unambiguously define the sum of any finite number of agents. If $X = \{B_1, ..., B_n\}$, then we define $\sum_{i=1}^{n} B_i$ to be $B_1 + B_2 + \cdots + B_n$.

12.5.3 Proposition

Suppose $B <= \sum_{i=1}^{n} g_i.B_i$ and $C <= \sum_{j=1}^{m} g'_j.C_j$, then:

$$\begin{aligned} B \mid C \approx & \sum_{i=1}^{n} g_i.(B_i \mid C) \\ & + \sum_{j=1}^{m} g'_j.(B \mid C_j) \\ & + \sum \tau.(B_i[E/x] \mid C_j) \; g_i = \alpha x \text{ and } g'_j = \bar{\alpha}E \\ & + \sum \tau.(B_i \mid C_j[E/x]) \; g'_j = \alpha x \text{ and } g_i = \bar{\alpha}E \end{aligned}$$

The proof is in Milner (1980).

We may use these rules to begin an analysis of *Eratosthenes*. First of all, let us extend rule 5(b) slightly, to:

$$B_1 \approx B_2 \;\&\; B'_1 \approx B'_2 \Rightarrow B_1 \mid B_2 \approx B'_1 \mid B'_2$$

since

$$B_1 \mid B_2 \approx B'_1 \mid B_2 \; (5(b))$$

$$\approx B_2 \mid B'_1 \ (3(a))$$
$$\approx B'_2 \mid B'_1 \ (5(b))$$
$$\approx B'_1 \mid B'_2 \ (3(a))$$

Now define:

$$front(0) <= source(2)$$
$$front(n+1) <= front(n) \mid cell_{n+1}$$

Thus, $front(n) = source(2) \mid cell_1 \mid \cdots \mid cell_n$.
Define, $A_n = \{\alpha_0, ..., \alpha_n\}$. We claim that for all n:

$$Eratosthenes \approx (front(n) \mid rest(n+1)) \backslash A_n \qquad [12.19]$$

The proof is by induction. Certainly [12.19] is true if $n = 0$ (by [12.14]). Suppose true for n, we prove for $n+1$.

Let us note, first of all, that neither α_{n+1}, nor $\overline{\alpha}_{n+1}$ belong to $\Lambda(front(n))$. Thus, by 4(a) of 12.5.2:

$$front(n) \approx front(n) \backslash \alpha_{n+1} \qquad [12.20]$$

By definition [12.10], we also have:

$$rest(n+1) \approx (cell_{n+1} \mid rest(n+2)) \backslash \alpha_{n+1} \qquad [12.21]$$

So, by [12.20], [12.21] using [12.18], we have:

$$(front(n) \mid rest(n+1)) \backslash A_n \qquad [12.22]$$
$$\approx ((front(n) \backslash \alpha_{n+1}) \mid (cell_{n+1} \mid rest(n+2)) \backslash \alpha_{n+1})) \backslash A_n$$

But neither α_{n+1} nor $\overline{\alpha}_{n+1}$ belong to:
$\Lambda(front(n)) \cap \overline{\Lambda(cell_{n+1} \mid rest(n+2))}$ and so, by 4(d) of 12.5.2:

$$((front(n) \backslash \alpha_{n+1}) \mid (cell_{n+1} \mid rest(n+2)) \backslash \alpha_{n+1})) \backslash A_n \qquad [12.23]$$
$$\approx (front(n) \mid (cell_{n+1} \mid rest(n+2))) \backslash \alpha_{n+1} \backslash A_n$$
$$\approx (front(n) \mid (cell_{n+1} \mid rest(n+2))) \backslash A_{n+1}$$

Finally, by 3(b) of 12.5.2, we have:

$$front(n) \mid (cell_{n+1} \mid rest(n+2)) \qquad [12.24]$$

$$\approx (front(n) \mid cell_{n+1}) \mid rest(n+2)$$
$$\approx front(n+1) \mid rest(n+2)$$

Thus:

$$(front(n) \mid (cell_{n+1} \mid rest(n+2))\backslash A_{n+1} \approx (front(n+1) \mid rest(n+2))\backslash A_{n+1} \quad [12.25]$$

But, by [12.22], [12.23] and [12.24]:

$$(front(n) \mid rest(n+1))\backslash A_n \approx (front(n) \mid (cell_{n+1} \mid rest(n+2))\backslash A_{n+1} \quad [12.26]$$

and so from [12.25] and [12.26], it follows that:

$$(front(n) \mid rest(n+1))\backslash A_n \approx (front(n+1) \mid rest(n+2))\backslash A_{n+1} \quad [12.27]$$

The induction step is now easy, for if *Eratosthenes* $\approx (front(n) \mid rest(n+1))\backslash A_n$, then by [12.27] *Eratosthenes* $\approx (front(n+1) \mid rest(n+2))\backslash A_{n+1}$.

The reader may have noticed that $\approx$ has many of the properties of $=$. However, there is one property it does not have. If $B_1 \approx B_2$, it is *not* true in general that $B_1 + B \approx B_2 + B$. Milner gives the example $B_1 = NIL$, $B_2 = \tau.NIL$, $B = \alpha.NIL$.

In technical terms, $\approx$ is not a congruence.*

The following relation, which is stronger than observational equivalence, *is* a congruence.

12.5.4 Definition

Let B_1, B_2 be expressions. We shall say that they are *strongly congruent* (and write $B_1 \sim B_2$) if $B_1 \sim_n B_2$, for all natural numbers n, where:

* Roughly speaking, a congruence is an equivalence relation that *respects* the operations of an algebra. For example $=$ $(mod\ n)$ is a congruence on the integers, because it respects addition and multiplication that is, if $a_1 = a_2\ (mod\ n)$, then $a_1 + a = a_2 + a\ (mod\ n)$ and $a_1 \times a = a_2 \times a\ (mod\ n)$. The equivalence relation associated with a given SP partition may also be considered a congruence.

(a) we always have $B_1 \sim_0 B_2$.
(b) $B_1 \sim_{n+1} B_2$ if and only if;
  (i) if $B_1 \to^{\mu} B'_1$ then there exists B'_2 such that $B_2 \to^{\mu} B'_2$ and $B'_1 \sim_n B'_2$
  (ii) if $B_2 \to^{\mu} B'_2$ then there exists B'_1 such that $B_1 \to^{\mu} B'_1$ and $B'_1 \sim_n B'_2$.

12.5.5 Proposition

$\sim$ satisfies all the properties of $\approx$ given in propositions 12.5.2 and 12.5.3 except 6. In addition:
(a) $B_1 \sim B_2 \Rightarrow B_1 \approx B_2$
(b) $B_1 \sim B_2 \Rightarrow B_1 + B \sim B_2 + B$.

$\sim$ is still rather strong; every τ action counts in establishing strong congruence. In particular, we would not have *Eratosthenes* $\sim$ *primes*, since the former has τ actions while the latter does not.

The following relation mediates between the two. It disregards 'harmless' τ actions but is still a congruence.

12.5.6 Definition

Define $\approx^c$ to be the smallest congruence bigger than $\approx$. If $B \approx^c B'$ then B and B' will be said to be *observationally congruent*.

12.5.7 Proposition

$B_1 \sim B_2 \Rightarrow B_1 \approx^c B_2 \Rightarrow B_1 \approx B_2$.

$\approx^c$ satisfies all the properties of $\sim$ given in proposition 12.5.5. In addition, it satisfies the following four τ Laws. If g is a guard, then:
(a) $g.\tau.B \approx^c g.B$
(b) $B + \tau.B \approx^c \tau.B$
(c) $g.(B + \tau.C) + g.C \approx^c g.(B + C)$
(d) $B + \tau.(B + C) \approx^c \tau.(B + C)$.

NOTES

At the time of writing, the only text on CCS outside of learned journals is Milner (1980). The book was based on a series of lectures given to postgraduates at Aarhus University and is accordingly a very readable introduction to the calculus.

Appendix

Sets, Relations and Functions

There are self-styled *programmers* who imagine that Computing Science can get along without even the most elementary parts of Set Theory. In precisely the same way a donkey can get along without legs; it simply pulls itself forwards by its teeth.

F. X. REID (attrib.)

A.1 SETS AND SET OPERATIONS

The notion of a *set* is one of the most fundamental in mathematics. Most objects in mathematics may be regarded as sets in some form or other (a rather complicated form, perhaps). It is not uncommon to find the definition of some new entity beginning, 'Let X be a set', or containing phrases such as 'where A, B and C are sets'. See the definition of Mealy automata, for instance.

A.1.1 Definition

A set is a collection of entities called the *elements* or *members* of the set.

If a set is small enough, we may describe it by giving a list of its elements between braces '{' and '}'. Thus, the set of all positive integers from 2 to 5 inclusive is written $\{2,3,4,5\}$.

If x is an element of a set X, we write $x \in X$.

Thus, we have $5 \in \{2,3,4,5\}$.

A.1.2 Example

We shall frequently be using the following example to illustrate set theoretic ideas.

The University of Dystopia is divided into five colleges named after famous historical personages, namely Attila the Hun, Ghengis Khan, Timur the Lame, Count Dracula and Dr F. X. Reid. If C denotes the set of all colleges at the University of Dystopia, then we have:

$$C = \{Attila, Ghengis, Timur, Dracula, Reid\}$$

Let S denote the set of all students at the university, let M denote the set of all male students, let F denote the set of all female students and let X denote the set of all other students.

Each student belongs to exactly one of the colleges. Let A, G, T, D and R denote the sets of all students at Attila, Ghengis, Timur, Dracula and Reid respectively.

A.1.3 Definition

Two sets are considered equal (we use the normal "=") precisely when they have the same elements.

Formally, equality is defined:

$$A = B \text{ if and only if } x \in A \Leftrightarrow x \in B$$

Here '$\Leftrightarrow$' is logical equivalence. The statement $p \Leftrightarrow q$ is true if and only if either both p and q are true or p and q are false.

Note that from the definition, we have $\{x, y\} = \{y, x\}$, that is, the order in which the elements are written is not important.

One set crops up very frequently, and that is the *empty* or *null* set, the set with no elements, usually denoted by $\varnothing$.

A.1.4 Definition

If every element of a set A also belongs to a set B, then we say that A is a *subset* of B or that A is included in B. We write $A \subseteq B$ to denote this. Formally:

$$A \subseteq B \text{ if and only if } x \in A \Rightarrow x \in B.$$

Here, '$\Rightarrow$' is logical implication. $p \Rightarrow q$ is true either if both p and q are true or if p is false. Since:

$$p \Leftrightarrow q \text{ if and only if } p \Rightarrow q \ \& \ q \Rightarrow p$$

we can conclude that:

$$A = B \text{ if and only if } A \subseteq B \ \& \ B \subseteq A.$$

'&' is being written here for logical 'and'.

If $A \subseteq B$ and $A \neq B$ then we say that A is a proper subset of B and write $A \subset B$.

A.1.5 Examples

Returning to our previous examples, we see that $M \subseteq S$, $F \subseteq S$, $X \subseteq S$, $A \subseteq S$, $G \subseteq S$, $T \subseteq S$, $D \subseteq S$ and $R \subseteq S$. It is also the case that $\varnothing \subseteq X$ for every set X. Let us see why this is true. By definition A.1.4, $\varnothing \subseteq X$ if and only if:

$$x \in \varnothing \Rightarrow x \in X \qquad \text{[A.1]}$$

Now, $x \in \varnothing$ is always false – because $\varnothing$ is empty – and as we have said, p'$\Rightarrow$'q is true when p is false. Thus, [A.1] is true.

A.1.6 Definition

Let A and B be sets, then there exists a set called the *intersection* of A and B, written $A \cap B$, which consists of precisely those elements which belong to both A and B. Formally, we would write:

$$A \cap B = \{x \mid x \in A \;\&\; x \in B\}$$

The expression on the right of the equals sign reads 'The set of all x such that x is a member of A and x is a member of B'.

A.1.7 Remark

Intersection satisfies both the *commutative law*:

$$A \cap B = B \cap A$$

and the *associative law*:

$$A \cap (B \cap C) = (A \cap B) \cap C$$

from which it follows that we may define the intersection of an arbitrary number of sets without needing to specify the order in which the intersections are made. If $\mathbf{X}$ is a set of sets, then we would write:

$$\bigcap_{X \in \mathbf{X}} X$$

or just $\bigcap \mathbf{X}$ to denote the intersection of the sets in $\mathbf{X}$.

A.1.8 Example

Returning to our examples, we have $F \cap M = \varnothing$ (assuming that there are no hermaphrodite students in the University). We also have that for any two sets X, Y in the set $\{A, G, T, D, R\}$ that $X \cap Y = \varnothing$ or $X = Y$, because nobody belongs to two colleges. Other intersections we might construct are $R \cap F$, the set of all female students belonging to Reid, or $D \cap M$, the set of male students in Dracula.

We also have $F \cap S = F$ and $M \cap S = M$. In fact, these last two equations are instances of a general result which says that for any two sets A and B:

$$A \subseteq B \Leftrightarrow A \cap B = A$$

If A and B are sets and $A \cap B = \varnothing$, then the sets A and B are said to be *disjoint*. Thus, the sets M and F in our example are disjoint.

A.1.9 Definition

Let A and B be sets, then there exists a set, called the *union* of A and B and written $A \cup B$ which contains every element of both A and B.

$$A \cup B = \{x \mid x \in A \vee x \in B\}$$

Here, '$\vee$' is the *inclusive* or.

A.1.10 Remark

Union satisfies both the *commutative law*:

$$A \cup B = B \cup A$$

and the *associative law*:

$$A \cup (B \cup C) = (A \cup B) \cup C$$

from which it follows that we may define the union of an arbitrary number of sets without needing to specify the order in which the unions are made. If **X** is a set of sets, then we would write:

$$\bigcup_{X \in \mathbf{X}} X$$

or just $\bigcup \mathbf{X}$ to denote the union of the sets in **X**.

A.1.11 Example

In our example, $M \cup F \cup X = S$ and $A \cup G \cup T \cup D \cup R = S$. Since the intersection of two sets or the union of two sets is also a set, we may combine these. Thus x is a member of $(F \cap (D \cup R)) \cup A$ if either x is a female student of either Dracula or Reid or x is a student (of any type) of Attila.

Note also that $M \cup S = S$ and that $F \cup S = S$. Again, these are instances of a general result, which says that:

$$A \subseteq B \Leftrightarrow A \cup B = B$$

A.1.12 Remark

Union and intersection obey the *distributive laws*:

$$A \cap (B \cup C) = (A \cap B) \cup (A \cap C)$$
$$A \cup (B \cap C) = (A \cup B) \cap (A \cup C)$$

Thus, for example:

$$(F \cap (D \cup R)) \cup A = ((F \cup D) \cap (F \cup R)) \cup A$$
$$= (F \cup D \cup A) \cap (F \cup R \cup A)$$

A.1.13 Definition

Let A and B be sets. The *difference* of A, B, written $A - B$ is defined:

$$A - B = \{x \in A \mid x \notin B\}$$

Here $x \notin B$ reads 'x is not a member of B'.

When forming sets, one has to be a little careful about using $\notin$. For example, if we were allowed to define $\mathbf{E} = \{x \mid x \notin \emptyset\}$ and then $\mathbf{U} = \underline{P}(\mathbf{E})$, then **U** would be the set of all sets, an object which cannot exist, because of *Russell's Paradox*.

The argument goes as follows. Suppose **X** is some set of sets, then it is perfectly legal to define $\tilde{\mathbf{X}} = \{A \in \mathbf{X} \mid A \notin A\}$. There is nothing wrong with this definition, and for 'ordinary' sets, it is usually the case that

$\tilde{\tilde{\mathbf{X}}} = \mathbf{X}$.

However, if **U** is a set, then $\tilde{\mathbf{U}} \neq \mathbf{U}$, since, **U** being a set of all sets, $\mathbf{U} \in \mathbf{U}$. However, there is something strange about $\tilde{\mathbf{U}}$.

For if $X \in \tilde{\mathbf{U}}$, then $X \notin X$ and so if $\tilde{\mathbf{U}} \in \tilde{\mathbf{U}}$, then $\tilde{\mathbf{U}} \notin \tilde{\mathbf{U}}$, a contradiction. Thus we cannot have $\tilde{\mathbf{U}} \in \tilde{\mathbf{U}}$ and so $\tilde{\mathbf{U}} \notin \tilde{\mathbf{U}}$. But, for any set X, if $X \notin X$, then $X \in \tilde{\mathbf{U}}$ and thus, in particular, since $\tilde{\mathbf{U}} \notin \tilde{\mathbf{U}}$ it follows that $\tilde{\mathbf{U}} \in \tilde{\mathbf{U}}$, another contradiction.

It follows that the **U** is not a set.

A.1.14 Definition

Let A be a set, the set of all subsets of A (and remember that both $\varnothing$ and A are subsets of A) is called the *powerset* of A. We shall denote it by $\underline{P}(A)$. Note that $\underline{P}(A)$ is a set whose members are themselves sets (we shall meet more examples of such sets later), and that:

$$X \subseteq A \Leftrightarrow X \in \underline{P}(A)$$

As an example, consider the set $A = \{1,2,3\}$. $\underline{P}(A)$ has eight elements, namely:

$$\varnothing, \{1\}, \{2\}, \{3\}, \{1,2\}, \{1,3\}, \{2,3\}, A$$

A.1.15 Definition

Let A be a set. A *partition* of A is a set of subsets of A such that every element of A belongs to exactly one of these subsets. We call these subsets the *blocks* of the partition and say that the blocks partition A.

Formally, a partition is a set $\pi \subseteq \underline{P}(A)$ such that:

(a) $\bigcup_{X \in \pi} X = A$.

(b) If X, $Y \in \pi$ then either $X = Y$ or $X \cap Y = \varnothing$. We shall write $\Pi(A)$ to denote the set of all partitions of a given set A.

A.1.16 Examples

We have already seen some examples of partitions. For example $\pi_{sex} = \{M, F, X\}$ and $\pi_{coll} = \{A, G, T, D, R\}$ are both partitions of the set S, since every student belongs to exactly one of the colleges and every student is either male or female...or whatever (but only one of each). Another partition, which we may obtain from the two above, is:

$$\pi_{both} = \{M \cap A, M \cap G, M \cap T, M \cap D, M \cap R, F \cap A, F \cap G,$$
$$F \cap T, F \cap D, F \cap R, X \cap A, X \cap G, X \cap T, X \cap D, X \cap R,\}$$

each student belonging to precisely one sex and precisely one college. Note that this partition is in some sense 'finer' than the two others, in that it divides the student body into a larger number of smaller sets. In fact, as we shall see, it is the 'largest' such refinement of the two. What we mean by 'larger' in this context will be explained in the next section (see A.2.6).

A.2 RELATIONS

Mathematics abounds in relations. Roughly, we may say that a relation is something that may or may not hold between two or more elements of a set or sets. Consider the set of positive whole numbers $\{0,1,2,...\}$ (usually denoted by **N**). Among the relations that may be defined on **N** are equality ($x = y$), inequality ($x \neq y$), the relation of being less than or equal to ($x \leq y$) and the relation 'divides' ($x \mid y$), which holds if $x.z = y$ for some $z \in$ **N**. We have also seen relations on sets, equality, inclusion and proper inclusion. In the set S of all students, we could define relations:

$=_{sex}$, *by* $x =_{sex} y$ *if and only if* x and y *are of the same sex.*

$=_{coll}$, *by* $x =_{coll} y$ *if and only if* x and y *are in the same college.*

Strictly speaking, these are all examples of binary relations, that is, they hold between two elements. We could also construct higher order relations. For example, the relation 'x lies between y and z', for points on a line, is a trinary relation.

Nor is it necessary that all the components in a relation be the same type. One practical use of relations is in the study of databases. A database may be considered a relation of the form 'x,y,z...' all are values in the same record, where x,y,z need not be of the same type.

But we have not yet said what a relation actually is. Let us consider the relation '<' on **N**. We have complete knowledge about this relation as we know exactly for which pairs x,y that $x < y$ is true. Of course, it is not sufficient to give merely the set of all such pairs; to say that x and y are in relation '<' does not tell us whether $x < y$ or $y < x$, and only one of these can be true. We must give the set of all such pairs in the right order.

Similarly, for higher order relations, we give lists of the n elements for which that relation holds. Such lists manifest themselves in a programming language as instances of a *record* type. Let us now try to formalize these ideas. Relations are sets of 'n-tuples' and n-tuples are elements of 'Cartesian products'.

A.2.1 Definition

The collection of all ordered pairs (a,b) where $a \in A$ and $b \in B$ is called the *Cartesian product* of A and B and is denoted $A \times B$.

For example, the set of points in the Cartesian plane is the Cartesian product of two copies of the real line. This is in fact the origin of the name; 'Cartesian' refers to the French philosopher and mathematician, René Descartes, the discoverer of coordinate geometry.

More generally, let $A_1, ..., A_n$ be sets, then the Cartesian product of the A_i, written $A_1 \times ... \times A_n$ is the set of all n-tuples $(a_1, ..., a_n)$, where $a_i \in A_i$, each i.

A.2.2 Definition

Let A be a set, then a (binary) relation R on A is a subset of $A \times A$. We usually write $x \; R \; y$ instead of $(x,y) \in R$.

A.2.3 Examples

We may now define the relations on S more precisely (or at least more correctly) by:

$$=_{sex} = \{(x,y) \in S \times S \mid \{x,y\} \subseteq M \vee \{x,y\} \subseteq F \vee \{x,y\} \subseteq X\}$$

$$=_{coll} = \{(x,y) \in S \times S \mid \{x,y\} \subseteq A \vee \{x,y\} \subseteq G$$
$$\vee \{x,y\} \subseteq T \vee \{x,y\} \subseteq D \vee \{x,$$

There are four properties of relations which are most frequently used.

A.2.4 Definition

Let A be a set and R a relation on A, then :

(a) R is *reflexive* if and only if $x \; R \; x$ for all $x \in A$.

(b) R is *asymmetric* if and only if $x \; R \; y \;\&\; y \; R \; x \Rightarrow x = y$, for all $x, y \in A$.

(c) R is *symmetric* if and only if $x \; R \; y \Rightarrow y \; R \; x$, for all $x, y \in A$.

(d) R is *transitive* if and only if $x \; R \; y \;\&\; y \; R \; z \Rightarrow x \; R \; z$, for all $x, y, z \in A$.

A.2.5 Definition

Let X be a set, R a relation on X, then:

(a) R is a *partial order* if it is reflexive asymmetric and transitive.

(b) R is an *equivalence relation* if it is reflexive, symmetric and transitive.

A.2.6 Examples

The order relation on numbers '$\leq$' is the prime example of a partial order.

Suppose A is a set, then the pair $(\underline{P}(A), \subseteq)$ is also a partially ordered set.

Another example is $(\mathbf{N}, |)$, where $x \mid y$ is to be read 'x divides y'.

For a final example of a partially ordered set, consider any set A and the set $\Pi(A)$ of all partitions of A. We may order these as follows:

$$\pi_1 \leq \pi_2 \Leftrightarrow X \in \pi_1 \Rightarrow X \subseteq Y, \ some\ Y \in \pi_2$$

For the partitions defined in A.1.15, we have $\pi_{both} \leq \pi_{coll}$ and $\pi_{both} \leq \pi_{sex}$.

We prove in Chapter 9 that $\leq$ is a partial order on partitions.

A.2.7 Examples

Equality '=' is certainly an equivalence relation (transitivity is equivalent to the axiom in Euclid that two things equal to a third thing are equal to each other).

Another example is that of equality modulo some number as a relation on the integers (positive and negative whole numbers). Say that $x = y\ mod(n)$ if $y - x$ is divisible by n. Certainly, 0 is divisible by n, and so $x = x\ mod(n)$; if $x - y$ is divisible by n then so is $y - x$, and so we have symmetry. Finally, if $x - y$ and $y - z$ are divisible by n, then so is $x - z = (x - y) + (y - z)$, and so we have transitivity.

The two relations $=_{sex}$ and $=_{coll}$ defined in A.2.3 are also equivalence relations.

The reader may have spotted a relationship between these two relations and the partitions π_{sex} and π_{coll} of A.1.15. Two persons are equivalent under $=_{coll}$ if and only if they belong to the same block of the partition π_{coll}. This is an instance of a general result, which we now state.

If R is a relation on a set X and $x \in X$, then we define $<x>_R$ to be the set of all y such that x is in the relation R to y.

$$\langle x \rangle_R = \{ y \in X \mid x \; R \; y \}.$$

$\langle x \rangle_R$ is called the 'R-class of x'.

Write X/R to denote the set of all $\langle x \rangle_R$ for $x \in X$.

A.2.8 Lemma

Suppose R is an equivalence relation on a set X, and let $x,y \in X$, then $x \in \langle y \rangle_R \Leftrightarrow \langle x \rangle_R = \langle y \rangle_R$.

Proof

First, suppose that $x \in \langle y \rangle_R$. If $u \in \langle x \rangle_R$, then by definition, $x \; R \; u$. Since $x \in \langle y \rangle_R$, we also have $y \; R \; x$. From $y \; R \; x$ and $x \; R \; u$, we have $y \; R \; u$ by transitivity of R. But $y \; R \; u$ implies $u \in \langle y \rangle_R$, by definition.

Thus $u \in \langle x \rangle_R \Rightarrow u \in \langle y \rangle_R$ and so $\langle x \rangle_R \subseteq \langle y \rangle_R$.

Now suppose that $u \in \langle y \rangle_R$, then $y \; R \; u$. Since $x \in \langle y \rangle_R$, we again have $y \; R \; x$ and hence $x \; R \; y$, by symmetry of R. Thus $x \; R \; y$ and $y \; R \; u$, whence $x \; R \; u$, by transitivity of R. But this means that $u \in \langle x \rangle_R$.

Thus $u \in \langle y \rangle_R \Rightarrow u \in \langle x \rangle_R$ and so $\langle y \rangle_R \subseteq \langle x \rangle_R$. Since we already know that $\langle x \rangle_R \subseteq \langle y \rangle_R$, it follows that $\langle y \rangle_R = \langle x \rangle_R$.

Conversely, suppose $\langle y \rangle_R = \langle x \rangle_R$. Since $x \; R \; x$, it follows that $x \in \langle x \rangle_R$. Since $\langle y \rangle_R = \langle x \rangle_R$, we must have $x \in \langle y \rangle_R$.

A.2.9 Proposition

(a) Let X be a set and R be an equivalence relation on X, then X/R is a partition. The sets $\langle x \rangle_R$ are called *equivalence classes* of the relation R.

(b) Let X be a set and π a partition on X, then the relation equiv(π), defined:

$$x \; equiv(\pi) \; y \textit{ if and only if } \{x,y\} \subseteq A, \textit{ some } A \in \pi$$

is an equivalence relation on X. Instead of writing $x \; equiv(\pi) \; y$ we shall write $x = y \; (\pi)$.

Proof

(a) First, we show that $\bigcup X/R = X$. Certainly $\bigcup X/R \subseteq X$. We must therefore show that $X \subseteq \bigcup X/R$. But if $x \in X$, then $x \in \langle x \rangle_R$, by reflexivity of R. Thus $x \in \bigcup X/R$ and we are done.

Next suppose $\langle x \rangle_R \cap \langle y \rangle_R \neq \emptyset$. We show that $\langle x \rangle_R = \langle y \rangle_R$. Indeed, if $z \in \langle x \rangle_R \cap \langle y \rangle_R$, then by lemma A.2.8, $\langle x \rangle_R = \langle z \rangle_R = \langle y \rangle_R$.

(b) Since $\bigcup \pi = X$, for every $x \in X$, we must have $x \in A$, some $A \in \pi$. But, this means that $\{x, x\} = \{x\} \subseteq A$ and so $x = x\ (\pi)$ for all $x \in X$. Thus *equiv* (π) is reflexive.

If $x = y\ (\pi)$, then $\{x, y\} \subseteq A$, some $A \in \pi$. Thus $\{y, x\} \subseteq A$ and so $y = x\ (\pi)$. Thus $x = y\ (\pi) \Rightarrow y = x\ (\pi)$ and *equiv* (π) is reflexive.

Finally suppose that $x = y\ (\pi)$ and $y = z\ (\pi)$ then there exists $A, B \in \pi$ such that $\{x, y\} \subseteq A$ $\{y, z\} \subseteq B$. But $z \in A \cap B$ and so $A = B$, since π is a partition. Thus $\{x, z\} \subseteq \{x, y\} \cup \{y, z\} \subseteq A \cup B = A$ and hence $x = z\ (\pi)$. Thus *equiv* (π) is transitive, and we are done.

A.3 FUNCTIONS

The reader will have met functions in the study of the calculus, but they may be defined between any pair of sets. Informally, if A and B are sets, then a function f is a rule that associates, to each element $a \in A$, a unique element $f(x)$ of B.

Formally, a function is made up of three things; A, its so called *domain*, B, its so-called *range* and a set Γ of ordered pairs $(a, b) \in A \times B$, where b is the element of B determined by a. (This set is called the *graph* of the function. By thinking of graphs of functions such as $\sin x$, see if you can see why.) The graph Γ is thus a relation.

A.3.1 Definition

A function is a triple (A, Γ, B), where A and B are sets and $\Gamma \subseteq A \times B$ satisfying:

(a) $a \in A \Rightarrow (a, b) \in \Gamma$, some $b \in B$;

(b) $(a, b_1) \in \Gamma\ \&\ (a, b_2) \in \Gamma \Rightarrow b_1 = b_2$.

If $f = (A, \Gamma, B)$ is a function we write $f : A \to B$ to indicate that f is a function with domain A and range B (or 'from A to B'), and write $f(x) = y$ to denote that y is the unique element of B such that $(x, y) \in \Gamma$.

Let A and B be sets and suppose $f : A \to B$ is a function.

A.3.2 Definition

If every element of A is sent to a *distinct* element of B, then f is said to be *injective* or *one-to-one*. Formally, f is injective if and only if:

$$\text{for all } x,\ y \in A : f(x) = f(y) \Rightarrow x = y$$

A.3.3 Example

The exponential function exp is injective as is log. The function:

$$f(x) = x^2$$

is not injective as a function from the reals to the positive reals, since we have $f(x) = f(-x)$, but it is as a function from the positive reals to the positive reals.

A.3.4 Definition

If every element of B equals $f(x)$, some $x \in A$, then f is said to be *surjective* or *onto*. Formally, f is surjective if and only if:

$$f(A) = B,\ \textit{where } f(A) = \{f(x) | x \in A\}$$

A.3.5 Examples

exp is not surjective considered as a function from the reals to the reals, since for no x is $exp(x)$ negative, but it is considered as a function from the reals to the positive reals.

A.3.6 Definition

If a function is both injective and surjective, then it is *bijective*.

It is not hard to see that there is a bijection between two finite sets if and only if they have the same number of elements. In fact, when one counts a finite set, one is implicitly establishing a bijection between that set and and initial segment of the natural numbers.

A.3.7 Definition

Suppose that A, B and C are sets and f, g are functions $f: A \to B$ and $g: B \to C$.

The *composite* of the functions f and g, written $g.f$, is the function $g.f: A \to C$ given by:

$$g.f(x) = g(f(x)).$$

If f is a bijection, then there is a function called its *inverse* and written f^{-1}, satisfying:

$$f(x) = y \Rightarrow f^{-1}(y) = x.$$

f^{-1} has the property that if $f: A \to B$ is bijective, then:

$$f.f^{-1} = id_A \text{ and } f^{-1}.f = id_B$$

where id_A is the *identity map* on A:

$$id_A(x) = x$$

A.3.8 Examples

Returning to the examples A.1.15 we see that the function $g_{coll}: \pi_{coll} \to C$ defined:

$$g_{coll}(A) = Attila$$

$$g_{coll}(G) = Ghengis$$

$$g_{coll}(T) = Timur$$

$$g_{coll}(D) = Dracula$$

$$g_{coll}(R) = Reid$$

is bijective.

There is a relationship between functions and equivalence relations which we shall find useful. Consider the function $f_{coll}: S \to C$ which maps each student to the college to which they belong. Formally:

$$f_{coll}(s) = x \Leftrightarrow S \in g_{coll}(x)$$

The reader will note that $f_{coll}(s) = f_{coll}(s') \Leftrightarrow s =_{coll} s'$. This is an instance of a general result that we now quote.

A.3.9 Proposition

Let $f: X \to Y$ be a function, then the relation $Ker(f)$, defined:

$$x \; Ker(f) \; y \Leftrightarrow f(x) = f(y)$$

is an equivalence relation. Conversely, if R is an equivalence relation, then it equals $Ker(f_R)$ where:

$$f_R : X \to X/R$$

is defined by $f_R(x) = \langle x \rangle_R$.

Proof

Certainly, $f(x) = f(x)$ and so $x \; Ker(f) \; x$ and $Ker(f)$ is reflexive.

If $x \; Ker(f) \; y$, then $f(x) = f(y)$ and so $f(y) = f(x)$ and hence $y \; Ker(f) \; x$ and so $Ker(f)$ is symmetric.

Finally, suppose $x \; Ker(f) \; y$ and $y \; Ker(f) \; z$, then $f(x) = f(y)$ and $f(y) = f(z)$ and so $f(x) = f(z)$ implying that $x \; Ker(f) \; z$. Thus $Ker(f)$ is transitive. $Ker(f)$ has now been shown to possess all three properties of an equivalence relation.

Now, suppose R is an eqivalence relation, then:

$$\begin{aligned} x \; R \; y &\Leftrightarrow \langle x \rangle_R = \langle y \rangle_R \\ &\Leftrightarrow f_R(x) = f_R(y) \Leftrightarrow x \; Ker(f_R) \; y \end{aligned}$$

Thus $R = Ker(f_R)$ as required.

EXERCISES

1 Prove that $A \subseteq B \Leftrightarrow A \cap B = A \Leftrightarrow A \cup B = B$.

2 Prove A.1.7. Hint: show that $A \cap B \subseteq B \cap A$ and $B \cap A \subseteq A \cap B$.

3 Prove A.1.10.

4 Prove A.1.12.

5 Let A, B, C be sets. Prove the following equalities:

(a) $(A \cup B) - C = (A - C) \cup (B - C)$;
$(A \cap B) - C = (A - C) \cap (B - C)$

(b) $A - (B \cap C) = (A - B) \cup (A - C)$;
$A - (B \cup C) = (A - B) \cap (A - C)$

(c) $(A - B) \cap B = \varnothing$;
$(A - B) \cup B = A$.

6 Let A and B be sets. The *symmetric difference* of A and B, denoted $A \Delta B$ is defined:

$$A \Delta B = (A - B) \cup (B - A)$$

Let X be a set and let $A, B, C \in \underline{P}(A)$. Show the following:

(a) $A \Delta (X - A) = X$; $A \Delta X = (X - A$

(b) $A \Delta A = \varnothing$; $A \Delta \varnothing = A$

(c) $(A \Delta B) \Delta C = A \Delta (B \Delta C)$

(d) $(A \Delta B) \cap C = (A \cap C) \Delta (B \cap C)$.

7 A relation R on a set X is a pre-order if it is reflexive and transitive. Show that the relation $e(R)$, defined:

$$x \; e(R) \; y \Leftrightarrow x \; R \; y \;\&\; y \; R \; x$$

is an equivalence relation.

8 Show that '|' (divides) is a pre-order in the set of all integers (positive and negative whole numbers). What are the equivalence classes of e(|) ?

References

Arbib, M.A. (1968) *Algebraic Theory of Machines, Languages and Semigroups*. Academic Press.

Brams, G.W. (1983) *Reseaux de Petri: Theorie et Practique*. Masson.

Brauer, W. (Ed.) (1979) Net theory and applications. *Springer Lecture Notes in Computer Science*, vol. 84.

Conway, J.H. (1971) *Regular Algebra and Finite Machines*. Chapman and Hall.

Genrich, H.J., Lautenbach, K., & Thiagarajan, P.S. (1983) Elements of general net theory. In *Reseaux de Petri: Theorie et practique*. Masson.

Hartmanis, J. (1966) *Algebraic Structure Theory of Sequential Machines*. Prentice-Hall.

Hofstadter, D.R.(1980) *Godel, Escher, Bach: An Eternal Golden Braid*. Penguin.

Holcombe, W.M.L. (1982) *Algebraic Automata Theory, Cambridge Studies in Advanced Mathematics*, vol. 1. Cambridge University Press.

Hopcroft, J.E. & Ullman, J.D. (1969) *Formal Languages and Their Relation to Automata*. Addison-Wesley.

Milner, R. (1980) A calculus of communicating systems. *Springer Lecture Notes in Computer Science*, vol. 92.

Peterson, J.L. (1981) *Petri Net Theory and the Modelling of Systems*. Prentice-Hall.

Rayward-Smith, V.J. (1983) *A First Course in Formal Language Theory*. Blackwell Scientific Publications.

Rayward-Smith, V.J. (1986) *A First Course in Computability*. Blackwell Scientific Publications.

Salomaa, A. (1973) *Formal Languages*. Academic Press.

Shields, M.W. (1985) Concurrent machines. *Computer J.*, vol. 28, no. 5.

Stoy, J.E. (1979) *Denotational Semantics: The Scott-Strachey Approach to Programming Language Semantics*. MIT Press.

Index